◎湖南警察学院专著出版基金资助成果
◎2023年度湖南省教育科学“十四五”规划项目（XJK23BGD041）阶段性成果
◎2023年度湖南省教育厅科学研究项目“党的二十大精神研究专项”（23A0768）阶段性成果

国际传播视域下的
跨文化交际能力培养研究

朱剑虹 / 著

On the Cultivation of **Intercultural Communication Competence** in the Context of International Communication

湖南师范大学出版社 · 长沙

图书在版编目(CIP)数据

国际传播视域下的跨文化交际能力培养研究 / 朱剑虹著. --长沙:湖南师范大学出版社，2024.12. --ISBN 978-7-5648-5676-2

Ⅰ.H319.3

中国国家版本馆 CIP 数据核字第 2024PA9115 号

国际传播视域下的跨文化交际能力培养研究

GUOJI CHUANBO SHIYU XIA DE KUA WENHUA JIAOJI NENGLI PEIYANG YANJIU

朱剑虹　著

◇出 版 人:吴真文
◇责任编辑:李　航　孙雪姣
◇责任校对:张晓芳
◇出版发行:湖南师范大学出版社
　　　　　地址/长沙市岳麓区　邮编/410081
　　　　　电话/0731-88873071　88873070
　　　　　网址/https://press.hunnu.edu.cn
◇经销:新华书店
◇印刷:长沙雅佳印刷有限公司
◇开本:710 mm×1000 mm　1/16
◇印张:17.5
◇字数:480 千字
◇版次:2024 年 12 月第 1 版
◇印次:2024 年 12 月第 1 次印刷
◇书号:ISBN 978-7-5648-5676-2
◇定价:69.00 元

Contents

Chapter 1
Introduction

The 20th National Congress of the Communist Party of China emphasizes the need to enhance the dissemination power and influence of Chinese civilization. It underscores the importance of upholding the position of Chinese culture, extracting and showcasing the spiritual symbols and cultural essence of Chinese civilization, accelerating the construction of Chinese discourse and narrative system, telling China's story well, spreading China's voice, and presenting a reliable, admirable, and respectable image of China. In the past 10 years of the new era, the Party and the country have undergone historic transformations and achieved historic accomplishments, providing a solid foundation for constructing Chinese discourse and narrative system. However, telling China's story still faces "communication barriers." The world can hear China's voice, but may not fully understand China's story. In short, our shortcomings lie not in the "story" itself, but in intercultural communication. Therefore, cultivating the intercultural communication competence (ICC) of university students is not only a key intersection of national strategy, talent development, and foreign language teaching in higher education institutions but also an important component of building China's soft power by creating new concepts, categories, and expressions that facilitate the integration of Chinese and foreign cultures.

As China increasingly steps onto the world stage, universities play an important role in cultural exchanges and become a crucial component of the country's international communication efforts. By telling China's story, they contribute to bridging the gap between China and other countries. Since the establishment of the People's Republic of China, the country's education system has expanded its international presence, both in terms of its reach and scope, as well as the quality of education and management services provided. This expansion has made significant contributions to China's economic and social development. The Chinese government has issued relevant documents to promote international understanding and the development of ICC through education.

In the context of China, intercultural education aims to strengthen students' cultural identity and belief in Chinese culture, while deepening their understanding of other cultures. This ultimately enables them to become global citizens with ICC and responsible Chinese citizens.

In 2010, the Ministry of Education of the People's Republic of China (MOE) issued the *Outline of National Medium- and Long-Term Program for Education Reform and Development (2010-2020)* (MOE of the PRC, 2010)①, asserting that schools and universities in China should enhance international understanding education, promote intercultural exchanges, and increase students' awareness and understanding of different countries and cultures. The *Core Competencies and Values for Chinese Students' Development*, released in 2016, presents the necessary framework of key abilities and fundamental qualities that students should possess to promote lifelong personal development and adapt to social changes. National identity and international understanding are explicitly included and elaborated upon in the core competences. The framework aims to strengthen the identification with national citizenship and cultural identity, respect the diversity and differences of world cultures, and actively participate in cultural exchanges. In 2017, the State Council of China issued the *13th Five-Year Plan for National*

① 教育部.(2010-07-29).国家中长期教育改革和发展规划纲要(2010—2020年).中华人民共和国教育部政府门户网站. Retrieved June 6, 2023, from http://www.moe.gov.cn/jyb_xwfb/s6052/moe_838/201008/t20100802_93704.html.

Education Development (MOE of the PRC, 2017)[①], emphasizing the cultivation of cultural identity and cultural confidence among young students, as well as the enhancement of multiculturalism, international understanding education, and the improvement of ICC. *The Opinions of the Ministry of Education and Seven Other Departments on Accelerating and Expanding the Opening up of Education in the New Era* (MOE of the PRC, 2020)[②] was formulated and issued by China's Ministry of Education in response to the new era and the new situation. This document proposes that "we should actively strengthen mutual learning, mutual accommodation and communication with other countries in the world to form a more comprehensive, broader, and more hierarchical educational system. There is no need to state the obvious when it comes to the importance of ICC, which is one of the essential characteristics that international talents should have. Without a shadow of a question, the primary educational objective of college English education in China has evolved into the cultivation of diversified, compound, and innovative international talents.

In response to the policies of the Chinese government and relevant departments, China has implemented reforms in foreign language education at all levels of education. The *College English Teaching Guide*, also known as *Guide 2020* for short, and other programmatic documents were published by China's Ministry of Education in the year 2020. These documents emphasized the importance and urgency of ICC from the perspective of national education decision-making and guidance. According to *Guide 2020*, one of the essential tasks of college English education is to carry out intercultural education...

---

① 教育部. (2017-01-10). 国务院关于印发国家教育事业发展"十三五"规划的通知. 中华人民共和国教育部政府门户网站. Retrieved June 6, 2023, from http://www.moe.gov.cn/jyb_xxgk/moe_1777/moe_1778/201701/t20170119_295319.html.

② 教育部. (2020-06-23). 教育部等八部门印发意见加快和扩大新时代教育对外开放. 中华人民共和国教育部政府门户网站. Retrieved June 6, 2023, from http://www.moe.gov.cn/jyb_xwfb/s5147/202006/t20200623_467784.html.

cultivate ICC (NACTELHE, 2020)[①]. This is made abundantly clear in the aforementioned passage. Therefore, college English education should cultivate and reserve outstanding talents who have an international vision and a great ICC, are familiar with international rules, and are proficient in international negotiations, in order to advance China's social and economic development, strengthen China's ability to fulfill its international obligations, and increase China's participation in global governance.

It is worth noting that merely having proficiency in a foreign language is far from sufficient to establish practical connections between China and the outside world. In-depth research on the history, culture, and current situation of other regions, a profound understanding of Chinese history, culture, and reality, as well as a comprehensive understanding and grasp of the world as a whole and its systemic nature, are essential self-cultivation for foreign language learners to develop their ICC. To enhance the effectiveness of international communication, we need to break through the single political persuasion framework based solely on strong effect orientation and gradually enrich our ability for intercultural dialogue in the face of diverse and differentiated groups. This will help us achieve a civilization exchange that transcends cultural barriers, a cultural assimilation that goes beyond cultural conflicts, and a coexistence of civilizations that surpasses the notion of cultural superiority. Ultimately, it will promote trust, connection, and value recognition in human society.

Despite 60 years of research on intercultural communication, significant research gaps remain. Firstly, existing studies largely focus on theoretical frameworks and specific skill development for intercultural communication, lacking systematic empirical research to verify the applicability of these theories to Chinese students. Secondly, past research has rarely emphasized

---

① 高等学校大学外语教学指导委员会(The National Administrative Committee on Teaching English Language in Higher Education, NACTELHE). 2020. 大学英语教学指南(2020 版). 高等教育出版社.

the uniqueness and importance of Chinese culture in intercultural communication, leading to a homogeneous and less targeted training model. Particularly, current studies are often based on Western cultural contexts, neglecting the intercultural communication needs and challenges faced by Chinese students in a globalized context. Furthermore, existing research often lacks effective application and evaluation mechanisms for ICC in practical teaching. It has not comprehensively explored how to systematically integrate the cultivation of ICC into higher education. This disconnect between theory and practice makes it difficult for current teaching models to truly enhance students' ICC, and they fail to effectively support the national strategy for international communication.

In view of this, this study aims to fill the existing research gaps by constructing theoretical and practical models for cultivating ICC. It proposes methods that meet the needs of Chinese students, improving their effectiveness and adaptability in international exchanges. This study not only holds significant academic value but also provides practical guidance for college foreign language teaching and supports the national strategy for international communication by preparing competent personnels.

1.1 Background of the Study

China needs the world, and the world also needs China. Present-day China cannot isolate itself from the world and thrive independently. Since the implementation of the reform and opening-up policy, China has made tremendous strides in its economy and has become a global leader in comprehensive national strength. Its all-around, broad-based, and multi-level pattern of opening-up continues to advance, and its importance in the globalized economic system is increasing. China plays an increasingly significant role in various international affairs. Where there is interaction, friction can occur. Only by understanding the differences between countries, ethnic groups, and various races, recognizing the root causes of cultural conflicts, and learning to think and handle issues from a intercultural perspective, can we overcome barriers in communication and interaction. Only through this can China further understand the world, and the world can have a better understanding of China.

1.1.1 Globalization and Interculturality

With rapid advancements in science and technology in fields such as communication, transportation, and information technology, the process of globalization is accelerating at an unprecedented pace. The world is indeed shrinking into a "global village", where people are more interconnected and interdependent than ever before. Cultural diversity and interculturality encounters have become a reality of modern life (UNESCO, 2009)①. Globalization is usually interpreted as a deep integration and interaction in multiple dimensions such as economy, politics, technology, and culture on a global scale. This process breaks down traditional geographical barriers, making the connections between different countries and regions increasingly close. Driven by globalization, various resources, information, technologies, and cultures flow globally, promoting the rapid development of human society. However, globalization does not simply point towards homogenization or unification; rather, it is a form of diversified development achieved based on respecting diversity and embracing differences. Therefore, in this process, interculturality, as the cornerstone of dialogue and interaction between different cultures, is particularly crucial. Through intercultural interaction and exchange, new meanings are constructed, and cultural innovation and development are realized. Different cultures collide and merge in exchanges, jointly constructing discursive subjects. While maintaining their cultural uniqueness, they also actively absorb the essence of other cultures, forming a

---

① UNESCO. (2009). World report No. 2: Investing in cultural diversity and intercultural dialogue. UNESCO. Retrieved June 6, 2023, from http://www.unesco.org/en/world-reports/cultural-diversity.

dynamic cultural reorganization. This cultural exchange and integration not only enrich the connotations of culture but also demonstrate its true meaning and value. Against the backdrop of globalization, cultural diversity and intercultural communication will continue to be important forces driving world progress.

However, intercultural communication is not an easy task. Different cultures face multiple obstacles, such as differences in value systems and cultural concepts, when articulating their identities and constructing their images. These obstacles often bring unexpected difficulties and problems to communication, with misunderstandings, confusion, conflicts, and even clashes occurring from time to time. The "self" realizes reflection and introspection on its own culture and identity through the process of otherizing and objectifying its own culture, absorbing beneficial elements from differentiated perspectives (Jia & Liu, 2018)①, and ultimately achieving a dialectical compatibility between cultures.

Whether people from different cultural groups can coexist and work together to address a range of human survival issues and pursue development largely depends on whether they can effectively communicate and gradually achieve mutual understanding. Mutual understanding can ultimately dissolve inherent prejudices, reduce conflicts and antagonisms between diverse cultures, and achieve a harmonious coexistence. Therefore, ICC, often considered one of the most important skills for talent in the 21st century (Byram & Wagner, 2018)②, is crucial not only for personal development but also closely related to a nation's overall strength. As China's economy integrates into the globalization process, our interactions with countries around the world are increasing, and China is playing an increasingly important role on the global economic and political stage. China's image is not

---

① 贾文山 & 刘杨. (2018). 跨文化传播的诠释学视角:以中国语境为例. 西安交通大学学报(社会科学版), (03), 123-129.

② Byram, M., & Wagner, M. (2018). Making a difference: Language teaching for intercultural and international dialogue. *Foreign Language Annals*, 51, 140-151.

constructed and interpreted as an object by a single subject from a self-centered cultural perspective; rather, it emerges from the interactive relationships among multiple subjects (Yin & Fang, 2023)①. This requires interculturality and the intercultural dialogue and cooperation among various civilizations. Therefore, China needs a large number of talents who not only understand international economic rules and possess global thinking but also hold ICC.

1.1.2 International Communication and Intercultural Communication

The present era is an era of great power competition. Whether we acknowledge it or not, whether we are willing or unwilling, we have already entered an era of great power competition. In addition to political, economic, and military hard power, winning hearts and minds and achieving victory in the competition of soft power is even more crucial. Language serves as the foundation of soft power; it is a constituent element of other forms of soft power and serves as a guarantee for cultural or ideological influence. At the individual level, cultural soft power refers to the understanding and comprehension of others, as well as insights and self-awareness based on that understanding, thereby enabling harmonious interactions with others. At the group level, cultural soft power refers to the ability to engage in intercultural communication, blending different cultural norms and backgrounds. At the societal level, cultural soft power represents the capacity to bridge social divides and conflicts, maintaining a balance of cultural diversity. For nations and the international community, cultural soft power is the ability to construct an open, non-violent intercultural space. With the advancement of economic globalization and information networking, cultures are experiencing the largest and most widespread contact in history, and intercultural communication has become an unavoidable phenomenon and mode of exchange in today's world. In the context of globalization, intercultural communication is crucial for

① 阴雅婷 & 方宇森. (2023). 基于文化间性的中国国家形象传播维度与路径研究. 新闻爱好者, (09), 53-56.

enhancing cultural soft power and achieving effective communication and cooperation.

In reality, the essence of international communication is intercultural communication. Intercultural communication is both an ancient cultural phenomenon in human history and a modern way of life and important skill for individuals. It is also one of the main driving factors behind the development and prosperity of national cultures and world cultures. Positive intercultural communication is beneficial for building a cultural community based on respecting the diversity of world cultures and achieving a deep integration of the community with a shared future for mankind. Over the years, the "politicized" dissemination of China-related topics by Western media has repeatedly led to "misinterpretations" and "distortions" of China's national image. This further exacerbates the cultural misunderstandings between the East and the West and deepens China's "discourse predicament". To break through the current predicament of international communication, we must face the "communication gap" caused by cultural differences, confront the increased difficulties in external communication due to intensified clashes of civilizations, and fundamentally deconstruct the similarities and differences between the East and the West. We need to rediscover, explore, and interpret the wisdom of the East, represented by Chinese culture, and extract and create new concepts, categories, and expressions that embody a world recognition with Chinese characteristics.

The purpose of China's international communication is not simply to let Chinese elements, Chinese voices, and Chinese stories "go global," but rather to ensure that Chinese discourse and Chinese wisdom are better understood and accepted in dialogical contexts and become global wisdom embraced by people from different cultural backgrounds. This requires us to engage in dialogue between the East and the West, and even dialogue among diverse cultures, avoiding the tendency of "talking to oneself" or being constrained by binary thinking. We should avoid falling into the pitfalls of cultural narcissism and self-sufficiency, but instead transcend the limitations of different civilizations, achieve "convergence of perspectives", gain a broader vision, and while pursuing the integration of the East and the West, always maintain a local and regional perspective. By allowing the West to rediscover, explore, and interpret the East, we can contribute power to the construction of a human community with a shared future.

At present, China is at a historical juncture of unprecedented global changes and the overall strategic goal of the great rejuvenation of the Chinese nation. The intertwined development of these two major trends will inevitably bring about changes in the balance of power among major countries and alterations in mutual perceptions. The external world's understanding and judgment of China will evolve along with changes in China's discourse and behavior. China should accurately grasp the global trends and characteristics of the times, continuously strengthen its discourse capacity building, explore methods that are more in line with the national and international situation, and make China's external communication more targeted, timely, influential, and penetrating. It is essential for outstanding intercultural talents to not only view themselves and their connection to the world from a Chinese perspective but also have the ability to observe China from different corners of the world, seeking and discerning the unique and distinctive aspects of China in its interaction with the world. In other words, within the scope of international communication, ICC encompasses a sustained and strong curiosity and thirst for knowledge about diverse cultural traditions, as well as an enduring passion for China's local culture and spiritual heritage.

1.1.3 Higher Education and Intercultural Communication

Global competition for national strength ultimately boils down to the competition for talent, particularly innovative talent. As China's international status rises, its external exchanges and cooperation in politics, economy, culture, and other fields have become more frequent. International interactions in industries such as technology, judiciary, environmental protection, and finance are rapidly growing, creating an urgent demand for intercultural human capital. This type of capital, characterized by sensitivity to cultural differences, intercultural consciousness, and communication skills, is essential in the new era of globalization.

The changing demand for talents has led to changes in education, and globalization has brought new requirements and challenges to higher education in China. In the 1980s and 1990s, although China had entered the era of reform and opening up, there were relatively limited exchanges with the outside world, and the society as a whole remained relatively closed. Students learning foreign languages (especially English) mainly treated it as a regular course in higher education institutions or pursued it out of personal interest to cultivate their own qualities and accomplishments. In terms of teaching objectives, traditional foreign language teaching focused on developing learners' abilities to read in the target language and communicate with speakers from the target language community. The language competence of native speakers of the target language was the standard that foreign language teachers and students aspired to achieve. Traditional college English curricula tend to neglect teaching students how to use English effectively in intercultural communication situations in favor of focusing on imparting students' specific language knowledge such as words, grammar, sentence patterns, etc., and strengthening language skills such as listening, speaking, reading, writing, and translating. This is, in reality, an unfair method. Students will not be able to adjust to the rapid growth of international exchanges with just language training alone. Students will struggle to comprehend and respond appropriately to problems in intercultual communication scenarios in their future lives and careers if they have not been adequately prepared for them. This will lead to misunderstanding and the failure of intercultural communication. As a result, it is becoming increasingly important for instructors of English in universities to place an emphasis on helping their students develop their ICC to produce globally-minded, successful professionals.

The globalization context calls for new educational concepts to guide the talent development in Chinese higher education. In today's globalized world, it is necessary for China's talent development strategy in higher education to take a global perspective. China's higher education can no longer develop in isolation but should be integrated into the global economic and social cycles. Talent development needs to adapt to the requirements of the knowledge-based economy and economic globalization, the global mobility of talents, the global economic and trade markets, as well as China's external communication needs. It is crucial to cultivate talents at different levels who possess the ability to participate in international competition. The development of higher education is strongly influenced by economic globalization and cultural globalization. Under the concept of new human capital, it is incumbent upon education today to cultivate new compound talents capable of working in intercultural environments. The cultivation of internationally-oriented talents with intercultural competencies has become an urgent task.

The development of foreign language education needs to be strengthened to meet the demands of social, political, and economic development. In turn, the development of foreign language education will promote social and economic progress and the process of global integration. Research conducted by Wang Kefei, as cited by Li (2019) ①, on the status and policies of foreign language education in thirteen representative countries and regions (including France, Germany, Russia, the European Union, Romania, Greece, Japan, the Republic of Korea, Malaysia, Thailand, Israel, Mexico, and Brazil) found that foreign language education and social-economic development have a mutually beneficial interaction and demand. Foreign language education reflects a country's level of openness and socio-economic development. The level of foreign language proficiency indicates a country's degree of internationalization and its citizens' international awareness. Foreign language education should not be limited to language teaching; instead, the focus should be on cultivating internationally competent professionals proficient

① 李霄翔. (2019). 我国大学英语课程建设的历史进程与未来走向. 外语教学与研究, 51(6), 814-818.

in foreign languages. McCloskey, as cited by Taskiran (2019) ①, points out that foreign language proficiency, global awareness, and intercultural communication skills are increasingly recognized as essential qualities for active participation in the economic, political, and social domains of the 21st century.

The national development strategy, the objective demands of an information-based society, and the need for innovative talent have placed new requirements on foreign language education, leading to corresponding changes in its purpose and tasks. As foreign language teaching continues to evolve, the target requirements for language learners have also been updated. Initially, the focus was solely on language proficiency, then it expanded to include communicative competence, and now it encompasses intercultural communication skills. Higher education institutions must prioritize the cultivation of international awareness among students, their understanding of different cultures of nations and ethnicities, and their proficiency in using foreign languages to undertake the responsibility of international communication. They should also foster students' understanding and interpretation abilities of Chinese culture to serve the external dissemination of Chinese culture (Xiang, 2020) ②. Therefore, strengthening foreign language education and enhancing students' cultural literacy have become important teaching tasks for universities. Foreign language teaching should play a positive role in the social development process and contribute to the goals of international communication.

1.2 Research Questions

Based on the importance of ICC in the context of globalization, the demand for intercultural talents in China's international communication

---

① Taskiran, A. (2019). Telecollaboration: Fostering foreign language learning at a distance. *European Journal of Open, Distance and E-Learning* (*EURODL*), 22(2), 87-97.

② 向明友. (2020). 顺应新形势，推动大学英语课程体系建设——《大学英语教学指南》课程设置评注. 外语界, (04), 28-34.

strategy, the corresponding changes in higher education talent development concepts, as well as the goals and tasks of foreign language education, researchers focus on the cultivation of ICC in foreign language teaching in Chinese universities. Drawing on relevant theories, concepts, and models from both domestic and international sources, the research aims to explore and demonstrate the concept of ICC development and investigate various models and methods for cultivating ICC. The research mainly focuses on four aspects: ICC frameworks, the status of ICC among Chinese undergraduates, ICC development models both in theory and in practice, and the application of ICC development models.

The first key research point is the study of ICC frameworks. There are diverse opinions among experts, both domestic and foreign, regarding the components of ICC. The researchers will analyze the principles, characteristics, and changes in ICC, review and summarize the characteristics of existing ICC frameworks at home and abroad, consider the realistic needs of China's international communication, and utilize grounded theory to thoroughly explore the specific components of ICC as well as the relationships between these components. The aim is to construct a comprehensive framework for ICC in context of China.

The second key research point is to conduct a panoramic scan of the current status of ICC among university students. Previous studies have often focused on exploring various dimensions within the framework of intercultural communication, overlooking the influence of demographic factors. This study aims to describe the demographic profile of the students and to identify the level of competence. Specifically, it seeks to answer the following questions. What is the profile of the student-respondents in terms of age, gender, year level and major①. What is the level of ICC in terms of the categories in the

① 12 majors are covered in line with the fields of disciplines of conferring academic degrees by China's MOE, namely philosophy, economics, law, education, literature, history, science, engineering, agriculture, medicine, management, and art.

framework constructed in this study? Is there a significant difference between the demographic profile of the student-respondents and the level of ICC? Is there a significant relationship between the demographic profile of the student-respondents and the level of ICC? What are the challenges encountered by the student respondents to become intercultural competent?

The third key research point is the construction of models for cultivating ICC. Building upon the framework of ICC, the researcher will integrate empirical research findings on the status of ICC development among Chinese university students. It aims to construct theoretical models in foreign language education and practical models in foreign language classroom. Detailed elaboration will be provided on the concepts, goals, principles, and content of ICC development, as well as the specific aspects and stages of ICC development in foreign language classroom.

The fourth key research point is the specific application of models for cultivating ICC. This involves exploring how the theoretical model and practical model can be applied in various aspects of foreign language education in Chinese universities, including classroom instruction, extracurricular activities, foreign language teaching faculty, foreign language textbooks, and the application of modern information technology. The aim is to implement ICC development in specific components, integrating and synergizing various aspects and elements of foreign language education to comprehensively develop and enhance students' ICC. This research ultimately seeks to enable students to engage in intercultural communication appropriately and effectively, leading to sustained improvement in their ICC.

1.3 Significance of the Research

The significance of the research lies in addressing the pressing issue of cultivating ICC, which is closely aligned with the pulse of the times and the goals of foreign language education in higher education institutions. This study aims to construct a framework for ICC, examine the current status of

ICC development among Chinese undergraduates, develop theoretical models and practical models for cultivating ICC, and further propose strategies for the specific application of these models in practice.

1.3.1 Theoretical Significance

This study further develops the theory of ICC from the perspective of foreign language education in Chinese universities. Various fields such as linguistics, education, psychology, cultural studies, and communication studies have been exploring the definition, components, competency structure, evaluation dimensions, and assessment tools of ICC. Previous research has focused on various groups such as overseas immigrants, residents, international students, overseas workers, business professionals, students majoring in foreign languages. However, due to the different core competencies and competency levels required in ICC for each group, it is necessary to study ICC from specific perspectives based on their unique needs. Therefore, this study will start from relevant theories of ICC and combine them with the practical requirements of China's international communication to redefine the elements of ICC. With this premise, the study will demonstrate the interrelationships among the various elements of ICC and establish its fundamental structure. Based on the survey results of undergraduates' ICC status, a theoretical model for foreign language education and a practical model in foreign language classroom will be constructed, providing practical guidelines for cultivating ICC in foreign language teaching. The application and interpretation of the ICC cultivation model in foreign language education will demonstrate its concrete implementation. The research findings will not only enrich the theory of ICC development but also provide a theoretical basis for practical research.

1.3.2 Practical Significance

The following communities or subsets of society will benefit from the findings of this study:

Collegiate students. This article describes methods of training that are both scientific and effective. When successful training strategies are put into action, it is inevitable that each student will be provided with additional chances for learning and practice, that the overall ICC of the student group will improve, and that the students' sense of self-efficacy will grow. It will also have a beneficial effect on their potential employment opportunities and efficiency in intercultural communication in the future. Students in higher education institutions will also further support Sino-foreign exchanges and social development on a larger stage.

University teachers. The current state of ICC research is predicated primarily on theory and speculative research, but there is a lack of relevant empirical research. The correlation between many different variables is analyzed using a scientific approach in this study. University teachers may be able to evaluate their students' ICC objectively and suggest effective and persuasive methods for their students to enhance their ICC. The theoretical model and practical model proposed in the research have strong guiding and operational capabilities. University teachers can creatively conduct teaching based on the ICC model according to their teaching realities. This approach ensures the foundation of teaching while meeting the needs of personalized instruction, thereby maximizing teaching effectiveness.

Universities. This study provides a comprehensive analysis of the overall situation of ICC among Chinese college students. It also obtains some first-hand information and data, which can provide data support for the formulation of international talent training goals within colleges and universities. In addition, the findings of this research could give institutions access to valid information, as the implementation of its findings will result in the proposal of improvements.

Ministry of Education of the People's Republic of China (MOE of the PRC). This study provides a powerful reference for the selection, appointment, and performance evaluation of international talent, which is of significant practical significance. The study evaluates the ICC of Chinese college students. It not only provides a reference for the cultivation of foreign language international talents and related ICC courses in colleges and universities, but also provides a reference for the cultivation of international talents in related ICC courses, so as to better serve the needs of China's international communication.

Future researchers. ICC studies both here in China and overseas are on the rise. This research builds an ICC model tailored to the realities of Chinese college students and the demand for China's international communication strategy, offers a wealth of data on the topic, and charts a fresh course of inquiry for scholars interested in this area.

1.4 Structure of the Research

Chapter 1 provides an overview of the background of the study, outlines the research questions and approach, discusses the purpose and significance of the research, and presents the structure of the thesis.

Chapter 2 is the literature review. This chapter serves as the theoretical foundation of the study and defines the scope of the research and key concepts involved. It primarily focuses on three aspects: (1) the relationship between language, culture, and communication; (2) ICC; and (3) the cultivation of ICC in foreign language education. Specifically, it includes the definition and characteristics of language, culture, and communication, as well as the relationship between language, culture, and communication. It also discusses the definition of ICC, classic models, measurement tools, and the theoretical rationale for integrating the cultivation of ICC into foreign language education objectives.

Chapter 3 introduces the ICC framework in foreign language education. The first section is the theoretical framework, which analyzes theories closely related to this research and provides theoretical basis and support for the study, specifically referring to Byram's ICC Model. The second section presents the research design derived from the ICC framework and provides detailed explanations of the research methods, including method selection, sample selection, and analysis strategies. The third section describes the specific implementation of the grounded theory research method, elucidating open coding, axial coding, selective coding, and the Saturation Test. The fourth section explains the analysis and interpretation of each element of the ICC framework, including intercultural consciousness, intercultural knowledge, intercultural skills, and intercultural behavior.

Chapter 4 focuses on an empirical study of the current status of ICC. A questionnaire survey is conducted with nearly 600 undergraduates from five universities in Hunan Province. The study primarily examines the differences and relationships between demographic factors and ICC levels, aiming to provide evidence for differentiated teaching and predictive relationships in future ICC education. Additionally, the chapter delves into an in-depth analysis of the challenges encountered by student respondents in developing ICC, which serves as a basis for constructing the ICC development model.

Chapter 5 integrates the results of theoretical and empirical research to construct theoretical and practical models for ICC development. Firstly, it provides a detailed exposition of the concepts, principles, and objectives involved in constructing the model in foreign language education. Then, it elaborates on the content and stages of ICC development. Finally, this chapter constructs a theoretical model in foreign language education and a practical model in foreign language classroom.

Chapter 6 focuses on the applied research of the ICC development models in foreign language education, specifically investigating the specific aspects of ICC in Chinese university foreign language teaching. It thoroughly examines the practical application of the ICC development model from five aspects: foreign language classroom teaching, extracurricular activities, foreign language teaching faculty, foreign language teaching materials, and integration of information technology.

Chapter 7 concludes the research by summarizing its findings, identifying limitations, and providing prospects for future research. The chapter aims to offer valuable insights and references for further studies in intercultural foreign language teaching.

1.5 Summary

This chapter begins by discussing the background of the research from three perspectives: globalization and interculturality, international communication and intercultural communication, and foreign language education and intercultural communication. It then clarifies the research approach and provides a brief introduction to the four research focal points. Furthermore, the significance of the research is explained from both theoretical and practical perspectives. Finally, the chapter outlines the structure of the thesis and highlights the key points of each chapter.

The next chapter is the literature review, where the researcher will review theories and literature closely related to the research, aiming to provide solid theoretical guidance and support for the research.

Chapter 2
Literature Review

This chapter reviews research and literature in the field to understand the current status and establish a theoretical foundation for future studies on ICC. It begins with definitions of language, culture, and communication, exploring their interconnectedness. Next, it provides an overview of the definition of ICC, including classic models and measurement tools. The final section discusses the rationale and practical requirements for fostering ICC within the context of foreign language teaching.

2.1 Language, Culture, and Communication

Globalization and cultural diversity have created a thriving environment for intercultural communication, connecting people from different countries more closely. In international interactions, the ability to understand and embrace diverse cultural patterns has become crucial for effective communication. Consequently, the demand for cultivating ICC has become integral to foreign language teaching. The interplay between language, culture, and communication is evident within and across various languages and cultures. Therefore, examining foreign language learning and teaching through the lens of intercultural communication is essential to fully embrace the unique characteristics of language, culture, and communication.

2.1.1 Language

1. Definition of Language

The definition of language is fundamental to language research, as it underpins all related inquiries and directly influences foreign language teaching principles and methods. Structuralism, notably advanced by Swiss linguist Ferdinand de Saussure, posits that language is both a symbolic and structural system. It involves relationships between symbols (syntax), symbols and their referents (semantics), and symbols and language users (pragmatics). Language units do not exist in isolation but in contrast and opposition to other units, much like chess pieces, which hold specific meanings and capabilities within the game's rules. Disconnected from the structural relationships of the chess game, these units become meaningless blocks or stones.

Edward Sapir, an anthropologist, emphasizes the instrumental and human-created nature of language. He asserts that language is a uniquely human, consciously constructed symbolic system for conveying ideas, emotions, and desires. Language, according to Sapir, is a non-instinctual method of communication conveying ideas, emotions, and desires, created and socialized by humans. Despite the influences of instinctual behavior and the natural environment on certain language components, and regardless of instinctual tendencies (physical or otherwise) shaping language expression, human language itself has no instinctive foundation.

Noam Chomsky, a prominent American linguist, views language as a finite system with infinite potential. He considers it an innate capacity for producing grammatically correct sentences that are comprehensible within one's community. According to Chomsky, language reflects the actual discourse of a given period and is shaped by human brain mechanisms and instincts. He defines language as the set of all possible sentences due to its infinite range, with grammar rules distinguishing between sentences and non-sentences.

Functionalism, as represented by British linguist Michael A. K. Halliday, highlights three key aspects of language: it is a social process, a system, and functional. Language plays a crucial role in life, serving as a process of meaning creation and being simultaneously shaped and influenced by context and culture. Language is not only a symbolic system that combines sound and meaning but also a cultural code. Through its own system of symbols (including speech and writing), language assigns meaning to objects, events, human experiences, and emotions in the external world. Even when encountering the same objects or events, people from different cultures may have different experiences and emotions. Therefore, language serves social and cultural functions and possesses cultural and social characteristics. Through prolonged processes of production, life practices, and the solidification of various emotions and experiences through the language symbol system, different language symbol systems and the meanings they express inevitably vary.

Over sixty definitions of language emerged from the early 19th to the early 20th century, reflecting diverse scholarly perspectives. However, scholars unanimously agree that language is the means and process through which humans perceive and express the world (Pan, 2001) ①. This underscores that language, which evolves alongside human society, serves as both a communication tool and a medium integrating individuals with culture. Language is deeply intertwined with human society and culture.

2. Functions of Language

Language functions can be broadly categorized into cognitive and communicative aspects. The cognitive function reflects how the human brain uses language to actively engage with objective reality, representing intellectual and psychological processes. Conversely, the communicative function involves explicit and interactive ways in which individuals use language to communicate and negotiate with others (Nida, 2001, as cited in Junining & Kusuma, 2020) ②.

Language is both a tool for thought and a carrier of culture. It reflects cognitive activities and cultural development, serving as a code for cultural

---

① 潘文国. (2001). 语言的定义. 华东师范大学学报 (哲学社会科学版), (01), 97-108+128.

② Junining, E., & Kusuma, V. A. M. C. (2020). Translation strategies for translating a news article. *LINGUA*, 15(1), 79-90.

information (Rönnberg et al., 2019)①. Language not only facilitates understanding of the external world but also shapes thinking and reasoning. Variations in language can lead to different thinking patterns, and linguistic diversity can stimulate creative thinking and drive social innovation.

Language serves as the fundamental tool for human interaction and comes to life through communication. It is both an inherent and social attribute of humans, reflecting our nature as cultural and social beings (Baker & Sangiamchit, 2019)②. Language, education, and society are deeply interconnected, forming the foundation for human social progress (Wang, 2011)③.

2.1.2 Culture

1. Concept of Culture

Culture is a core concept in intercultural communication, and defining it is essential for studying the field. The term "culture" is inherently complex, multifaceted, and often ambiguous.

Edward Burnett Tylor, a key figure in cultural anthropology, defined culture in his 1871 book *Primitive Culture* as including knowledge, beliefs, art, morals, laws, customs, and other skills and habits acquired by individuals in society (as cited in Nasir et al., 2020) ④. Edward T. Hall, a pioneer in intercultural communication, argued in *The Silent Language* that culture and communication are inseparable (Feine et al., 2019)⑤. He described culture as comprising diverse components and acting as a bridge for

---

① Rönnberg, J., Holmer, E., & Rudner, M. (2019). Cognitive hearing science and ease of language understanding. *International Journal of Audiology*, 58(5), 247-261.

② Baker, W., & Sangiamchit, C. (2019). Transcultural communication: Language, communication and culture through English as a lingua franca in a social network community. *Language and Intercultural Communication*, 19(6), 471-487.

③ 王克非. (2011). 外语教育政策与社会经济发展. 外语界, (01), 2-7.

④ Nasir, N. I. S., Lee, C. D., Pea, R., & McKinney de Royston, M. (Eds.). (2020). *Handbook of the cultural foundations of learning* (*1st Edition*). Routledge.

⑤ Feine, J., Gnewuch, U., Morana, S., & Maedche, A. (2019). A taxonomy of social cues for conversational agents. *International Journal of Human-Computer Studies*, 132, 138-161.

human interaction. Hall identified three levels of culture: the visible, the invisible, and the technical. He also distinguished between explicit culture, which is observable, and hidden culture, which remains unseen and challenging to discern, even for trained observers. The hidden aspects are often more significant than what is readily apparent, and even insiders may struggle to recognize these concealed elements.

Hendon, as cited by Pasang et al. (2023) ①, distinguishes between "Culture with a capital C" and "culture with a small c." The former includes broad aspects of civilization like politics, economy, literature, art, music, architecture, philosophy, and technology. The latter refers to daily life elements such as dietary habits, customs, behavioral norms, and social traditions. Additionally, culture encompasses thoughts and values tied to its historical development, systematically explaining people's communicative behavior.

According to Hu (1999)②, culture includes beliefs, values, customs, knowledge, tangible objects, and tools. At its core, culture's values differentiate distinct cultural systems and guide human actions, shaping behavior and influencing every word and action. Culture is acquired through socialization, not innate. It carries inherited elements from the past while evolving with societal changes. Once formed, culture remains stable yet dynamic, continually adapting to time and societal shifts. Jiang et al. (2010)③ note that frequent interactions between cultures lead to mutual influence, where cultures permeate and accommodate each other. This process seeks common ground for communication and exchange while preserving unique differences. Ethnic cultures contribute to the global culture, forming a mosaic

---

① Pasang, S., Ramiana, R., Harbi, A. A., & Amaluddin, A. (2023). The Role of Attitude in Language Learning as a Part of Cultures. *Edumaspul: Jurnal Pendidikan*, 7(1), 66-74.

② 胡文仲.(1999). 跨文化交际学概论. 外语教学与研究出版社.

③ 蒋晓萍,康兆春,罗赛群,霍明杰 & 张黎琴. (2010). 跨文化教学之重:外语教学的跨文化诠释. 广东人民出版社.

of diverse elements. Dai (2011) ① describes culture with five characteristics: regionalism, historicity, social construction, systematicity, and fluidity. These traits contribute to the complexity and diversity of culture, fostering communication and integration.

Culture has unique national characteristics, with distinct value orientations. It is not hierarchical, and intercultural dialogue promotes mutual learning and complementarity, enhancing cultural diversity. A dynamic developmental perspective and an inclusive, respectful attitude are essential for effective intercultural communication, especially in globalization.

2. Functions of Culture

Culture serves diverse functions, providing spiritual nourishment, promoting social harmony, driving economic development, and fostering creativity. It helps individuals accurately understand the world. As anthropologist William Haviland, cited by Zeitzen (2020)②, noted, "people maintain cultures to deal with problems or matters that concern them." Culture evolves to offer a predictable worldview, aiding individuals in comprehending their environment and facilitating appropriate interactions.

Culture preserves historical legacies, including societal development, traditions, and values. As the collective memory of society, it transmits experiences and knowledge across generations, helping people understand their past and present while preparing for the future. Cultural inheritance preserves and innovates ethnic cultures (Mei & Meng, 2022)③, aiding in understanding cultural roots and identity, and reinforcing social cohesion (Tian, 2020)④.

Culture imparts significance to human existence, providing guidance for

---

① 戴晓东. (2011). 跨文化交际理论. 上海外语教育出版社, 2011.

② Zeitzen, M. K. (2020). *Polygamy: A cross-cultural analysis*. Routledge.

③ 梅萍 & 孟恒艳. (2022). 中华优秀传统美育文化的价值意蕴及弘扬. 社会主义核心价值观研究, 8(1), 45-53.

④ 田丰. (2020). 优秀文化记忆与大学生社会主义核心价值观培育. 中国青年社会科学, 39(3), 79-86.

actions, thoughts, and choices through values, beliefs, and customs. From its birth, culture shapes behavior by teaching societal norms. Influenced by our own culture, we internalize its thinking patterns, worldviews, values, customs, lifestyles, behavioral norms, moral standards, and communication modes, enabling us to adapt within a social context. Culture allows us to draw on the accumulated wisdom of human evolution, fostering wise interactions with others, society, and nature, and equipping us to face environmental challenges (Yu, 2022)①.

Culture nurtures social harmony by embodying shared beliefs, values, and norms. While differences across cultures can lead to conflicts, cultural dialogue, understanding, exchange, and cooperation promote diversity and inclusiveness, reducing conflicts, strengthening social connections, and enhancing cohesion and stability. In globalization, culture acts as a bridge, fostering mutual understanding and respect, and driving social harmony. Thus, promoting cultural dialogue, intercultural exchange, and innovation is essential for ensuring social harmony and development.

2.1.3 Communication

1. Concept of Communication

The term "communication" derives from the Latin word "communicare," meaning "common" or "together." It involves creating shared understanding and connection through exchanging and transmitting information. Effective communication relies on a shared cultural framework. Due to the complexity of communicative behavior, scholars have diverse interpretations of the concept.

Communication is a form of social interaction characterized by its unpredictability and creativity. It occurs within specific discourses and socio-cultural contexts, serving a purpose and utilizing authentic materials and their

① 余华. (2022). 人类文明新形态的内涵，特征与实践向度. 观察与思考，(11)，24-34.

outcomes to gauge its success (Harsch & Malone, 2020)①. Samovar et al. (2000)② define communication as a dynamic and systematic process in which humans employ symbols to create and reflect meaning. It involves the exchange of information, mutual influence, and the collective construction of meaning and identity. Communication is the exchange of information between individuals or groups, encompassing the creation, transmission, and interpretation of messages to establish relationships, coordinate activities, and solve problems. Floyd and Weber (2020)③ assert that communication is the process of transmitting and receiving information, ideas, and emotions through diverse channels and media, such as language, facial expressions, and technology.

The concept of communication is intricately connected to the understanding of communicative competence. It emerged in the late 1960s and early 1970s, with influential discussions led by scholars such as Habermas, Campbell and Wales, and Hymes. Among them, Hymes, as cited by Tulasi & Murthy (2022) ④, stands out as the most influential American sociolinguist. Hymes introduced the concept of communicative competence as a response to Chomsky's theory of linguistic competence. He argued that language users possess abilities that surpass the boundaries set by Chomsky, extending beyond the mere identification of grammatically correct sentences. Hymes emphasized the importance of judging the appropriateness of utterances within communicative contexts. Communicative competence, according to Hymes, encompasses practical language use, involving judgments related to grammar,

---

① Harsch, C., & Malone, M. E. (2020). Language proficiency frameworks and scales. In P. Winke, & T. Brunfaut (Eds.) *The routledge handbook of second language acquisition and language testing* (pp. 33-44). Routledge.

② Samovar, L. A., Porter R. E., & Stefani, L. A. (2000). *Communication between cultures*. Foreign Language Teaching and Research Press, Brooks/Thomson Learning Asia.

③ Floyd, K., & Weber, R. (Eds.). (2020). *The handbook of communication science and biology*. Routledge.

④ Tulasi, M. L., & Murthy, N. S. R. (2022). A review of linguistic and communicative competence: An ESP approach. *The Review of Contemporary Scientific and Academic Studies*, 2(3), 1-4.

psychology, sociocultural factors, and probability. It involves applying one's knowledge and skills to language. Canale and Swain, as cited by Kimura (2023)①, proposed a three-dimensional model of communicative competence, comprising grammatical competence, sociolinguistic competence, and strategic competence. On the other hand, Van EK, as cited by Dildora (2022)②, presented a more comprehensive model consisting of six dimensions: linguistic competence, sociolinguistic competence, discourse competence, strategic competence, sociocultural competence, and social competence. Lin and Xie (2005)③ stated that communicative competence results from the integration of knowledge structure, psychological qualities, and communicative practices.

Researchers believe that communication is a shared process of symbolic activity and information exchange, influenced by social, cultural, psychological, and pragmatic factors. "Sharedness" is fundamental to communication, with symbolic activity and information exchange as its core attributes. Social, cultural, and psychological factors are essential for effective communication.

2. Functions of Communication

Communication is vital for human social life, essential for survival, development, relationships, social harmony, and cultural transmission. Its primary function is to transmit information and knowledge, allowing individuals to share thoughts, experiences, and perspectives, thereby fostering understanding and trust. This broadens knowledge, enhances cognitive abilities, and includes both written and nonverbal forms, such as body language and facial expressions. Another key function is emotional expression and exchange. Communication enables individuals to convey feelings, emotions, and attitudes, encoding and decoding thoughts and

---

① Kimura, D. (2023). Diverse conceptualizations of "competence" in second language research and teaching. *LEARN Journal: Language Education and Acquisition Research Network*, 16(1), 18-27.

② Dildora, M. (2022). The six components of communicative ability: Van Ek (1986). *Involta Scientific Journal*, 1(12), 43-45.

③ 林大津 & 谢朝群. (2005). 跨文化交际学：理论与实践. 福建人民出版社.

symbols. This process enhances expressive abilities, empowering effective interaction with others. Communication also helps establish new social relationships, strengthening friendships and promoting social interaction. Through dialogue, individuals understand others' thoughts and values, building relationships based on mutual respect, reducing suspicion, and fostering trust. This contributes to stable, harmonious social networks.

2.1.4 The Relationship Between Language, Culture, and Communication

Language, culture, and communication are inseparable, mutually influencing and depending on each other. Language is the primary tool for communication, conveying cultural content and characteristics while being shaped by cultural backgrounds, which in turn mold communication styles and habits.

First and foremost, language is an integral component of culture, and conversely, culture influences language. Language serves as the principal medium for human expression and communication, conveying thoughts, emotions, knowledge, and values. However, language does not exist in isolation and it is constrained and influenced by cultural contexts. To a certain extent, language reflects the thoughts, values, and lifestyles of individuals within a specific culture. As a product of human civilization, language encompasses a nation's history and cultural background, embodying its worldview, values, customs, and thought processes. It serves as a reflection of a nation's distinctive features. Language not only carries culture but also encapsulates a nation's cultural development. Analyzing various cultural phenomena through language proves to be more convenient and transparent than directly analyzing culture. Scholars like Boas, Humboldt, Sapir, and Whorf have used language to uncover thought patterns and cultural customs, suggesting that language mirrors cognitive development (Chen, 2014)①. Language is central to culture, and learning a language is an effective way to understand and appreciate a nation's culture. It facilitates understanding of

① 陈桂琴.(2014).大学英语跨文化教学中的问题与对策[博士学位论文,上海外国语大学].

foreign cultures, cultural differences, and intercultural communication skills.

Furthermore, culture and communication are intricately linked. Culture fundamentally shapes communication, while communication is the primary means for disseminating and exchanging culture. Edward Hall (2010)① notes that culture is embedded in communication, which itself is an expression of culture. Howard Sypher emphasizes that understanding the relationship between culture and communication is central to intercultural communication research (Lee & Ostwald, 2019)②. This means culture comprises shared behavior patterns (communication) and systems of meaning (language). Essentially, language, communication, and culture are inseparable. Social verbal behavior is influenced by cultural norms and appropriateness, with cultural values shaping communication styles. Both verbal and nonverbal communication reflect these values, expressing beliefs directly or indirectly.

Additionally, language and communication are closely intertwined. Language serves as the foundation of communication, enabling the conveyance of information and expression of meaning. Communication, in turn, is the process of exchanging information and interacting using language and other modalities. Communication relies on language, which facilitates efficient and accurate interaction. Language is both the basis and manifestation of communication. Through social interactions, individuals acquire language and cultural competence, as language and culture are shared through communicative activities.

In summary, language, culture, and communication form the framework of human activities. Language is a crucial mode of communication, culture provides its context, and communication transmits information. Language use reflects values, lifestyles, and thinking patterns, while sociocultural contexts shape the evolution of language. Communication bridges language and culture,

---

① 爱德华·霍尔著；何道宽译.(2010). 无声的语言. 北京大学出版社.

② Lee, J. H., & Ostwald, M. J. (2019). Measuring cognitive complexity in parametric design. *International Journal of Design Creativity and Innovation*, 7(3), 158-178.

enabling cultural sharing through language. Thus, language, culture, and communication are inseparably linked.

2.2 Intercultural Communication Competence

2.2.1 Concept of ICC

ICC research, which has been going on since the 1960s, has made some significant advances over the years. Researchers need to have a firm grasp on the various words associated with the concept of ICC if they are to grasp the various ways in which academics have conceptualized this intricate idea. Different terms from ICC have been used by researchers, such as "intercultural adaptability" "intercultural sensitivity" "cross-cultural competence" "cross-cultural communication competence" "globalization competence" "international competence" "international cognition" "international citizenship" "cultural competence" and "cross-cultural regulation". In this article, however, we use the term "intercultural communication competence" (ICC) because of its widespread use in the field of ICC studies today. Due to the multifaceted nature of ICC, the study looks back over the last 60 years to examine the most important and authoritative definitions of the concept.

When Chen first started talking about ICC, he defined it as the ability to "communicate appropriately and effectively in a specific environment and let the other person respond according to their own intentions" (Senyshyn, 2019)①. The term puts an emphasis on open dialogue and efficient operation.

Additionally, Chen and Starosta defined ICC as the capacity for effective and appropriate communication that results in the anticipated response in a

---

① Senyshyn. R. M. (2019). A first-year seminar course that supports the transition of international students to higher education and fosters the development of intercultural communication competence. *Journal of Intercultural Communication Research*, 48(2), 150-170.

given situation (Ilie, 2019)[①]. Interlocutors can behave in negotiation with each other's cultural identity to reach the goal. Clearly, they began to realize the problem of respecting each other's cultural identity in ICC, and proposed that the definition of ICC should emphasize the communication interaction and cultural identity between the two sides of communication, as well as stress the importance of effective and appropriate communication and environmental factors.

In a similar vein, Rogers and Steinfatt suggested that intercultural competence is one's level of proficiency in communicating with people from a variety of cultural backgrounds (Gu, 2017)[②]. Many academics, including Spitzberg, concur that the two-pronged test for ICC should be whether or not it is appropriate and whether or not it is effective in a given context (Kim et al., 2022)[③]. According to Wiseman, intercultural competence is "the ability to work effectively and appropriately with people from diverse cultural backgrounds" (Zhang & Zhou, 2019)[④]. Kupka proposed that the ICC engages in impression management by helping people from various cultural systems become more self-aware of their similarities and differences and by helping them reach consensus on the meanings of different symbol systems, leading to more harmonious relationships (Zhu & Feng, 2021)[⑤].

Byram, a researcher and educator in the field of second language acquisition, defined linguistic competence as "the ability to interact with people of another nation and culture in a foreign language," highlighting the relevance of intercultural competence (or ICC) to second language learning

---

① Ilie, O. (2019). The intercultural competence. Developing effective intercultural communication skills. *International Conference Knowledge-Based Organization*, 25, 264-268.

② 顾晓乐. (2017). 外语教学中跨文化交际能力培养之理论和实践模型. 外语界, (01), 79-88.

③ Kim, S., Kim K., & Hwang, Y. (2022). Examining the intercultural competence of early-childhood teachers. *European Early Childhood Education Research Journal*, 31(2), 287-303.

④ Zhang, X., & Zhou, M. (2019). Interventions to promote learners' intercultural competence: A meta-analysis. *International Journal of Intercultural Relations*, 71, 31-47.

⑤ Zhu, X., & Feng, A. (2021). ICC nurturing strategies in the context of Sino-foreign institutes. *Theory and Practice in Language Studies*, 11(9), 1072-1079.

(Jackson, 2020)[①]. Rather than taking monolingualism as the default code between intercultural speakers, it calls for interlocutors to have the knowledge, attitudes, and skills to work through differences.

Deardorff used the Delphi method to examine the nebulous meaning of ICC. To paraphrase what she found, "the ability to communicate effectively and appropriately based on personal intercultural knowledge, skills, and attitudes and shown in IC practice" is how ICC researchers typically describe ICC (Yuan, 2022)[②]. Deardorff believes that one's own efforts determine one's success, while the actions of others determine one's suitability.

Yan (2009)[③] defined the connotation of ICC as "the process of communicating information between people, that is, the communication process in which individuals use verbal or nonverbal information to communicate opinions, convey ideas, and express feelings and needs."

According to Lustig and Koester, ICC cannot be achieved without adequate knowledge, appropriate motivation, and well-trained behavior (Li & Dong, 2021)[④]. ICC refers to the characteristics of individual communication, not the characteristics of individuals.

Perry and Southwell believe that ICC refers to the ability to communicate effectively and appropriately with people from various cultural backgrounds (Martin et al., 2021)[⑤].

There are a variety of expressions and emphases for these ideas. According to Hu (2013)[⑥], ICC has a very complex connotation. Diverse individuals have divergent views on how to cultivate it. Therefore, it is

---

① Jackson, J. (2020). *Introducing Language and Intercultural Communication*. Routledge.

② 袁靖. (2022). 非英语专业学生跨文化交际能力量表的构建 [博士学位论文，黑龙江大学].

③ 严明. (2009). 跨文化交际理论研究. 黑龙江大学出版社.

④ Li, F., & Dong, L. (2021). Cultivation of intercultural communication competence for business English majors. *Open Journal of Business and Management*, 09(02), 752-760.

⑤ Martin, T. J., Esteve-Faubel, J. M., & Esteve-Faubel, R. P. (2021). Developing intercultural citizenship competences in higher education by using a literary excerpt in an English as a Foreign Language (EFL) context. *Intercultural Education*, 32(6), 649-666.

⑥ 胡文仲. (2013). 跨文化交际能力在外语教学中如何定位. 外语界, (06), 2-8.

necessary to elucidate some fundamental ideas. Numerous scholars have attempted to define intercultural communication, but none of their definitions has been widely acknowledged. However, almost all of them emphasize effective and appropriate communication between people of different cultures. These definitions provide a theoretical basis for analyzing the ICC elements and establishing a theoretical framework.

Based on the research of renowned intercultural experts from home and abroad, this study defines ICC as the comprehensive ability to communicate and interact with people from different languages and cultures in a variety of intercultural contexts through the effective use of personal intercultural resources, such as awareness, knowledge, skills, and behavior.

2.2.2 Theoretical Models of ICC

Researchers studying ICC used interviews and focus groups to identify psychological traits shared by those who excel in intercultural interactions. They later employed quantitative techniques to explore ICC further, leading to the development of theoretical models. These models abstractly express behaviors and phenomena through in-depth logical thinking, covering key elements and typical characteristics. They reflect behavior mechanisms, derive relationships between elements, and express complex behaviors concisely.

1. Theoretical Models of ICC Outside China

Compositional models, co-orientational models, developmental models, adaptive models, and causal models are just some of the well-known types of models seen in academic settings (Spitzberg & Changnon, 2009)①. These five distinct models are not exclusive of one another, and it is likely that other typological frameworks exist that could also yield fruitful outcomes. Here the researcher only lists the most influential ones in line with the categories.

---

① Spitzberg, B. H., & Changnon, G. (2009). Conceptualizing intercultural competence. In *The sage handbook of intercultural competence* (pp. 2-52), Thousand Oaks, Sage.

(1)Compositional Models

Compositional models are useful for identifying hypothesized components of competence but not for defining their relationships. These models serve as "lists" of qualities, features, and abilities constitutive of competent interaction. Deardorff, using a Delphi expert survey, defined intercultural competence as the ability to communicate effectively and appropriately based on intercultural knowledge, skills, and attitudes, as demonstrated in IC practice (Gefei & Kulich, 2019)①.

Based on this, Deardorff developed a pyramid model of intercultural competence, in which the base is meant to strengthen the top. There are four distinct levels to the model. The bottom of the tower is a necessary attitude: respect, openness, curiosity and discovery; The second level is knowledge, comprehension and skills. There is an interactive relationship between them: the deeper the understanding and perception of cultural awareness, cultural knowledge, cultural information, social language awareness, etc., the faster the improvement of intercultural ability, and vice versa; The third level is the desired internal outcome: adaptability, flexibility, enthnorelative and empathy. Effective and appropriate intercultural communication sits atop the pyramid as an externally focused goal. Successful and appropriate interaction across cultural boundaries is the model's external (visible) goal, while the representation of a conception of fundamental elements and an implicit ordering of those elements is the model's internal (invisible) purpose.

(2)Co-orientational Models

Co-orientational models primarily conceptualize the interactional attainment of intercultural understanding, focusing on criteria like perceptual accuracy, empathy, perspective-taking, clarity, and shared meaning systems. These models emphasize communicative mutuality and shared meanings

① Gefei, S., & Kulich, S. (2019). Applying a Delphi process towards assessing the status and conceptualization of intercultural communication studies in China. *Global Media and China*, 4(3), 381-396.

between parties. The co-orientational model developed by Byram and colleagues, a cornerstone in this field, serves as the theoretical framework for this research (Ömer, 2023)①. Detailed explanations will be provided in Chapter 3.

According to Naoua and Ghedeir (2022)②, Fantini summarized key components involved in linguistic processes necessary for co-orientation. When two people interact, their selective perceptions are "translated" into concepts and thoughts, broken down into semantic clusters, and then into expression-based units (morphology and syntax), finally becoming overt actions (phonology, graphemes, signs, etc.). Fantini describes ICC from multiple perspectives, agreeing that traits identified in componential models—such as flexibility, humor, patience, openness, curiosity, empathy, tolerance for ambiguity, and suspending judgment—facilitate interlocution. These traits are likely organized along four dimensions: awareness, attitudes, knowledge, and skills. Thus, proficiency in a second language and various levels of longitudinal acculturation are likely beneficial.

(3) Developmental Models

Developmental models emphasize progression over time, specifying stages through which competence evolves. Bennett's Developmental Model is a widely used theoretical framework in foreign language education, explaining how people develop intercultural sensitivity through six stages (as cited by Yuan, 2022)③. The first three stages—denial, resistance, and minimization—are ethnocentric, while the last three—acceptance, adaptation, and integration—are ethnorelative. As individuals move from ethnocentrism to ethnorelativism, their ability to cope with cultural differences improves.

---

① Ömer, E. R. E. N. (2023). The explanatory power of intercultural communicative competence among EFL teacher candidates. *Ege Eğitim Dergisi*, 24(1), 29-38.

② Naoua, M., & Ghedeir, B. M. (2022). Investigating the impact of pragmatics on communicative competence models: A historical-descriptive study. *Journal of Al-Shamel for Educational and Social Sciences*, 5,323-5,333.

③ 袁靖. (2022). 非英语专业学生跨文化交际能力量表的构建[博士学位论文，黑龙江大学].

During the denial stage, individuals believe their culture is the only valid one and show little interest in others. In the defensive phase, they recognize cultural contrasts but reject similarities. In the minimization stage, they acknowledge surface differences but emphasize universal human similarities. In the adaptation stage, individuals change their perspectives and behaviors to be culturally appropriate. In the integration stage, they construct multicultural identities and switch between cultures easily. This model effectively explains the dynamic development of intercultural sensitivity, significantly influencing training and research.

(4) Adaptational Models

Adaptational models consider multiple interactants and emphasize their interdependence through a recursive adjusting process. These models can be categorized into two types, with the primary focus being the idea that competence arises from the reciprocal alteration of behaviors, attitudes, and understandings through interactions with individuals from other cultures. Thus, adaptation itself is viewed as a criterion of competence.

Intercultural adaptation is defined by Kim as the process in which an individual establishes (or reconstructs) a relatively stable, mutually beneficial, and effective relationship with a new, unfamiliar, or changing cultural environment after migration. This definition highlights the fact that intercultural adaptation is a process rather than an outcome. She developed a complex adaptation model in which the individual's dispositions (such as cultural/ethnic background, openness, and resilience) enable the interactor to use interaction and mass communication experience to inform the ability to interact with representatives of another culture. Specifically, the model posits that an individual's dispositions (such as cultural/ethnic background, openness, and resilience). By leveraging interpersonal and social sources, individuals can gain deeper insights during the adaptation process. This process is influenced by factors such as pressure to adapt to the dominant culture and the host culture's tolerance of alternative methods. Adaptation involves adjusting one's behavior to align with another participant's cultural perspective. It is a dynamic process where individuals or groups change to maintain internal and external balance in response to environmental fluctuations. The central idea is achieving a "fit" between individuals and their environments to maximize social life possibilities.

(5) Causal Process Models

Models of causal processes reflect the interrelationships among their components in a reasonably specified manner. Moreover, these models are the ones that can be most naturally formalized from or translated into testable propositions. Typically, these models take the shape of a "path model," in which a clear chain of distal-to-proximal ideas leads to a final set of results that serve as a benchmark or criterion of proficiency. To put it another way, one way to think of these models is as constituting a standard for measuring competence.

For instance, Arasaratnam contends (as cited by Nadeem et al., 2018)① that a person who is competent for intercultural communication possesses something in his or her own that enables him or her to be competent for various forms of intercultural communication. This idea was presented in the context of intercultural competence. He argues that empathy fosters competence in two ways: directly, by encouraging participation in intercultural and interpersonal contacts; and indirectly, by influencing involvement in interactions and global perspectives. It is anticipated that these collective variables will influence individuals' motivation to communicate competently, which will in turn influence individuals' competence. As a result, two different theoretical routes can be taken to arrive at competent interaction.

2. Theoretical Models of ICC in China

The concept of ICC was introduced to China in the 1980s. Prominent

---

① Nadeem, M. U., Rosli, M., & Syarizan, D. (2018). An overview of dominant research approaches to measure intercultural communication competence (ICC). *International Journal of Educational Research Review*, 3(4), 141-149.

scholars such as Hu Wenzhong, Gu Jiazu, Guan Shijie, Jia Yuxin, Xu Lisheng, Wang Hongyin, Lin Dajin, Liu Runqing, Chen Guoming, Sun Youzhong, Gao Yihong, and Wang Fuxiang have contributed significantly to the field by publishing numerous books and papers exploring the intricate relationship between language and culture, as well as the importance of cultural education in language teaching (Wu, 2014:7)①.

Although research on ICC in China began in the mid-1980s, its theoretical construction emerged in the 1990s. Scholars have analyzed ICC from the perspective of foreign language teaching, proposing theories by critically absorbing Western perspectives (Dai, 2019)②. Lin (1996)③ discussed ICC's behavioral capacity from three angles: behavioral, structural hierarchy, and ethical perspectives, and elaborated on the required knowledge structure and psychological qualities. Xu (1997)④ identified four levels of ICC: sociolinguistic, textual, grammatical, and strategic, noting that grammatical and strategic levels are less culturally constrained and more universal. Gao (1998)⑤ distinguished between "principles" (essence) and "tools" (peripherals) of ICC, addressing the efficacy-centered research tendency. Principles refer to sound personality and productive communication orientation, while tools include knowledge, skills, and effectiveness. Although these studies have not formed a systematic ICC model, they significantly contribute to China's theoretical development of ICC. Chinese scholars have integrated Western theories with China's specific conditions, providing a preliminary theoretical framework and research methods. After 2000, theoretical construction in China progressed, driven by non-Western theories, with domestic research still focused on foreign language teaching but adopting broader perspectives and refined models.

---

① 吴卫平.(2014).中国大学生跨文化能力综合评价研究[博士学位论文,华中科技大学].

② 戴晓东.(2019).跨文化能力理论发展六十年:历程与展望.外语界,(04),58-66.

③ 林大津.(1996).跨文化交际能力新探.福建师范大学学报(哲学社会科学版),(03),58-62.

④ 许力生.(1997).交际能力与跨文化交际.浙江大学学报(社会科学版),(03),105-110.

⑤ 高一虹.(1998).跨文化交际能力的"道"与"器".语言教学与研究,(03),39-53.

(1)"Going Across" and "Going Beyond" Model

Building upon the "principles" and "tools" framework, Gao (2002)① further proposed the concept of "going across" and "going beyond" as two dimensions of ICC. "Going across" refers to acquiring knowledge and communicative skills of the target culture, as well as the shift in perspective, emotions, and behavioral patterns from one's native culture to the target culture. In contrast, "going beyond" emphasizes the recognition of cultural differences or stereotypes without being constrained by them, enabling one to engage in intercultural communication in an open, flexible, and effective manner, while constructively forming self-identity in the process. "Going across" represents the most direct and superficial level of ICC, mainly manifesting as skills and performance, akin to the "tools." "Going beyond," on the other hand, is the deeper and ultimate ICC level, representing a higher level of cultural understanding and inner growth, similar to the "principles."

The distinction between "going across" and "going beyond" is tailored specifically to the characteristics of English language teaching in China. Chinese learners, coming from developing countries, require special attention to their cultural self-identity in their native language. "Going across" can be viewed as a preparatory stage for "going beyond." When learners encounter a new culture, they often start with widely held cultural stereotypes. With a deeper understanding of the target culture, learners with an open mindset and a reflective consciousness will gradually comprehend the multilayered nature of culture, making choices from numerous possible factors and integrating them into their self-identity. However, the development of ICC can stagnate at the "going across" stage. In particular, learners with a "non-productive orientation," such as those with a "hoarding orientation" who are satisfied with accumulating cultural knowledge or a "market orientation" who are focused on exchanging cultural knowledge and skills for practical benefits, may appear "effective" externally but struggle to achieve inner growth.

---

① 高一虹. (2002). 跨文化交际能力的培养:"跨越"与"超越". 外语与外语教学, (10), 27-31.

(2)ICC Model Based on the Syllabus 2000

Yang and Zhuang (2007)① argue that ICC should be the ultimate goal of foreign language teaching, while the improvement of comprehensive language proficiency is a primary task, serving as a means and foundation for achieving ICC. Ultimately, ICC is demonstrated through effective communication and the fulfillment of specific communication goals. Based on the relevant requirements of the *Syllabus for English Teaching in Colleges and Universities* (*2000*), they constructed a framework for ICC in foreign language teaching, comprising four interconnected and indispensable systems of abilities: global mentality, cultural adaptation, knowledge, and communication management.

These four abilities exist in a hierarchical relationship. Firstly, global mentality serves as the foundation of ICC. Having global mentality and sensitivity to cultural differences is a prerequisite for cultural adaptation and the acquisition of cultural knowledge. Secondly, cultural adaptation ability is the second tier of ICC. Based on global mentality, learners cultivate psychological adaptation and flexibility, gradually achieving cultural adaptation. Thirdly, the acquisition of knowledge is built upon global mentality and cultural adaptation. Learners need to possess global mentality and cultural adaptation ability to approach cultural differences with the correct mindset and better grasp intercultural knowledge through comparing and identifying different cultures, understanding and analyzing culture with an intercultural mindset. Finally, communication management represents the highest level of ICC. Through effective communication management, learners can integrate global mentality, cultural adaptation, and cultural knowledge, demonstrating the comprehensiveness and depth of ICC in actual communication.

(3)Progressive-Interactive ICC Model

Based on the new requirements for communicators' intercultural personality in the context of globalization, Xu & Sun (2013)② proposed a progressive-

---

① 杨盈 & 庄恩平. (2007). 构建外语教学跨文化交际能力框架. 外语界, (04), 13-21+43.

② 许力生 & 孙淑女. (2013). 跨文化能力递进—交互培养模式构建. 浙江大学学报(人文社会科学版), (04), 113-121.

interactive ICC model. This model takes the context of globalization as its backdrop and aims to cultivate open intercultural personalities with a multicultural awareness as the ultimate goal of ICC cultivation. In terms of content, this model covers three levels: emotional, cognitive, and behavioral, which are transformed into three educational categories: knowledge, motivation, and skills. Through a progressive approach of knowledge acquisition, motivation cultivation, and skill training, learners develop a tolerant and open attitude towards cultural differences based on their mastery of linguistic and world cultural knowledge, ultimately achieving mutually understandable and acceptable intercultural communication outcomes in interactive communication. This model incorporates five elements: motivation, knowledge, skills, context, and effect, exploring the relationship between motivation, knowledge, and skills, emphasizing the interactive nature of communication, and placing the entire process of ICC cultivation in the context of communication with globalization as its realistic foundation. It should be noted that while knowledge acquisition, motivation cultivation, and skill training are progressive, this does not mean that ICC cultivation is a linear process. Knowledge is the foundation, motivation is the prerequisite, and skills are the key. Learners need to possess a certain level of linguistic and cultural knowledge to establish correct attitudes in cultural comparisons, thereby cultivating positive communication motivation. Meanwhile, with corresponding linguistic and cultural knowledge and positive motivation, learners can effectively adjust and adapt in communication to achieve the desired communication goals.

(4)Chinese-Teacher Perspective ICC Model

Dai (2022)① emphasizes that ICC is context-dependent, referring to the ability to communicate appropriately and effectively in intercultural situations. Through three rounds of questionnaire surveys among 84 teachers from 46 universities in China and 68 intercultural experts from 8 countries, Dai

---

① 戴晓东.(2022).中国教师视角的跨文化能力模型建构.外语界,(05),20-28.

constructed a theoretical ICC model from the perspective of Chinese teachers, encompassing five dimensions: attitude, knowledge, awareness, skills, and expected goals.

The first dimension, attitude, involves the communicator's emotional tendencies such as respect, openness, prudence, and empathy. The second dimension, knowledge, refers to understanding cultural information and communication behaviors, including one's own cultural knowledge, other countries' cultural knowledge, social linguistic knowledge, and communication strategy knowledge. The third dimension, awareness, emphasizes a clear understanding of held knowledge and beliefs, and the ability to self-monitor, adjust, and reflect, including cultural self-awareness, diversity awareness, self-and-others awareness, and growth-oriented reflective awareness. The fourth dimension, skills, involves the behavioral ability to use the first three dimensions to engage in intercultural communication and complete communication tasks, including listening and observation skills, adjustment and adaptation skills, language and non-verbal skills, and interactive management skills. The fifth dimension, expected goals, refers to the results the communicator aims to achieve, such as a global mindset, inclusive mutual understanding, appropriate and effective behavior, and narrowing cultural gaps. These dimensions are interrelated and work together to achieve the expected goals of intercultural communication, and achieving these goals further promotes the improvement of attitude, knowledge, awareness, and skills, leading to progressive ICC development.

(5) IMCSICD Model

Zhang and Yao (2020)① proposed a "4-3-2-1" theoretical framework for ICC development, integrating four perspectives (communicative behavior, interpersonal relationship, cultural conflict, and identity), three levels (cognitive understanding, emotional attitude, and behavioral skills), two

① 张红玲 & 姚春雨. (2020). 建构中国学生跨文化能力发展一体化模型. 外语界, (04), 35-44+53.

contexts (work and life), and one platform (foreign language education). They further developed the Integrated Model for Chinese Students' Intercultural Competence Development (IMCSICD), tailored to the needs and characteristics of Chinese students.

The IMCSICD model emphasizes three core levels: cognitive understanding, emotional attitude, and behavioral skills. At the cognitive understanding level, it involves recognizing the world's complexity, understanding the relationship between culture, individuals, and society, and having a profound grasp of one's own culture and other cultures. The emotional attitude level focuses on fostering qualities such as respect, tolerance, understanding, and appreciation, along with values like national identity, global perspective, and international understanding. Finally, the level of behavioral skills is about developing basic skills such as listening, observation, description, and comparison, and practical skills such as communication, conflict management, reflection evaluation, and learning innovation.

This model emphasizes the synchronous development of ICC and foreign language proficiency, ensuring that this ability can run through the entire education process from primary school to university. Through the IMCSICD model, we can clearly see the importance of cultivating ICC and its practical path in education, helping Chinese students better showcase their talents on the global stage and contribute Chinese wisdom to the world's development.

3. Synthesis

Foreign scholars have proposed various ICC models, each with unique features and limitations. Deardorff's Pyramid Model details ICC components but has a simple research procedure and overlapping ideas. Fantini's Intercultural Interlocutor Competence Model includes various linguistic capabilities and non-linguistic variables, but its detailed language components are impractical. Bennett's Developmental Model outlines the progression from ethnocentric to ethnorelative stages but lacks discussion on the concept of intercultural competence. Kim's Adaptational Model focuses on assimilation or cultural integration, aligning with mainstream ideology but neglecting individual and group needs in intercultural adaptation. Arasaratnam's Causal Process Model emphasizes the cognitive level but inadequately covers behavioral aspects and stages of intercultural competence.

Chinese scholars, while critically absorbing Western theories, have proposed theories with Chinese characteristics. Gao's "Going Across" and "Going Beyond" Model distinguishes between superficial and deep levels of ICC, but students often stagnate at the "Going Across" stage, making it difficult to reach the "Going Beyond" stage. The ICC framework constructed by Yang and Zhuang emphasizes four levels of ICC, but in practice, it is challenging to implement and assess the development of these competencies. Xu and Sun's Progressive-Interactive ICC Model gradually develops ICC through knowledge acquisition, motivation cultivation, and skill training, but it lacks effective methods for concrete implementation. Yang's School Education ICC Model, while systematic, requires further research on its application at different educational stages. Dai's Chinese-Teacher Perspective ICC Model emphasizes contextual relevance and effective communication ability, but the specific implementation path remains unclear. The IMCSICD Model proposed by Zhang and Yao emphasizes the simultaneous development of ICC and foreign language proficiency, but its effectiveness is yet to be validated.

Despite significant progress in ICC research, current theoretical models still need improvement in terms of systematization, comprehensiveness, and cultural adaptability. Especially in China, a country with rich cultural heritage and a unique educational environment, it is crucial to develop an ICC model that both aligns with Chinese cultural characteristics and meets the practical needs of contemporary university students. Constructing a theoretical ICC competence model suitable for Chinese university students not only expands and deepens existing theories but also further refines the theoretical system of ICC. This model will integrate the essence of both domestic and international research, deeply considering the cultural background, cognitive characteristics, and practical needs of Chinese university students in international communication. This approach aims to establish a systematic and practical theoretical framework. With this framework, we can provide more precise theoretical guidance for foreign language education, especially for foreign language education aimed at international communication, thereby promoting the standardized and systematic development of ICC education. Meanwhile, theory must be translated into practice to realize its true value. Therefore, developing a practical model suitable for Chinese foreign language classroom teaching is equally crucial. This model will integrate the latest theoretical research with practical experience, providing foreign language teachers with a set of effective, operable teaching strategies and methods. This ensures that the cultivation of ICC goes beyond theoretical discussions and is genuinely integrated into daily teaching, thereby enhancing students' ICC. This exploration and attempt will contribute beneficially to the reform and innovation of foreign language education in China.

In conclusion, this study asserts that developing theoretical and practical ICC models for Chinese university students holds significant academic and practical value. The goal is to enhance students' ICC, improve their international communication abilities, and advance foreign language education. This research aims to offer scientific and systematic theoretical support and practical guidance for ICC education, fostering the cultivation of talents with international vision and ICC in China.

2.2.3 Evaluation Tools of ICC

Prior to the 1990s, few researchers devised research scales for intercultural competence. Notable examples include the Behavioral Assessment Scale for Intercultural Competence (BASIC) (Ruben & Kealey, 1979, cited in Chen & Gabrenya, 2021)① and the Intercultural Sensitivity Inventory (ISCI) (Bhawuk & Brislin, 1992, cited in Morales, 2017)②. The

① Chen, X. W., & Gabrenya, W. K. (2021). In search of cross-cultural competence: A comprehensive review of five measurement instruments. *International Journal of Intercultural Relations*, 82, 37-55.

② Morales, A. H. (2017). Intercultural sensitivity, gender, and nationality of third culture kids attending an international high school. *Journal of International Education Research*, 13(1), 35-44.

ISCI is a self-report method evaluating individuals based on their ability to communicate and describe their behaviors when interacting with people from other cultures. Researchers use the BASIC scale to assess ICC through behavior, analyzing necessary skills such as respect for others, knowledge orientation, and empathy. According to Chen and Gabrenya (2023)①, Koester and Olebe developed a fundamental measure incorporating traditional standards like skills, knowledge, and attitude, and introducing new elements like respect for others, task-appropriate behavior, tolerance for ambiguity, and interactive attitude.

The Intercultural Development Inventory (IDI) by Hammer and Bennett (1998) and the Intercultural Adaptability Inventory (CCAI) by Kelley and Meyers (1995) are two widely cited methods. The IDI, based on the intercultural sensitivity model, includes a 44-item descriptive scale primarily used to evaluate ICC development. In the past decade, assessment techniques like the Intercultural Sensitivity Index (ISI) and the Assessment of Intercultural Competence (AIC) have gained popularity. Fantini developed the Your Objectives Guidelines & Assessment (YOGA) method for ICC evaluation. The AIC evaluation scale comprises 90 descriptive items categorized into consciousness, attitude, abilities, knowledge, and second language proficiency.

Most current evaluation tools for ICC rely on self-reports, primarily in the form of questionnaires, emphasizing the general structure of ICC. The Intercultural Development Inventory (IDI) is another tool for assessing intercultural competence. Unlike other tools, the IDI focuses more on the continuity of the evaluation process rather than just the overall structure of ICC. However, some researchers question the credibility of certain evaluation tools, particularly those using self-report forms for indirect evaluation. Kohli Bagwe and Haskollar (2020)② noted that Altshuler, Sussman, and Kachur's

---

① Chen, X., & Gabrenya, W. (2023). Is there really any good way to measure cultural intelligence, and what exactly is it, anyway? In D. C. Thomas, & Y. Liao(Eds.) *Handbook of cultural intelligence research* (pp. 72-88). Edward Elgar Publishing.

② Kohli Bagwe, T., & Haskollar, E. (2020). Variables impacting intercultural competence: A systematic literature review. *Journal of Intercultural Communication Research*, 49(4), 346-371.

research revealed discrepancies between participants' self-perceptions of their intercultural awareness and sensitivity and their actual abilities. Researchers have long been skeptical about the reliability and honesty of self-assessments. Despite these potential flaws, self-report surveys remain the primary form of indirect evaluation due to their efficiency, speed, and convenience in data collection and analysis.

Existing ICC evaluation scales are varied, but applying these scales to this study is impractical. While these scales play an important role in assessing ICC levels and providing feedback, there were also some issues with the research scales. First, these scales vary in the theoretical basis for construction, and the contents of the scales are quite different. To prevent inappropriate use, it is essential to make a thoughtful selection of the scales that correspond to the evaluation contents and evaluation objectives prior to their application. Furthermore, some research scales were developed for particular populations, such as overseas employees, diplomats, foreign students, travelers, immigrants, and multinational corporations, making them inappropriate for determining the level of proficiency in foreign languages possessed by Chinese college students. In addition, the majority of the existing scales are intended in commercial settings, making it extremely costly to submit an application and challenging to find widespread application in the field of higher education in China. As a result, these scales are insufficient to provide necessary information for China's cultivation of international talents' ICC.

Research on ICC scales in China has only emerged in the past 10 years, and a unified, concrete national standard for ICC teaching has not yet been established. Wu (2014)① made a notable contribution by constructing an ICC evaluation scale with four main dimensions, divided into six factors: knowledge of one's own culture, knowledge of foreign cultures, attitudes, intercultural communication skills, intercultural cognitive skills, and awareness. Shen and Gao (2015)② developed the ICC Inventory for Chinese

① 吴卫平. (2014). 中国大学生跨文化能力综合评价研究[博士学位论文，华中科技大学].

② 沈鞠明 & 高永晨. (2015). 基于知行合一模式的中国大学生跨文化交际能力测评量表构建研究. 中国外语，(03)，14-21.

College Students (ICCICS), based on integrating knowledge and practice. The knowledge system comprises knowledge, awareness, and thinking modules, while the behavioral system includes attitude, intercultural communication skills, and communication strategy modules. Another important contribution is Sun's (2019)① work, which constructed a theoretical and element-based test for German majors' ICC through expert interviews, covering cognitive, emotional, and behavioral dimensions. Yuan (2022)② developed a scale for non-English majors' ICC, consisting of 99 descriptive statements organized into six subscales: psychological adaptability, cultural knowledge, cultural contrast awareness, global consciousness, critical thinking, and strategic ability. The scale is subdivided into three levels of difficulty—basic, intermediate, and advanced—aiming to accurately describe non-English majors' intercultural learning outcomes from entry to proficiency in university English courses.

These scales provide effective tools for assessing ICC of university students and play a crucial role in enhancing the quality of ICC cultivation in college English teaching. However, these scales still face certain limitations in their application. Firstly, the grade settings and evaluation criteria of the scales need to be further refined and clarified to ensure the accuracy and reliability of the assessment results. Secondly, the scales mainly focus on foreign language proficiency and communication skills in their measurement content, while overlooking the consideration of key abilities such as global perspective and critical thinking, which limits their application in comprehensively assessing the ICC of university students to a certain extent. Thirdly, existing scales are mostly based on foreign research results, which may lead to deviations in assessing Chinese university students and fail to accurately reflect their unique intercultural communication ability. To meet the diverse needs of university students in intercultural learning, the evaluation scale needs to cover various aspects such as language proficiency,

---

① 孙永春. (2019). 跨文化能力评价模式建构及测试. 外语学刊, (03), 73-78.

② 袁靖. (2022). 非英语专业学生跨文化交际能力量表的构建 [博士学位论文, 黑龙江大学].

communication skills, global perspective, and critical thinking, and it should also be able to conduct individualized assessments based on the characteristics and needs of each student. Therefore, we need continue to delve deeply into the connotation and assessment methods of ICC, explore a scientific system for ICC cultivation, and contribute to cultivating talents with ICC.

2.3 Cultivating ICC in Foreign Language Teaching in China

2.3.1 Intercultural Communication and Foreign Language Teaching

The previous definitions and descriptions of language, culture, communication, and ICC highlight the significance of language as a symbol. In foreign language teaching, it is crucial to have a clear understanding of the form, meaning, and rules governing the combination of language symbols. Language also functions as a symbol of culture. Comprehensive foreign language teaching should not only encompass the cultural background knowledge embedded in language structures, semantic systems, and usage but also consider the social and cultural factors of the language-speaking country, as well as the social and psychological factors of the learners. Communication involves the exchange of information among individuals from diverse cultural backgrounds, necessitating adherence to requirements such as "symbolic information commonality" and "cultural information sharing." Teaching itself is a form of communication. Thus, foreign language teaching must utilize language as a tool for intercultural communication to enable learners to genuinely master the target language. Foreign language teaching can be likened to a needle that threads and weaves language, culture, and communication together, providing a vital pathway for successful intercultural communication.

Furthermore, foreign language dissemination entails cross-border, cross-cultural, and cross-linguistic communication. Cross-border communication involves challenges related to politics and transmission. Cross-cultural communication grapples with the complex and diverse nature of cultural differences. Cross-linguistic communication revolves around language (both written and spoken) as a means of communication. Given the inseparable relationship between language and culture, numerous issues in this domain intertwine with intercultural problems. Therefore, it is evident that the central issues in foreign language dissemination revolve around language, culture, and communication.

In the early stages of foreign language learning, the primary focus of foreign language teaching was to teach the rules of language structure, and learners' goals were limited to language proficiency, particularly in grammar skills. However, in the 1960s and 1970s, the emergence of new linguistic schools like sociolinguistics and pragmatics led to a shift in the demands on foreign language learners from language proficiency to communicative competence. As society developed and global interactions became increasingly interconnected, cultural contact became more frequent. As a result, the goals of foreign language teaching expanded from communicative competence to ICC. In China, most researchers engaged in intercultural communication studies are university foreign language teachers, and the specific methods and approaches for cultivating ICC are closely intertwined with foreign language teaching.

Gao (2002)① discussed the cultivation of ICC from a philosophical perspective, highlighting the importance of "going across" and "going beyond" cultures. While "going across" is the focus of cultural teaching, "going beyond" should be considered a more significant educational objective. Zhuang (2006)② argued that the cultivation of ICC should be integrated throughout the entire process of foreign language teaching and incorporated into the development of each language skill. Zhang (2007)③ explored ICC cultivation

---

① 高一虹. (2002). 跨文化交际能力的培养:"跨越"与"超越". 外语与外语教学, (10), 27-31.

② 庄恩平. (2006). 跨文化能力:我国21世纪人才必备的能力——"2006跨文化交际国际学术研讨会"综述. 外语界, (05), 79-80.

③ 张红玲. (2007). 跨文化外语教学. 上海外语教育出版社.

by studying intercultural foreign language teaching syllabi, teaching principles and methods, teaching materials, testing, and teacher resources. Kang (2010)① suggested that intercultural awareness should be fostered through diverse educational activities, combining in-class immersion and out-of-class enrichment. Yan (2012)② emphasized the need to develop students' cultural literacy and help them overcome cultural barriers, bridging the "cultural divide" between Chinese culture and world culture to construct a "cultural bridge." Liu and Shan (2017)③ analyzed the shared core and differences in cultivating ICC in three types of courses: "general foreign languages," "special-purpose foreign languages," and "intercultural communication," using the theory of legitimation of language codes. Peng, et al. (2020)④ constructed a theoretical and practical model for intercultural foreign language teaching that reflects the inseparable relationship between experiential, speculative, and interactive learning, the language course platform, and the cultivation of intercultural competence in the Chinese context. Lv and Yu (2021)⑤ pointed out that incorporating a two-way cultural teaching approach, considering both the target language culture and the learners' native culture, is a promising solution to address the issue of "cultural aphasia" in foreign language learners and an effective pathway to meet the challenges of cultivating comprehensive intercultural communication talents.

In the 21st century, there is a growing need for diverse and internationally-oriented foreign language talents, highlighting the significance of ICC for university students. This demand necessitates the strong emphasis on cultivating ICC in the goals of university education, at both the macro and

---

① 康淑敏. (2010). 外语教育中的文化意识培养. 教育研究, (08), 85-89.

② 颜静兰. (2012). 英语专业学生作文能力与教学状况探析——以 2011 年英语专业四级考试作文分析为例. 外语测试与教学, (01), 11-20.

③ 刘承宇 & 单菲菲. (2017). 大学英语课程的跨文化交际能力共核与差异——基于合法化语码理论的《大学外语教学指南》解读. 外语界, (04), 79-87.

④ 彭仁忠,付容容 & 吴卫平. (2020). 新时代背景下跨文化外语教学理论模型和实践模型研究. 外语界, (04), 45-53.

⑤ 吕丽盼 & 俞理明. (2021). 双向文化教学——论外语教学跨文化交际能力培养. 中国外语, (04), 62-67.

micro levels. The MOE of the PRC recognizes the importance of developing ICC from the perspective of national development strategy. As early as 2007, the MOE of the PRC issued the *Teaching Requirements for College Foreign Language Courses*, which emphasized the goal of fostering students' comprehensive application of foreign languages, particularly their listening and speaking abilities, enabling them to effectively communicate in foreign languages for future studies, work, and social interactions. This approach also aims to enhance their autonomous learning skills and comprehensive cultural literacy to adapt to China's social development and international exchanges.

The *Medium- and Long-Term Education Reform and Development Outline* (*2010-2020*) explicitly stated the objective of nurturing a large number of internationally-minded talents who are familiar with international rules, capable of engaging in international affairs and competition. Cultivating foreign language talents with ICC has become a primary goal of modern foreign language teaching. The *Guide 2020* outlined requirements for intercultural education, aiming to foster students' intercultural awareness, deepen their understanding of different cultures, and enhance their ICC. These guidelines ensure that the content and scheduling of college foreign language courses incorporate intercultural communication and fulfill the demands of international perspectives and ICC necessary for international cooperation, international communication, and international influence.

Intercultural communication is a multidisciplinary and interdisciplinary field of research that encompasses language and culture, communication and culture, intercultural perception, and intercultural adaptation. Consequently, the cultivation of ICC is a complex process that necessitates close collaboration across different disciplines and the support of the social and educational environment.

2.3.2 Cultivation of ICC in Foreign Language Education

Education about other cultures is the most important part of learning a foreign language. The capacity to speak a foreign language and the cultivation of ICC are organically integrated through the study of intercultural foreign language education. Not only does it place a significant emphasis on the instruction of linguistic knowledge and abilities, but it also places an emphasis on the fundamental aspects of education in a foreign language, such as the construction of discourse, the interaction in cultural exchange, the expansion of one's vision, and the development of one's cultural identity. Education in conventional foreign languages lacks the depth and breadth of this subject's connotation and extension, both of which are vastly superior. In this new period, being able to cultivate international talents with Chinese sentiments and a global vision, proficiency in foreign languages, and the ability to communicate effectively across international boundaries has emerged as an important priority. Even though intercultural education in the realm of higher education should be integrated into all aspects of the learning process, it is not contingent on any one particular subject. However, because the actual condition of college foreign language education in China is as it is, the majority of intercultural education for college students is implemented in college English classes since these classes have the largest audience. College English is the main component of China's higher education in foreign languages and intercultural education. It is also an essential method for the cultivation of international talents in the new era, and it is connected to the future personal and professional development of each college student. College English is a public basic course that is required of all Chinese college students.

It is stated explicitly in the *Guide 2020* that college-level English classes are meant to help students develop ICC by helping them gain insight into other societies and cultures through the medium of English (NACTELHE, 2020)①. At the collegiate level, students can choose from courses of general English, English for specific objectives, or intercultural communication English. According to Liu and Shan's (2017) ② interpretation of the *Guide 2020*,

---

① 高等学校大学外语教学指导委员会(The National Administrative Committee on Teaching English Language in Higher Education, NACTELHE). 2020. 大学英语教学指南(2020 版). 高等教育出版社.

② 刘承宇 & 单菲菲. (2017). 大学英语课程的跨文化交际能力共核与差异——基于合法化语码理论的《大学英语教学指南》解读. 外语界, (04), 79-87.

grounded in the canon law theory of codes, all three varieties of college-level English classes require students to develop their intercultural communicative skills.

The *Guide 2020* proposes ICC-related instructional requirements (see Table 2-1). Table 2-1 on the following page demonstrates that the English curriculum at the college level requires students to be aware of cultural differences and to be able to employ communication strategies from the three levels of foundation, advancement, and development. However, these are insufficient to completely describe the ICC that college students should possess, nor can they provide ICC standards for college English courses. What type of ICC should college students acquire through the study of English education in order to participate in multicultural learning and work?

Table 2-1 Requirements for Intercultural Education of College English

Level	ICC Description	Target Students
Foundation	When communicating with people from different cultural backgrounds, they can observe the cultural and value differences between them, and can use basic communication strategies according to communication needs.	Most students with basic English learning needs.
Advancement	When communicating with people from different cultural backgrounds, they can better cope with the differences in culture and values with the other party, and can better use communication strategies according to communication needs.	Students who have a good English foundation and high learning needs at the time of enrollment.
Development	When communicating with people from different cultural backgrounds, they should be able to cope with the differences in culture and values with the other party, and be able to properly use communication strategies according to different communication situations, communication occasions and communication objects.	Students who are cultivated to the special needs of talent training plan and who can spare no effort in learning.

China's college foreign language education in the new era should take on the urgent mission of intercultural and international talent training as soon as possible. This is true whether one looks at the pressing need for talents from China in a holistic way or at the trend of development in global higher education. This is not only a once-in-a-lifetime chance, but also the zenith of foreign-language education in Chinese colleges, which has risen like a phoenix from the ashes.

Prior research has demonstrated the cognitive and socio-cultural benefits of foreign language education, but the majority of these studies view ICC as the individual characteristics of communicators and pay little attention to the connection between foreign language education and ICC. In addition, based on the results of an empirical study of foreign language education in China, language instructors have investigated and commented on the cultivation of ICC in language classes. However, there are not many studies that investigate the correlation between foreign language education and ICC. Consequently, ICC in foreign language education remains a neglected issue. In light of the practical issue of how to cultivate ICC in a foreign language classroom, the extant explanation, guidance, and evidence of research findings are insufficient. The cultivation of ICC in actual foreign language education contexts is still ungoverned, and ICC enchantment in universities is a test-driven development, which impacts the quality of foreign language education and the effectiveness of international talent training. Obviously, an ICC paradigm that is compatible with the context of chinese foreign language education must be developed immediately.

2.4 Summary

This chapter offers a comprehensive overview of the current research status and relevant theories in the field of study. The researcher begins by explaining the fundamental concepts and functions of language, culture, and communication, highlighting the intricate relationship among these elements, where they mutually influence and shape one another. This interplay establishes a crucial connection between intercultural communication and foreign language teaching. Subsequently, the researchers discuss the concept of ICC, classic models of intercultural communication, and assessment scales for evaluating ICC. Lastly, the chapter delves into the correlation between ICC and foreign language teaching in China, examining the theoretical framework of intercultural communication in language instruction and the cultivation of ICC. By examining the current research status and relevant theories, this analysis provides both practical evidence and theoretical guidance for determining research design and methods. The following chapter will present the theoretical foundation of this study and introduce the research design and methods.

Chapter 3
Construction of ICC Framework

This chapter aims to establish the theoretical basis, clarify the research questions, outline the design approach, and define the specific research methods employed in the study. It is organized into five sections. The first section provides the theoretical foundation, while the second section introduces both the overall and specific research questions. In the third section, the design approach is presented, including the principles of research design, the selection of research subjects, a description of the data collection and analysis methods, and a discussion on academic ethics. The fourth section utilizes tables to illustrate the specific research methods employed. Finally, the chapter concludes with a summary highlighting the key points discussed.

3.1 Theoretical Framework

The theoretical and empirical components of a study are interconnected; otherwise, it would be impossible to extract the essence of phenomena. The organization of the theoretical framework allows for a precise structure in the empirical section, providing guidance for research design and supporting the argumentation of the main research questions. In accordance with the research objectives and the needs of the core research questions, this study adopts Byram's ICC Model as the theoretical framework. This choice serves as a foundation for the exploration of ICC and its related aspects in the study.

The theory of intercultural communication has been constructed by scholars since the 1960s from a variety of perspectives, which has significantly improved our comprehension of it. According to Jackson (2020), Byram's ICC model is the most credible one when it comes to teaching a foreign language, which is why it was chosen to serve as the theoretical foundation for this particular research project.

Byram concentrates on language as the central component of his model and incorporates cultural identity and cultural comprehension into the conceptual definition of language. He broke ICC down into its four primary components, which are linguistic competence, sociolinguistic competence, discourse competence, and intercultural competence, the latter of which includes attitudes, knowledge, skills, and a variety of other components.

Apart from the elements of language, the ICC model pays attention to the specific contents of interculture competence as follows: A) Attitudes. They refer to the curiosity, openness, tolerance and acceptance of other cultures in the face of cultural differences, rather than the attachment to one's own culture. B) Knowledge. It encompasses, on the one hand, knowledge of the processes of interaction at the individual and societal levels, and, on the other, knowledge about social groupings and their cultures in one's own nation and the interlocutor's country. C) Skills of interpreting and relating. In order to decipher the allusions and meanings hidden inside a "document" (used here in its broadest sense) from another country, a reader needs both contextual information and a framework of background knowledge. D) Skills of discovering and interacting. Acquiring a new cultural perspective involves learning about a society and its norms, and then using what you've learned to communicate and interact effectively with others from that culture. E) Political education/critical cultural awareness. The ability to assess the practices and goods of one's own culture and those of other nations in light of unambiguous normative standards. There are five subelements: attitudes, knowledge, skills of interpreting and relating, skills of discovering and interacting, political education/critical cultural awareness. The factors of knowledge and attitude are preconditions, and the nature of intercultural communication processes is a function of the skills, which may be split into two broad categories that are related to one another: skills of interpreting and relating, and skills of discovering and interacting. In theory, these four facets of intercultural interaction can be learned through hands-on experience and reflection within a pedagogy that emphasizes the cultivation of critical cultural awareness with regard to both the learner's own culture and that of other nations.

This model takes into account linguistic competence, sociolinguistic competence, discourse competence, and intercultural competence. Its overarching goal is to develop "intercultural people" from language learners of other languages. By doing so, they may be given the ability to acknowledge the existence of cultural differences, to preserve their cultural identities throughout the process of dynamic intercultural communication, and to search for common ground while retaining their differences. Through active communication characterized by mutual respect and tolerance, the space for intercultural communication will be expanded, and the intuitive sense of intercultural experience will be transformed into ICC founded on critical thinking.

For characterizing ICC among college students, this model excels over alternatives. Firstly, the model categorizes ICC into four subcategories that are equally important and work together to improve ICC as a whole, which is in line with the widespread acceptance of ICC in the field of foreign language teaching. The model is a product of the interplay and merging of its parts. The above factors are acquired through experience and thought in the education of political philosophy and critical cultural awareness, and are manifested as intercultural curiosity, openness, and inclusiveness. In the end, it demonstrates successful and appropriate intercultural communication behavior. Classifying competence will prevent overlap between the dimensions at all levels and can greatly reduce ambiguity surrounding the idea of competence, making it an approachable framework for describing ICC. Thirdly, this model' aims to train communicators to be better able to appreciate, understand, and work with varying cultural contexts. Educating "talents with world vision, international awareness and ICC, who are familiar with international rules and are proficient in international negotiations" is a stated goal of the English curriculum at the university level (NACTELHE, 2020)①, and this aligns with the general understanding of what "ICC" means in the field of foreign language teaching. Finally, the model has been used in the study of the ICC scale. The scientific character and impact of the model are partially explained by the fact that it serves as the theoretical foundation for tools like the Intercultural Competence Assessment, which is used by the European Union's Leonardo da Vinci Program. Therefore, Byram's ICC model was used for this study.

3.2 Research Design

Building upon the previous sections, this chapter will employ the method of grounded theory's three-level coding to identify the components of the ICC framework. This research design aims to systematically analyze and categorize the data, allowing for a comprehensive understanding of the ICC framework.

3.2.1 Research Method

Grounded Theory was initially proposed by Barney Glaser and Anselm Strauss in their book *The Discovery of Grounded Theory* in 1967. It is a research method that extracts theories through the analysis and organization of raw data, without predetermined assumptions (Glaser & Holton, 2007)②. They explicitly established principles and procedures that encourage researchers to innovate theoretically based on the raw material. Grounded Theory is widely recognized because the theories generated through this method can be traced back to the original data, allowing for iterative testing

① 高等学校大学外语教学指导委员会(The National Administrative Committee on Teaching English Language in Higher Education, NACTELHE). 2020. 大学英语教学指南(2020版). 高等教育出版社.

② Glaser, B., & Holton, J. (2007). *The grounded theory seminar reader*. Sociology Press.

and continuous improvement of conclusions (Strauss, 1987) ①. Furthermore, since the conclusions are derived from the data, subjective influences are minimized. These characteristics make grounded theory a reliable and evidence-based qualitative research method.

Grounded theory emphasizes an iterative process, where theory formation is a continual comparison of literature, ideas, and concepts until it takes shape. It prioritizes theoretical sampling to achieve information saturation rather than relying on random sampling. Theoretical sensitivity guides literature review and data analysis. The process involves coding, memos, and concepts, analyzing data sentence by sentence to identify and generalize phenomena. Memos facilitate the transition from description to conceptualization. Constant comparison ensures theory emergence by comparing data with data, coding with coding, and concepts with literature. Theoretical saturation occurs when no new categories emerge, ensuring the theory's integrity. Grounded theory values fit, workability, relevance, and modifiability, with "fit" being foundational, meaning categories derive from data. "Workability" indicates the theory's ability to predict and explain phenomena. "Relevance" ensures the theory's connection to the research problem, while "modifiability" allows adaptation to new data. Grounded theory aims to provide theoretical explanations of fundamental social processes rather than universal laws (Jing, 2017) ②.

With these benefits, it is appropriate for the study of interpersonal interactions, personal processes, and the reciprocal impact of people's actions on wider societal processes (Charmaz, 1995)③. This study employs grounded theory to construct the central structure of the ICC model from existing relevant literature. Grounded theory codes, categorizes, and summarizes data, and converts them into concepts and categories, producing a clear analytic

---

① Strauss, A. L. (1987). *Qualitative analysis for social scientists*. Cambridge University Press.

② 景怀斌. (2017). 扎根理论编码的"理论鸿沟"及"类故理"跨越. 武汉大学学报:(哲学社会科学版), (06), 109-119.

③ Charmaz, K. (1995). Grounded theory. In Smith, J., Harré, R. & Langenhove, L. (Ed.), *Rethinking methods in psychology* (pp. 27-65), Sage.

result that allows researchers to examine the environment and background of Chinese college students and disclose the nature of their behavior and thoughts. In addition, grounded theory mandates researchers to maintain a neutral and objective stance throughout the research process, adopt a variety of data collection and analysis techniques, and in tandem cross-check and repeatedly verify the data to ensure the credibility and efficacy of the analysis results.

3.2.2 Sample Selection

Before applying grounded theory, selecting appropriate research samples is crucial. Unlike quantitative research, grounded theory does not prioritize sample size and randomness. Instead, it focuses on purposeful sampling, selecting representative samples rich in data and information for qualitative analysis.

In this stage, "intercultural competence", "cross-cultural competence" and "language" are leveraged as keywords to undertake literature retrieval on Web of Science, EBSCO, and Scopus. With the criteria of whether the recovered literature includes the influence of language on ICC, the obtained literature is filtered to the title, abstract, and full text. These key words are then converted into Chinese "跨文化能力" and "外语" or "英语、法语、日语、韩语、西班牙语" and other commonly used Chinese language names in order to prevent omission, and their Chinese equivalents have been searched in CNKI (China National Knowledge Infrastructure), the largest academic platform in China, using the same literature retrieval and screening methods. 182 articles are filtered and a database for open coding is generated. The coding adheres to the theoretical saturation concept.

3.2.3 Coding Analysis

1. Open Coding

Open coding is the initial stage of grounded theory, involving the decomposition, examination, comparison, conceptualization, and categorization of data. The basic steps include labeling, conceptualizing, and categorizing the data. Labeling entails assigning codes to the collected data, which can be done at the word or sentence level depending on the data volume. Most grounded theory studies adopt sentence-level coding to reduce researcher workload and ensure data integrity. Based on labeling, the researcher combines raw data with similar meanings into concise concepts and further categorizes a subset of concepts based on their similarities. Throughout the coding process, the researcher maintains a mindset of continuous comparison, constantly testing and enriching the developed categories.

2. Axial Coding

While open coding provides a sufficient number of categories, these categories may remain in a scattered state, primarily reflecting the objective aspects of the original data. Axial coding aims to identify connections between these categories and establish organic links among them. The logic of axial coding can stem from the researcher's own reflections and judgments about the data or be guided by a coding paradigm model, including: A) causal conditions (factors triggering the phenomenon), B) the phenomenon (general representation of the category), C) context (nature or dimension of the category), D) intervening conditions (factors influencing the occurrence of the phenomenon), E) strategies (actions taken in the event), and F) consequences (outcomes of the actions). The researcher reassembles categories and subcategories during axial coding (Li & Chen, 2016)①.

3. Selective Coding

Selective coding aims to identify one or several core categories through comparison and reflection. The researcher systematically connects these core categories to their supporting categories, verifies their relationships, and supplements incomplete categories with concepts. The core categories serve as the integration point for the main categories, establishing a comprehensive theoretical framework. Finally, the research findings are presented through a coherent narrative that showcases the logical progression of the research subject.

---

① 李方安 & 陈向明. (2016). 大学教师对“好老师”之理解的实践推理——一项扎根理论研究的过程及其反思. 教育学报, (2), 58-70.

3.3 Implementation of Grounded Theory

The previous section elaborated on the comprehensive operational methods for conducting research using Grounded Theory. The main task of this section is to apply the constructed research process to the collected data and, through specific analysis and research, explore and summarize the elements that the ICC should possess.

3.3.1 Open Coding

Open coding is a process of data collection and analysis in which concepts are initially refined and classified into categories. This research effectively classifies, labels, summarizes and encodes the 182 articles collected. Open coding process is divided into three steps: A) All text materials are read word by word and abstract concepts are annotated. B) Similar cases are summarized and concepts are initialized. 51 initial concepts summarized are shown in Table 3-1. C) These 77 initial concepts are abstracted to their connotation and extension, and 12 categories are formed.

Table 3-1 Open Coding Example (part)

Initial Category	Initial Concept	Primitive Statement
A1 Intercultural communication motivation	a1 Intercultural communication for practical reasons.	Individuals may need to communicate with people who speak different languages in their personal or professional lives. This can include communicating with family members, friends, colleagues, or clients who speak a different language.
	a2 Intercultural communication for career advancement.	Many companies are looking for employees who are proficient in more than one language. Individuals are motivated to carry out intercultural communication in the job market, particularly in fields such as international business, diplomacy, or translation.

(Continued)

Initial Category	Initial Concept	Primitive Statement
A2 Foreign language contributes to global perspective	a7 Foreign language expands world-view and understanding of global issues.	BP exposes individuals to diverse cultures and helps them to more easily access information, ideas, and perspectives from different cultures, which can expand worldview and understanding of global issues.
	a8 Foreign language promotes the awareness of cultural equality.	The National Curriculum for Languages in England maintains that studying languages provides pupils with an insight into other cultures and an opportunity to develop appropriate and effective ways to communicate..., a liberation from insularity... an opening to other cultures.
A3 Declarative knowledge	a12 Intercultural knowledge includes language knowledge.	Intercultural knowledge includes language knowledge, such as knowledge words, phrases, sentences and passages.
	a13 Intercultural knowledge includes values, social norms, etc.	Intercultural communication knowledge is embodied in the values, social norms, social customs, social system, history, religion, social system, etc. of a specific culture.
A4 Plurilingual skills	a17 Plurilingual skills are the correct application of language knowledge and language skills.	Plurilingual skills refer to the ability to speak or understand unprecedented and grammatical sentences, and to distinguish sentences with the same surface form but different actual semantics to master the application of language skills.
	a18 Plurilingual skills are the understanding and adjustment of pragmatic rules.	Multilingual skills are the " conscious " understanding of the pragmatic rules of one's own culture and those of the other's culture, and the adjustment of one's words and deeds according to the pragmatic rules of both sides.

(Continued)

Initial Category	Initial Concept	Primitive Statement
A5 Strategic knowledge	a19 Communicators get strategic knowledge to interpret and relate culture.	Communicators get the strategic knowledge to interpret a document or event from another culture, to explain it and relate it to documents from one's own.
	a20 Communicators use strategic knowledge to discover relationships and implement interactive knowledge.	Communicators use the strategic knowledge to understand their own language and language varieties, their own culture and the relationship..., and operate communication knowledge under the constraints of real-time communication and interaction.
A6 Communication & cooperation skills	a21 Intercultural communication maintains the smooth development of communication.	Intercultural communication stimulates the recognition of cultural differences, eliminates the interference of stereotypes, develops common sense, so as to maintain the smooth development of communication.
	a22 Intercultural communication helps build a good communication relationship.	Intercultural communication ensures the accurate understanding of each other in terms of semantics and pragmatics, so as to establish a good interpersonal relationship and improve communication efficiency.
A7 Pluricultural skills	a27 Intercultural communicators understand multiculturalism.	Being aware of one's own cultural background and biases, intercultural communicators are willing to tolerate the embarrassment caused by ambiguity and uncertainty... Respect cultural diversity and maintain multicultural coexistence.
	a28 Intercultural communicators promote cultural development.	Intercultural communicators absorb the new culture required by the times, spread the positive elements of foreign culture, and promote the development of national culture.

(Continued)

Initial Category	Initial Concept	Primitive Statement
A8 Adjustment & adaption skills	a31 Communicators should flexibly use knowledge and skills.	In intercultural communication, communicators should flexibly use all kinds of knowledge and skills to calmly cope with and reasonably handle various emergencies.
	a32 Communicators should implement adjustment.	In the face of cultural conflict, communicators should adjust their psychological state, reduce uncertainty, reduce stress, and achieve self-relaxation.
A9 Speculative training	a33 The level of bilingual ability depends on the level of speculative ability.	Language exists in discourse which is a meaning system composed of cultural elements and thinking elements; The level of bilingual ability depends on the level of speculative ability.
	a34 Speculative training can promote the acquisition of language and culture.	Language is not neutral and foreign language teaching can involve exposing students to a variety of texts and representations of a culture in order to develop students' speculative ability of the cultural aspects of language and cultural representations.
A10 Intercultural experience	a38 Intercultural communication can be acquired through bilingual class-room education.	Intercultural communication can also be taught across subjects as part of a school's mission.
	a39 Intercultural communication can be improved by studying abroad.	Study abroad has been shown to enhance intercultural understanding among university students. The magnitude of the change has been linked to students' goals and to the length of the stay.

(Continued)

Initial Category	Initial Concept	Primitive Statement
A11 Interactive practice	a42 Efficient intercultural interaction depends on language and paralanguage communication.	Efficient intercultural interaction depends not only on the correct use of social language, but also on the increased communicative effect of gesture, posture, facial expression, touch, space-time concept and other factors based on the cultural characteristics of the other party.
	a43 Intercultural interaction requires the use of communication strategies.	Intercultural interaction requires the proper use of communication strategies, including the use of synonyms, examples and other reporting strategies and code switching, language transfer and other compensation strategies.
A12 Intercultural communication awareness	a47 Intercultural communication awareness is the consciousness of adjusting language output.	Intercultural communication awareness includes the consciousness of adjusting one's own language understanding and language production according to the target language culture when using bilingual language.
	a48 Intercultural communication awareness is the emotion of pursuing culture.	People understand the connotation of culture and accept the influence of culture at the same time in the process of language learning, and IC awareness is imperceptibly internalized into an emotion of pursuing culture.

3. 3. 2 Axial Coding

Axial coding is the process of categorizing and abstracting the initial categories into the main categories by exploring the intrinsic relationship between categories. 12 categories are further refined and 4 main categories are summarized. The main categories and corresponding initial categories are shown in Table 3-2.

Table 3-2 Main Categories Formed by Axial Coding

Main Category	Initial Category	Category Connotation
M1 Intercultural Consciousness	F2 Global perspective	Every communicator is a ferry between different cultures.
	F12 Intercultural communication awareness	The awareness allows communicators to move between different languages, and better use of L1 and L2 to promote smooth communication.
	F1 Intercultural communication motivation	Positive motivation can enhance the willingness to use language and promote IC activities.
M2 Intercultural Knowledge	F3 Declarative knowledge	Declarative knowledge mainly required on memory, including linguistic knowledge, paralinguistic knowledge and cultural knowledge.
	F5 Strategic knowledge	It is a conscious, planned and dynamic measure to ensure smooth communication and achieve communicative purpose.
M3 Intercultural Skills	F4 Plurilingual skills	Plurilingual skills require critically absorbing repertoires (not just the first language) for communication, including application skills of linguistic and paralinguistic knowledge.
	F7 Pluricultural skills	Pluricultural skills are the sensitivity, insight, understanding and integration of the heterogeneous cultural roots behind language, behavior, psychology, attitude, etc.
	F6 Communication & cooperation skills	Communication & cooperation skills give full play to prevent communication friction, eliminate communication barriers, and improve the efficiency of bilingual use.
	F8 Adjustment & adaption skills	Adjustment & adaption skills help bilinguals to maintain balance in a confrontational environment in both original cultural identity and harmony with the new environment.

(Continued)

Main Category	Initial Category	Category Connotation
M4 Intercultural Behavior	F10 Intercultural experience	This experience awakens the perception of language and cultural exchanges, eliminate the impact of differences, and optimize the way of thinking and expression.
	F9 Speculative training	Speculative training on reflecting on one's own culture and rationally evaluating various cultures promotes the development of critical cultural awareness, and enhances the appropriateness and effectiveness of language practice.
	F11 Interactive practice	Interactive practice strengthens and deepens the language and integrates and creates a new culture.

3.3.3 Selective Coding

Selective coding is the process to find out core category, deal with the relationship between categories and form a comprehensive process. This stage differentiates the existing categories as core categories and secondary ones, and describes the materials around the "core category" as well. With the help of the developed main categories, the whole "story line", the main categories, and the initial categories are sorted out, and all categories are strung into a whole, thus forming a new substantive theoretical framework related to the theme.

This study takes ICC as the core category, on which the story line is structured. Factors as intercultural consciousness, knowledge, skills and behavior of intercultural communication are the four main categories. Among them, the consciousness is the trigger factor, which is the key to break the threshold of intercultural communication; knowledge serves as a tool which provides reserves for intercultural communication; skills, the technical elements, play the role of a guarantee for effective intercultural communication; behavior is fortifier in practical operation of intercultural communication.

3.3.4 Saturation Test

To ensure the scientificity of the grounded theory research process and the accuracy of the research results, this study takes the first step to conceptualize the implicit relationship between concepts or categories formed by open coding and axial coding according to Glaser and Strauss (1999)①. Then theory and concept initially constructed are constantly compared with the existing literature and concepts. After repeated comparison, it is found that there is no new concept dimension, so the theory and concept are saturated. The second step goes to saturation test for literature left (No. 26-81) through the same method as coding and analysis. The 55 documents are encoded and analyzed, and it is found that the analysis results of these documents are consistent with the previous relational attributes and conceptual dimensions. That is to say, no new category is obtained from the coding analysis conducted on the 55 documents, which are all extracted by the previous 4 main categories.

3.4 Model Interpretation

By encoding the pertinent literature, a complete story line is formed, and an ICC model is conceptualized as consisting of four components as intercultural consciousness, knowledge, skills, and behavior, which help individuals become more effective communicators and build stronger relationships across cultural boundaries.

3.4.1 Consciousness: Trigger for Intercultural Communication

Consciousness represents the underlying mindset that can both help and hinder effective intercultural communication. When cultivated and harnessed effectively, consciousness can be a powerful tool for building bridges across cultural boundaries and fostering greater understanding and empathy.

---

① Glaser, B., & Strauss, A. (1999). *Discovery of grounded theory: Strategies for qualitative research (1st Edition)*. Routledge.

However, when ignored or left unchecked, it can be a force that perpetuates stereotypes, biases, and misunderstandings, and undermines efforts to build more inclusive and diverse communities.

1. Global Perspective

Global perspective refers to the recognition by communicators that, in an era of globalization and diversity, all human beings are interconnected and interdependent as a unified entity, often referred to as "global citizens" (Risager, 2007)①, "global culture" (Kumaravadivelu, 2008)②, and "intercultural citizens" (Byram, 2008)③. Global perspective entails the ability of individuals to critically and objectively observe and evaluate each other's behavior, as well as engage in intercultural activities based on this capability. It encompasses self-identity consciousness, ethnic cultural confidence, and cultural equality consciousness (Jiang, 2017)④.

Self-identity consciousness pertains to the communicator's awareness of their social status, roles, obligations, responsibilities, and interpersonal relationships. A clear understanding of one's own identity aids in maintaining rational objectivity and self-assurance during communication, while facilitating the appropriate use of languages (Gu, 2017)⑤. Ethnic cultural confidence refers to the recognition that individuals residing within a specific cultural and historical context possess about their own culture. It involves a profound understanding of the role and significance of their culture, an accurate grasp of its developmental patterns, and an active commitment to the responsibility of advancing cultural heritage (Fei, 2004)⑥. By consciously employing ethnic cultural confidence, one can mitigate "cultural aphasia" in the face of

---

① Risager, K. (2007). *Language and culture pedagogy: From a national to a transnational paradigm* (Vol. 14). Multilingual Matters.

② Kumaravadivelu, B. (2008). *Cultural globalization and language education*. Yale University Press.

③ Byram, M. (2008). *From foreign language education to education for intercultural citizenship: Essays and reflections*. Multilingual Matters.

④ 姜英敏. (2017). 东亚国际理解教育的政策与理论. 高等教育出版社.

⑤ 顾晓乐. (2017). 外语教学中跨文化交际能力培养之理论和实践模型. 外语界, (01), 79-88.

⑥ 费孝通. (2004). 对文化的历史性和社会性的思考. 思想战线, (02), 1-6.

globalization, thus promoting the preservation, development, and innovation of ethnic cultures. Cultural equality consciousness entails approaching the ethnic cultures of other nations with an acknowledgement of "appreciating each other's beauty," an appreciation for "beauty in diversity," respect for "beauty and commonality," and an openness to "a harmonious world" (Su et al., 2022)①. It necessitates abandoning ethnocentrism in linguistic expressions, seeking commonalities while preserving differences, and serving as a bridge for the shared development of diverse civilizations (Fang, 2019)②.

A global perspective entails fostering local culture, successfully combating "aphasia" in international interactions, encouraging the transmission, growth, and production of language and culture, and acting as a ferryman for the shared development of many civilizations. It helps individuals to comprehend the original culture in depth and undertake historical responsibility for cultural growth, and examine cultural differences logically and realize the mutual penetration of the fundamental cultural traits of both sides.

2. Intercultural Communication Awareness

Intercultural communication awareness is a psychological attribute of language operation mechanism that communicators consciously pay attention to and reflect on language practice. It allows individuals to use language as a tool for communication and connection, rather than a barrier to understanding. The benefit lies in that it enables language switching to suit the communication context and boosts sensitivity to the nuances of different languages as well as the cognitive and social-emotional development, resulting in enhanced problem-solving skills, creativity, and social abilities. The interpretation is back by Ashton et al. (2022)③ who explored the efficacy of

---

① 苏健蛟,冯朝海 & 李印东.(2022). 新时代我国民族传统体育文化发展方位审视. 北京体育大学学报,(04), 134-144.

② 方杲.(2019). 人类命运共同体与自由人联合体的逻辑一致性. 吉林大学社会科学学报,(03), 179-186+235.

③ Ashton-Hay, S. A., Lamberton, G., Zhou, Y. N., & von der Heidt, T. (2022). Bilingual learning strategies to support Chinese EAL business students. *Journal of International Education in Business*, 15 (2), 290-310.

bilingual learning methodologies and discovered that the foreign language practice can assist both intercultural communication and in-depth learning. A study that may also linked with this is, Ashton and Pillay (2011)① noticed bilinguals enhance the efficiency of intercultural activities and reflect greater ICC while overcoming the issue of "translation time lag" brought on by cognitive overload from self-regulation and communication in the language of choice. Intercultural communication awareness is the recognition of the inherent and mutually dependent relationship between language and culture. Language, as a social symbol, serves as a source for transmitting and shaping a particular cultural framework, and language use is a microcosm of society (Kramsch, 1993)②. IC awareness enables bilingual individuals to navigate seamlessly between two languages and two cultures, facilitating effective intercultural communication (Ge & Wang, 2016)③. By being aware of LP, individuals can communicate more effectively, promote understanding and inclusivity, and enhance their IC.

3. Intercultural Communication Motivation

Intercultural communication can be challenging due to differences in language, cultural values, and communication styles. Motivation is essential to overcome these challenges and work towards effective communication. Therefore, intercultural communication motivation is the root of improving intercultural communication, which provides sufficient foreign language practice impetus. It can help individuals overcome linguistic and cultural barriers and promote more inclusive and respectful communication. Communication motivation can be intrinsic or extrinsic (Martin & Nakayama, 2010)④. Intrinsic motivation, driven by healthy curiosity and an open

---

① Ashton-Hay, S., & Pillay, H. (2011). Case study of collaborative learning in two contexts: What do students gain? In Russo, B. L. (Ed.), *Encyclopedia of teaching and teacher research*. *Nova Science Publishers*, United States of America (pp. 783-804), NOVA Science Publishers, Incorporated.

② Kramsch C. (1993). *Context and culture in language teaching*. Oxford University Press.

③ 葛春萍 & 王守仁.(2016). 跨文化交际能力培养与大学外语教学. 外语与外语教学, (02),79-86+146.

④ Martin, J. N., & Nakayama, T. K. (2010). *Intercultural communication in contexts* (*5th Edition*). McGraw-Hill.

mindset, promotes the voluntary and valuable process of using bilingual skills for intercultural communication. Extrinsic motivation, on the other hand, implies that the desire to engage in intercultural communication using bilingual skills is driven by external rewards such as money, power, or recognition.

Intercultural activities, cultural experience, and language development are the primary impetuses for the need for two language symbols and conventions to facilitate communication, exchange, and interaction between other languages and cultures. Motivation to learn about different cultures and languages can help individuals expand their knowledge and gain a deeper understanding of the world around them. This can lead to personal and professional growth and provide opportunities for new experiences. Motivation to understand and empathize with people from different cultures can help break down barriers and promote mutual understanding, and build stronger relationships. Therefore, maintaining positive and lasting communication motivation and encouraging smoother and more efficient intercultural communication require respecting the communicators' feelings toward their mother tongue, recognizing the equality of two languages and cultures, and ensuring the willingness and psychological preparation to communicate with each other.

3.4.2 Knowledge: Tool for Intercultural Communication

Knowledge provides individuals with the information and understanding necessary to navigate intercultural interactions successfully. With this tool, individuals can avoid misunderstandings, adapt their communication style to better suit the needs of their communication partners, and build stronger intercultural relationships.

1. Declarative Knowledge

Declarative knowledge is mainly used to answer the questions of what, why and how, pointing to the nature, characteristics and states of concepts. It includes linguistic knowledge, paralinguistic knowledge and cultural knowledge.

Linguistic knowledge refers to phonetics, vocabulary, grammar, discourse and pragmatic knowledge. A solid language foundation is beneficial for intercultural communication. Communicators should have a grasp of vocabulary, pronunciation, spelling, and other language features and patterns in both their native language and the target language. Language differences are one of the most significant barriers to effective intercultural communication. Without an understanding of the language of the people you are communicating with, it can be challenging to convey ideas accurately, understand their perspectives, or establish rapport. Different cultures may use language in different ways, such as the use of formal or informal language, direct or indirect communication styles, or the use of idioms and slang. Understanding these differences can help you navigate communication more effectively and avoid misunderstandings. Cultural vocabulary within words carries explicit ethnic cultural information and conceals deeper meanings of ethnic culture. Having a grasp of semantic knowledge facilitates the appropriate use of language. Different cultures give rise to different pragmatic rules, and language usage varies in different contexts. Intercultural communicators should possess an understanding of how culture influences language and communication styles, and master the pragmatic knowledge of using language appropriately and effectively based on different contexts.

Para-linguistic knowledge refers to the nonverbal aspects of communication, including tone of voice, facial expressions, gestures, and other body language. Different cultures have different norms and expectations around nonverbal communication, such as gestures, facial expressions, tone of voice and other body language. Without an understanding of these differences, intercultural communication can be challenging and may lead to misunderstandings or offense. Nonverbal cues can add additional layers of meaning to communication beyond the words themselves. For example, a smile can indicate friendliness or approval, while a frown can indicate disapproval or sadness. Understanding these cues can help you interpret the meaning behind the words and better understand the intentions of the speaker.

Nonverbal cues can also convey cultural values and attitudes, such as respect, deference, or assertiveness. By understanding these cues, you can gain insight into the cultural context of the communication and better navigate potentially sensitive or complex interactions. Being able to pick up on and respond appropriately to nonverbal cues can help establish rapport and build trust with people from different cultures. This can facilitate more effective communication and help bridge cultural differences.

Cultural knowledge is comprised of customs, religious beliefs, historical geography, world outlook, values, ways of thinking, conduct codes of different countries, and the knowledge of similarities and differences between different cultures.

Cultural knowledge encompasses both explicit surface culture and implicit deep culture (Simko & Olick, 2021)①. For intercultural communicators, cultural knowledge goes beyond surface-level aspects like customs, dietary habits, religious beliefs, geographical knowledge, historical knowledge, and taboos. It also includes a deeper understanding of cultural values and ways of thinking. The first level of intercultural awareness involves recognizing superficial cultural features. Values serve as the foundation of culture, and comprehending them allows communicators to grasp the essence and meaning of a culture. Scarino (2017)② emphasizes that language learners engaging in intercultural communication should not only learn their own language and culture but also understand the culture associated with the foreign language they are studying. Successful intercultural communicators should be acquainted not only with their own culture and the culture of the target language country but also with world cultures. In the globalized context, communicators may interact with people from diverse cultural backgrounds. Therefore, it is crucial to understand not only British or American culture but

① Simko, C., & Olick, J. K. (2021). What we talk about when we talk about culture: A multi-facet approach. *American Journal of Cultural Sociology*, 9, 431-459.

② Scarino, A. (2017). Developing assessment literacy of teachers of languages: A conceptual and interpretive challenge. *Studies in Language Assessment*, 6(1), 18-40.

also the cultures of other countries. A shared understanding of one's own culture and other cultures helps communicators develop an international perspective, fostering mutual understanding and facilitating the identification of common ground among different cultures. Familiarity with one's own culture enables accurate information conveyance, while knowledge of other cultures allows for the reception of information transmitted by others with high quality. Social knowledge encompasses understanding of politics, economics, laws and regulations, social etiquette in one's own and other countries, as well as relevant knowledge in sociology and psychology.

Based on concepts, declarative knowledge is a conscious and accurate understanding of various changes in language meaning in different contexts and the ways to use language appropriately to communicate with others in specific situations. It helps overcome misunderstanding, stereotype and ethnocentrism, so as to avoid failure in intercultural communication due to disappointment with expectations, preconception and single criteria.

2. Strategic Knowledge

Strategic knowledge encompasses a set of methods and techniques for effectively utilizing available resources to solve problems (Gao, 2016)①. It involves employing specific responses to overcome communication difficulties and establish mutual understanding. This knowledge is divided into two main categories: reduction strategies and achievement strategies (Faerch & Kasper, 1983)②. Reduction strategies, such as topic avoidance and linguistic form avoidance, help manage communication barriers. Achievement strategies include paraphrasing, seeking help, delaying responses, and using nonverbal cues to facilitate effective intercultural communication. Additionally, strategic knowledge involves the ability to adapt to various communication contexts, ensuring flexibility and effectiveness in diverse intercultural interactions. This

---

① 高永晨. (2016). 中国大学生跨文化交际能力现状调查与分析. 外语与外语教学, (02), 71-78+146.

② Faerch, C. , & Kasper, G. (1983). Plans and strategies in foreign language communication. In C. Faerch, & Kasper, G. (Ed.), *Strategies in interlanguage communication* (pp. 20-60). Longman.

involves understanding how communication styles may differ in different cultures or situations, and adjusting one's communication style accordingly. For example, in some cultures, indirect communication is preferred, while in others, direct communication is valued. Understanding these differences and adapting one's communication style can help facilitate effective communication and build positive relationships. Another important aspect of strategic knowledge is to manage conflict in intercultural communication. This involves recognizing and addressing potential sources of conflict, such as differences in values or expectations, and using effective conflict resolution strategies to resolve conflicts when they arise. This may include strategies such as active listening, compromise, and negotiation. Intercultural strategies invite learners to push themselves beyond their "comfort zone," stretch their capabilities, and make the most of their current interlanguage proficiency. In turn, this is likely to widen their resources, actively expand their (limited) competence, and last but not least, to develop a positive attitude by not "giving up" and by becoming accustomed to taking risks and tolerating language anxiety.

3.4.3 Skills: Techniques for Intercultural Communication

Skills are automatic action systems that people develop via training and depend on prior knowledge. They are the technical support of this stage, covering plurilingual skills, pluricultural skills, communication and cooperation skills as well as adjustment and adaptation skills.

1. Plurilingual Skills

Plurilingual skills contains the application of linguistic knowledge and paralinguistic knowledge. It requires critically absorbing students' language repertoires (not only their first language), cultural, and symbolic resources for communication, but does not demand that all languages be equally proficient (Galante et al., 2022)①. These skills go beyond simple languages

① Galante, A., Chiras, M., & dela Cruz, J. W. N., & Zeaiter, L. (2022). *Plurilingual guide: Implementing critical plurilingual pedagogy in language education*. Plurilingual Lab Publishing.

and involve the ability to use a range of languages to communicate in different contexts. They include skills such as code-switching (switch between languages) and translanguaging (using different languages to express fully and flexibly), and appreciation of linguistic diversity in a more inclusive and respectful communication. Byram demonstrated that language and culture produce the alternative concept of the world, which promotes the growth of intercultural communication (Byram, 2012)①. Intercultural communicators critically absorb multilingual, multimodal and multi symbol resources from repertoires, flexibly adjust the way and timing of language practice, and ensure the smooth progress of intercultural communication (Canagarajah, 2018)②.

2. Pluricultural Skills

Pluricultural skills complement plurilingual skills. Having pluricultural skills helps individuals to avoid misunderstandings, overcome cultural barriers and build relationships based on mutual respect and understanding. It also fosters empathy and an appreciation for different ways of thinking and living, leading to more effective and harmonious communication. These skills consist of cultural understanding skills and cultural integration skills. Cultural understanding skills include the discovery and comparison of cultural differences and similarities, the interpretation of cultural concepts and phenomena, and the overview and synthesis of cultural views. Cultural integration skills integrate cultural resources and language resources in a dynamic communication scenario, and incorporate language and communication content, language and culture, language and mind from the perspective of holism. Only with high-level cultural understanding skills can communicators deeply comprehend and master language, enabling them to effectively use languages for communication. Cultural integration skills aim to

---

① Byram, M. (2012). Language awareness and (critical) cultural awareness: Relationships, comparisons and contrasts. *Language Awareness*, (21), 5-13.

② Canagarajah, S. (2018). Translingual practice as spatial repertoires: Expanding the paradigm beyond structuralist orientations. *Applied Linguistics*, (39), 31-54.

integrate diverse cultural resources and language resources in a dynamic communicative context, with a holistic perspective that integrates language with communication content, language with culture, and language with thinking.

3. Communication and Cooperation Skills

Intercultural communication is often complicated by differences in language and cultural backgrounds. Communication and cooperation skills are those to positively orient opportunities and actively solve problems with language practice, including active intervention, effective dialogue implementation, internal element connection evaluation, and expression support. They can timely correct problems in exchanges, enhance mutual understanding, increase exchanges and complementarities between different cultures, and promote cultural development. Yonn and Kim (2017)① have proved that intercultural communication can be cultivated through bilingual cooperation, and meanwhile intercultural activities have also improved intercultural communication. Effective communication and cooperation involve the ability to understand and respect diverse perspectives, actively listen to others, and engage in constructive dialogue. Cooperation skills also involve involves being able to negotiate differences and find common ground, as well as being able to manage conflicts constructively. Therefore, these skills can prevent communication friction, eliminate communication barriers, improve the effectiveness of intercultural activities.

4. Adjustment and Adaptation Skills

Adaptive capacity refers to the communicators' ability to modify their behavior according to cultural characteristics in a intercultural environment, involving both social and psychological adjustments (Schumann, 1986)②. Intercultural communication serves as a visible means of cultural adaptation,

---

① Yonn, H-S., & Kim, J-R. (2017). The effects of online cultural collaboration on elementary school students' intercultural communicative competence and affective domain. *Journal of Foreign Studies*, (42), 575-604.

② Schumann, J. (1986). An acculturation model for second language acquisition. *Journal of Multilingual & Multicultural Development*, 7(5), 379-392.

as communicators are continuously involved in a progressive process of transitioning from non-adaptation to adaptation. The effectiveness of their language usage depends on the adaptability of communicators to the new culture. Social adaptation skills encompass assimilation, preservation, and accommodation. This entails being open-minded, flexible, and receptive to learning about new cultural practices and perspectives. It also involves understanding cultural norms, customs, and values, and adjusting one's own behavior accordingly. Psychological adaptation skills encompass the ability to navigate language conflicts, cultural conflicts, and ego-permeability, which refers to the capacity to navigate language boundaries effectively. This involves being open-minded, flexible, and willing to learn about new cultural practices and perspectives. This includes being aware of cultural norms, customs, and values, and being able to adjust one's own behavior accordingly. Psychological adaptation skills include the ability to navigate language conflicts, cultural conflicts, and ego-permeability, which refers to the capacity to negotiate language boundaries effectively. This involves being able to cope with the stress and anxiety associated with the unfamiliar and the unknown, as well as being able to find ways to connect with others and feel a sense of belonging. These skills involve the process that communicators adopt active strategies, abandon inappropriate language and cultural elements, change the nature of language and cultural elements, or selectively absorb foreign language and cultural elements, so as to achieve self-structural reorganization. Francis and Jean-François (2010)① discovered that adapting language to the target group is beneficial to the development of intercultural communication by examining the process of French university lecturers adjusting to Chinese pupils. It is clear that language practice is an explicit method of cultural adaptation, and the success of language practice will depend on how well intercultural communicators can adjust to the new culture.

---

① Francis, B., & Jean-François, B. (2010). Teaching French as a second language to Chinese students: Instructional staff adaptation and intercultural competence development. *International Journal of Intercultural Relations*, 34(6), 561-570.

3.4.4 Behavior: Fortifier for Intercultural Communication

Intercultural behavior represents the practical application of intercultural communication skills and knowledge in real-world intercultural contexts. It is practice to fortify cultural understanding, foster inclusivity, and enhance intercultural communication.

1. Intercultural Experience

Intercultural experience refers to personal experience when contacting another language in the form of classroom education, extracurricular activities, studying abroad, immigration, online communication and so on. It provides an effective way to directly acquire knowledge and skills through language. It offers a practical means of immediately acquiring information and skills through language. The goal of intercultural experience is to renew symbols, references, or situational connections in the course of intercultural communication between the two language systems, to comprehend the world of knowledge in the dialogue between various cultures, and to realize communication between cultures and individuals as cultural carriers. In order to reach the objective both internally and externally, intercultural experience can help to foster the understanding of many cultures, which can then be used to construct a "diversified and integrated" intercultural communication. Intercultural experience also helps individuals to develop an open-minded and empathetic attitude towards people from different cultural backgrounds. It can break down stereotypes and prejudices, and increase tolerance and acceptance towards diversity. Through intercultural experience, individuals can also learn to identify and understand cultural differences and similarities, as well as develop strategies to navigate and negotiate cultural differences in various contexts. Moreover, intercultural experience can also provide opportunities for individuals to develop intercultural networks and relationships. This can lead to increased opportunities for personal and professional growth, as well as enhance their ability to collaborate and work effectively with people from diverse backgrounds.

2. Speculative Training

The elements of intercultural critical thinking involve understanding diverse cultures, accepting and respecting heterogeneous cultures, organizing, analyzing, and evaluating received information, and integrating and connecting information from different cultures to expand and enrich one's own capabilities. It includes the ability to objectively analyze cultural phenomena or events, to engage in rational and objective evaluation free from biases, to make logical deductions based on relevant evidence, to reflect on one's own actions, to creatively use the target language, and to perceive new cultural insights through rational analysis, evaluation, reflection, and innovative language application (Gao, 2002)①. Byram (2012)② believed critical cultural awareness can motivate communicators to analyze, explain, and evaluate ideas, behaviors, and products from a multicultural perspective in order to break down communication barriers when intercultural misunderstanding develops. Esen (2021)③ summed out how critical thinking has influenced the growth of ICC. He believed that speculative training is an effective way to solve problems in intercultural communication. Through planned and purposeful speculative training, communicators can re-examine the original fixed language and cultural habits, reflect on their dynamic behavior, innovate the ability to use the target language, and creatively use the language on the basis of rational analysis, judgment and reflection, and understand the new cultural ideas.

3. Interactive Practice

Interactive practice is a social practice that respects the subjectivity of different cultures. It is a process of interaction and integration with various cultural subjects to generate meaning. Dialogicity is inherent to human

---

① 高一虹(2002). 跨文化交际能力的培养:"跨越"与"超越". 外语与外语教学,(10),27-31.

② Byram, M. (2012). Language awareness and (critical) cultural awareness: Relationships, comparisons and contrasts. *Language Awareness*, 21(5), 5-13.

③ Esen, M. (2021). Critical thinking and intercultural competence: Review, use, and classification of the 21st century skills in intercultural EFL education. *International Journal of English Language Teaching*, 8(1), 23.

thinking, and cooperation is fundamental to social activities. Language serves as a means of interactive behavior in which individuals participate collectively through symbolic means (Pickering & Garrod, 2021)①. Communicating parties engage in interactive discourse practices through rhetorical devices and the construction of multiple discourses. They shape language structures through various aspects of language and utilize multimodal resources, including both verbal and non-verbal elements, to achieve communicative intentions and conversational behaviors. The goal is to share meaning and bridge cultural divides. Interactive practice enables individuals to apply their linguistic and cultural knowledge in real-world communication situations. It is a social practice that respects the subjectivity of culture, and a process of mutual integration and generation of meaning with various cultural subjects. ICC is not the personal quality of communicators, but the competence to interact with members from other cultures. Intercultural interaction increases meaningful intercultural experience and makes a positive impact on ICC. To communicate meaning and close the culture gap, communicators can test their own language and cultural knowledge throughout the intercultural engagement and recreate knowledge in light of the tensions and inconsistencies that arise.

3.5 Characteristics of the ICC Model

With grounded theory, this study proposes a 4-element framework of ICC that not only emphasizes the cognitive level (such as intercultural consciousness, intercultural knowledge), but also explicitly emphasizes the behavioral components (such as intercultural skills and intercultural behavior). There are indications that the research object's temporal characteristics are reflected in some of the ICC framework's four components. It manifests primarily in the following ways:

First of all, the 4-element framework is founded on the multicultural

① Pickering, M. J., & Garrod, S. (2021). *Understanding dialogue: Language use and social interaction*. Cambridge University Press.

context of work and life as a starting point. The majority of people work and live in a multicultural environment because of the convenient mobility of the world's population and the shared virtual world brought about by information technology. As a result, they are forced to get along with people from different cultural backgrounds and work together, which is the real demand for ICC cultivation.

What's more, the framework accurately portrays the organic connection that exists between language, society, and communication. In Byram's model, intercultural competence includes four dimensions: knowledge, skills, attitudes, and political education/critical cultural awareness, which are independent of language competence, sociolinguistic competence, and discourse competence. Even though Byram emphasizes that these four dimensions are interrelated, he does not clearly explain how they are related. As a result, it is challenging to connect ICC with linguistic proficiency in educational practice. Consequently, instructors of languages other than English often consider ICC to be supplementary to language instruction. The linguistic and societal components of this study are woven throughout its four elements. That is to say, whether one is cultivating consciousness, constructing knowledge, training skills, or practicing intercultural exchange, language, culture, and communication are interwoven.

Additionally, it integrates globalization and localization in a dialectical manner. The consciousness element consists of a global perspective, which includes national cultural consciousness and cultural relative consciousness as sub-elements. It advocates for ending ethnocentrism and promotes reciprocal respect between different cultures while highlighting the importance of the original culture's perspective during communication. In the knowledge dimension, national and foreign cultural information are both considered sub-elements. It emphasizes that to construct intercultural knowledge, we should focus on the target language's culture and strengthen our understanding of our own culture. The skills include applying native culture knowledge and understanding other countries' cultures.

Last but not least, compared to representative intercultural communication models, both domestically and internationally, the new theoretical model is better suited for China's new era of foreign communication. In Byram's ICC model, critical thinking is an independent dimension. However, in practice, training in critical thinking skills falls under intercultural empowerment. Incorporating it as a behavioral dimension enhances the model's coherence and facilitates the implementation of tiered instruction in classrooms, allowing the gradual development of students' ICC from easy to complex.

3.6 Summary

This chapter follows the research logic of "preparation-implementation-analysis." Firstly, during the preparation stage, appropriate research methods and samples are selected, accompanied by an explanation of the rationale and basis for their selection. Secondly, during the implementation stage, grounded theory coding procedures, including open coding, axial coding, and selective coding, are used to organize and extract data. This process results in the formation of ICC framework, which comprises four major elements: intercultural consciousness, intercultural knowledge, intercultural skills, and intercultural behavior. Finally, during the analysis stage, the original data are combined to explain and elaborate on the four major elements and their subcategories.

The purpose of constructing the ICC framework is to provide theoretical support for identifying ways and methods to enhance ICC. This chapter establishes the groundwork for examining the current status of ICC and constructing innovative models for cultivating ICC. Chapter 4 will conduct a comprehensive survey of the current state of ICC among college students, providing empirical evidence for the development of models aimed at cultivating ICC.

Chapter 4
Status Quo of College Students' ICC

In this chapter, a panoramic scan of the current state of ICC among college students is provided. The primary objective is to gain insights into the influence of demographic implicit factors on the four dimensions of ICC. Additionally, the chapter explores the variations and relationships between demographic factors and ICC. The ultimate aim is to make informed predictions, facilitate timely adjustments in teaching practices, and establish a solid groundwork for the development of future models aimed at enhancing ICC.

4.1 Methodology

This section discusses the study design, population and sampling, participants of the study, study instrument and its validation, the data gathering procedures and finally, the statistical treatment.

4.1.1 Research Design

This study focuses on descriptive quantitative research design on the ICC of Chinese college students using a questionnaire. Descriptive research design helps in gathering information that will display relationships between variables without changing the environment (Creswell & Creswell, 2017)①. The questionnaire was conducted in two parts: the first part was the demographic

① Creswell, J. W., & Creswell, J. D. (2017). *Research design: Qualitative, quantitative, and mixed methods approaches*. Sage publications.

information of the respondents, including age, gender, year level, and major; the second part was the investigation of respondents' ICC on intercultural consciousness, intercultural knowledge, intercultural skills intercultural and behavior as well as the challenges encountered by the student respondents to become intercultural competent.

4.1.2 Population and Sampling

The study covered five universities located in Changsha, Hunan Province, China, namely Central South University (CSU), Hunan University (HNU), Hunan Normal University (HNNU), Hunan Agricultural University (HNAU), and Changsha University of Science and Technology (CSUST).

The inclusion of institutions from all levels—national, provincial, and municipal—in the selection above demonstrates that an inclusive scope was pursued. These five universities are among the most prominent in Changsha, with a significant number of students, placing them among the most representative of the city's higher education institutions. They all place a significant emphasis on international cooperation and collaboration, and they have developed fruitful relationships with nations located all over the globe. As a result, the ICC of these college students is an accurate representation of the degree of college students in Changsha, and the ICC of these college students also has a significant impact on the efficiency with which countries are communicated with. An in-depth analysis of these college students' ICC will not only contribute to a better comprehension of college students' ICC in general but will also assist in better preparing these students for future international experiences and interactions.

The subjects of this research were undergraduates from the aforementioned five universities via stratified sampling. The subjects were seventeen thousand and twenty-four (17024) college students from CSU, ten thousand six hundred and fifty-five (10655) from HNU, twelve thousand six hundred and seventy-eight (12678) from HNNU, nine thousand nine hundred and eighty-six (9986) from HNAU, and eleven thousand six hundred and fifty-seven (11657) from CSUST, a total of sixty-two thousand (62000) college students.

After careful consideration, the scholar concluded that the aforementioned sample size was too great to be practical. In order to save time and money, the researcher selected a small subset of the population and then used Stratified Random Sampling to select samples from the population.

Table 4-1 Frequency Distribution of the Respondents

University	Total Population of College Students (Undergraduate Only)	Respondents	
	Frequency	Sample Size	Percent
CSU	17024	164	0.97%
HNU	10655	103	0.97%
HNNU	12678	123	0.97%
HNAU	9986	97	0.97%
CSUST	11657	113	0.97%
Total	62000	600	0.97%

Table 4-1 displays the distribution of the respondents from 5 universities. By using the formula $n=Z^2\times[P\times(1-P)]/E^2$ with a 95% confidence interval ($Z=1.96$), error margin ($E=5\%$), and probability value ($P=0.5$), the sample size was calculated as 384 from a population of 62, 000 college students. To avoid skewed data, the sample size was increased to 600 undergraduates, spanning all academic years. The sampling process involved four steps: First, divide the population into five strata: CSU, HNU, HNNU, HNAU, and CSUST. Then, determine the sampling ratio: 600 : 62,000 = 0.97%, meaning one student per 103 students. Third, allocate the number of respondents from each stratum proportionally: 164 from CSU, 103 from HNU, 123 from HNNU, 97 from HNAU, and 113 from CSUST. Next, Simple Random Sampling was used to select individuals from each stratum. The selected students formed the final sample.

In this study only the undergraduates from CSU, HNU, HNUU,

HNAU, and CSUST were considered for participation in survey. Electronic survey questionnaires were disseminated to student respondents via WJX. CN① platform.

4.1.3 Research Instrument

The questionnaire for this study was based on the ICC model from Chapter 3, ensuring alignment with the theoretical framework and enhancing the model's empirical validity.

1. Pilot Questionnaire

The pilot questionnaire structure and content were primarily guided by the ICC model detailed in Chapter 3, focusing on dimensions relevant to Chinese college students. References included Byram's multi-dimensional ICC model (1997, cited in Jackson, 2023)②, and ICC evaluation scales like YOGA and IDI, which were used to supplement and validate questionnaire items within our ICC model framework. Descriptive items from these scales were merged and classified to fit the context and needs of Chinese college students as defined in Chapter 3. Three ICC research experts with over a decade of experience refined the questionnaire, and feedback from five college students ensured its relevance. The final questionnaire consisted of 60 descriptive items and an open-ended question.

2. Small Scale Test & Analysis of the Pilot Questionnaire

The pilot questionnaire was conducted on July 2, 2022, in freshman class 1 and junior class 3 at Hunan Police Academy, where the researcher works. The researcher personally distributed the questionnaire with the help of head teachers, addressing student questions to ensure quality responses. The questionnaire description emphasized its use for research only, with no impact on students or the academy. Students were also reminded to avoid missing

---

① WJX. CN is a professional online questionnaire survey, evaluation and voting platform in China. Compared with the traditional survey methods, the WJX. CN has obvious advantages of being fast, easy to use and low-cost, and it has been widely used in China. (https://www.wjx.cn/)

② Jackson, J. (2023). *Introducing language and intercultural communication* (*3rd Edition*). Routledge.

answers. 43 questionnaires were distributed, with 7 removed as unqualified, resulting in 36 valid responses.

Unfortunately, SPSS 21 exploratory factor analysis indicated unclear dimension design. Student feedback revealed three main issues: First, too many questions led to impatience and inaccurate responses. Second, lack of clear dimension separation made it difficult to answer and distinguish between different aspects. Third, the open-ended question often resulted in vague responses.

3. Questionnaire Modification

The questionnaire was redesigned to address issues from the first trial. The new Chinese college students' ICC evaluation questionnaire consists of two parts: the respondents' profile (gender, grade, age, major, intercultural experience, etc.) and the ICC evaluation scale, which includes four dimensions: consciousness, knowledge, skills, and behavior. Each dimension has 8-10 questions, totaling 38 multiple-choice questions and one closed question (see Appendix).

The researcher collaborated with experts in intercultural communication and college students to refine the questionnaire. This involved repeated review, understanding, modification, and improvement of the questions. The goal was to ensure the questions aligned with ICC training theory and the intercultural communication experiences of Chinese college students, while also making them easy to understand.

4. Validation of the Research Instrument

After the pilot questionnaire test and analysis, the researcher made substantial modifications and finalized the questionnaire design. From July 10-20, 2022, a pilot test of the revised questionnaire was conducted, collecting twenty (20) pilot survey responses via the WJX. CN platform (https://www.wjx.cn/). The validation of the research instrument was based on this data, which provides robust empirical support for the theoretical foundation and enhances the model validity of the study.

(1) Scale Reliability Analysis

The small sample data obtained from the survey were analyzed with SPSS 21, and the results are shown below.

Table 4-2 Reliability Statistics of the Pilot Questionnaire

Cronbach's Alpha Reliability Analysis (Simplified Format)		
Number of items	Sample size	Cronbach's alpha coefficient
38	20	0.929

Table 4-2 shows that the Cronbach's alpha of the scale is 0.929. Referring to Cronbach's alpha coefficient criteria and judgment instructions, the coefficient of the scale is greater than 0.9, which means that the scale has highly desirable reliability and passes the reliability test.

(2) Scale Validity Analysis

In this study, exploratory factor analysis was chosen to analyze the validity of the scale structure and to test the scale validity by comparing it with the constitutive dimensions designed by the researcher.

Table 4-3 KMO and Bartlett's Test of the Pilot Questionnaire

KMO and Bartlett's Test		
KMO value		0.855
Bartlett's test of sphericity	Approximate chi-square	122.472
	df	28
	p-value	0.00

The approximate chi-square values of Bartlett's sphericity test were 122.472 and the p-value is less than 0.05, which reached the significant level. The above data indicate that the measurement scales are suitable for factor analysis.

Based on these findings, the reliability and validity of the questionnaire were confirmed. These results strengthen the empirical support for the study's theoretical foundation and enhance the validity of the ICC model constructed in Chapter 3, thereby increasing the persuasive power of the research's theoretical basis and model validity.

4.1.4 Data-Gathering Procedure

For quantitative data collection, the following steps were used: A) preparation and modification of the questionnaire, B) validation of questionnaire reliability and validity, C) distribution of valid electronic questionnaires through WJX. CN platform starting from September 2022, and D) questionnaire retrieval were done within October 2022 to November 2022 to consolidate and record the results.

4.1.5 Statistical Treatment of Data

Statistical analysis was planned to be performed with the SPSS 21, taking into account the 95% confidence interval. Cross-tabulations is displayed and examined. Descriptive and inferential statistics were used to analyze the collected data. Demographic characteristics were expressed as frequencies and percentages. College students' perceptions of ICC characteristics were compared based on mean scores.

Frequency, Percentage, Mean, independent-Samples T-test, One-Way Analysis of Variance (ANOVA), Pearson R Coefficient of Correlation was used as formulas to identify and test the validity of this study. The following methods were used in this study to analyze and interpret the collected data.

Frequency Distribution and Percentage. These tools were used to determine the number of cases and its respective representation out of the whole in the profile variables of age, gender, year level, major, and intercultural experience of college students.

Mean. This tool was employed to measure the level of ICC in terms of consciousness, knowledge, skill and behavior to students.

Independent-Samples T-test. It was used to determine the difference between the demographic profile (gender and major) and the level of ICC. Only the items that reached a significant level of $P<0.05$ were considered relevant for this study.

One-Way Analysis of Variance (ANOVA). It was used to determine the difference between the demographic profile (age and year level) and the level of ICC.

Pearson R Coefficient of Correlation. Pearson correlation analysis is a simple and easy method to measure the relationship between quantitative data. It can analyze the relationship between variables and the strength of the relationship, such as the correlation between gender and intercultural consciousness; the correlation between age and intercultural knowledge.

4.1.6 Ethical Considerations

Protecting the privacy, confidentiality, and anonymity of co-participants is a top priority. Co-participants will not face expected risks or discomfort, receive direct benefits, additional credit, or incentives. Non-participation will not affect them adversely.

An informed consent form, detailing the purpose, procedures, risks, benefits, confidentiality, contact information, and voluntary participation, will be sent to potential co-participants. Participation is voluntary, requiring a signed consent form if they choose to join. Co-participants can withdraw at any time without giving a reason, and their data will be returned or destroyed.

Identities will be kept confidential and pseudonyms used in reports. Co-participants can contact the researcher with any questions or concerns. The informed consent forms will be read and signed, and six participants will be interviewed over the next three weeks.

4.2 Data Presentation, Analysis and Interpretation

This section summarizes the findings, analyses, and interpretations of the data acquired for this study. It includes demographic information on respondents, the level of ICC manifested, and the analysis of significant differences and relationships between the demographic profiles of student-respondents and their level of ICC. The proposed model is presented in the final part. Electronic survey questionnaires were distributed to student respondents via the Questionnaire Star platform (WJX. CN). Out of 600 completed questionnaires, two were deemed invalid: one was completed in less than 30 seconds (far below the average of 209 seconds), and the other had identical responses for every item (all valued at 3). After removing these two responses, 598 valid responses remained, resulting in a response rate of 96.92%. The collected data were processed using SPSS 21. Given the larger final sample size compared to the pilot survey, a thorough examination of the questionnaire's reliability and validity was conducted before data presentation and analysis.

4.2.1 Reliability and Validity Testing

1. Reliability Analysis

SPSS 21 software is used to conduct reliability analysis on the ICC scale as a whole and four dimensions, the corresponding Cronbach's Alpha coefficients are shown in the table below.

Table 4-4 Reliability Statistics of the Large-Scale Questionnaire

Cronbach's Alpha Reliability Analysis (Simplified Format)			
Variables	Number of items	Sample size	Cronbach's alpha coefficient
Intercultural Consciousness	10	598	0.913
Intercultural Knowledge	10	598	0.926
Intercultural Skills	10	598	0.917
Intercultural Behavior	8	598	0.927
ICC (overall scale)	38	598	0.951

According to the reliability analysis results in above table, the ICC scale corresponds to a total of 38 measurement questions, which are divided into 4 sub-dimensions. All the Cronbach's Alpha coefficients for the latent variables, with overall ICC scale ($\alpha = 0.951$), Intercultural Consciousness ($\alpha = 0.913$), Intercultural Knowledge ($\alpha = 0.926$), Intercultural Skills, and Intercultural Behavior ($\alpha = 0.927$). meet the basic standard of being greater than 0.7. It can be seen that the survey questionnaire used in this study has good reliability.

2. Validity Testing—Confirmatory Factor Analysis (CFA)

Confirmatory Factor Analysis (CFA) is a statistical analysis method used in survey data to test whether the relationship between a particular factor and its corresponding observed variables conforms to the theoretical relationship pre-established by the researcher.

Table 4-5 Fit Index of the Large-Scale Questionnaire

X^2/df	GFI	AGFI	NFI	IFI	CFI	NNFI(TLI)	RMSEA
2.864	0.858	0.840	0.873	0.914	0.913	0.908	0.056

Table 4-5 shows the X^2/df value is 2.864, less than 3, and the RMSEA is 0.056, less than the standard level of 0.08, indicating a good fit. The GFI is

0.858, AGFI is 0.840, NFI is 0.873, IFI is 0.914, CFI is 0.913, and TLI is 0.908. All of the fit indices meet the general standards, indicating that the Confirmatory Factor Analysis (CFA) model established in this study is effective and matches the collected data well.

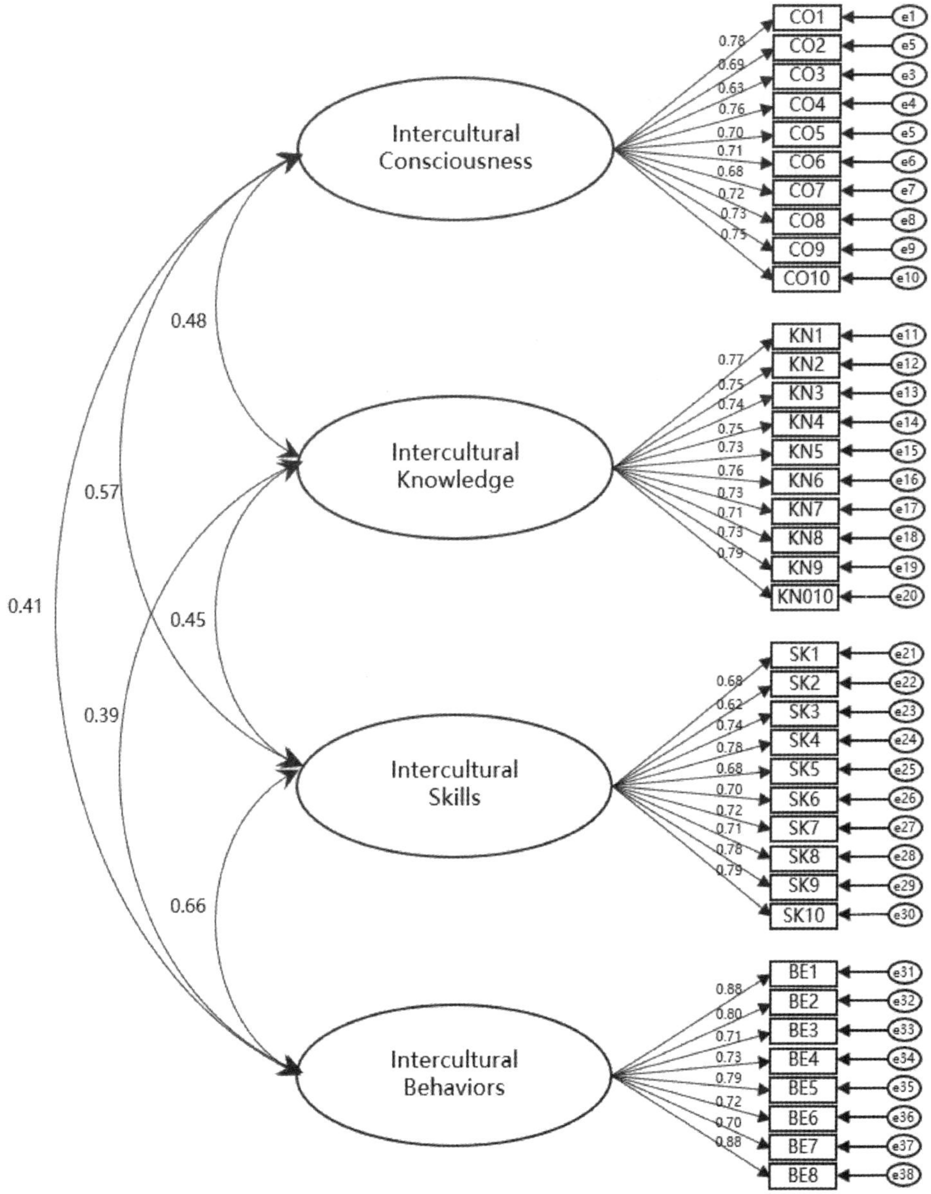

Figure 4-1 Confirmatory Factor Analysis (CFA) Model Diagram

As shown in figure 4-1, the standardized factor loadings for each item are all greater than 0.5, indicating that each item can be well explained by its corresponding dimension and demonstrating good questionnaire validity. The composite reliability (CR) is greater than 0.7 for each latent variable, indicating that all the measurement items in each latent variable can consistently explain that variable. The convergent validity for each dimension, as measured by the average variance extracted (AVE), is above the standard value of 0.5, indicating that the questionnaire in this study has good convergent validity.

4.2.2 Profile of Student-Respondents

1. Overall Profile of the Student-Respondents

Table 4-6 Profile of the Student-Respondents

Variables	Age	Frequency	Percent
Age	Below 18 years	27	4.5
	18 to 20 years old	394	65.9
	20 to 22 years old	159	26.6
	Above 22 years	18	3.0
Gender	Male	194	32.4
	Female	404	67.6
Year level	Freshman	166	27.8
	Sophomore	172	28.8
	Junior	149	24.9
	Senior	111	18.6
Major	Social Science	402	67.2
	Natural Science	196	32.8
Total		598	100

2. Profile of the Student-Respondents in Terms of Age

Among the 598 student respondents, a very small proportion ($f=27$, 4.5%) are under the age of 18, the majority ($f=394$, 65.9%) are between the ages of 18 and 20, some ($f=159$, 26.6%) are between the ages of 20 and 22, and a few ($f=18$, 3.0%) are over the age of 22.

The age distribution in this study is consistent with a normal distribution, indicating that this study's sampling followed a normal distribution in terms of age. According to China's compulsory education system which includes six years of primary school and six years of secondary school, the majority of undergraduate students complete their studies between the ages of 19 and 22. However, some students choose to take a gap year, work, or study abroad after graduating from high school and then reapply for undergraduate studies, resulting in a small percentage of undergraduate students aged 22 and older.

3. Profile of the Student-Respondents in Terms of Gender

The survey revealed that out of 598 teacher respondents, 404 ($f=404$, 67.6%) are female students and the remaining 194 ($f=194$, 32.4%) are male students. The number of female student respondents are significantly higher than that of male student respondents.

"The number of female college students exceeds the number of male college students" reflects the development of higher education in China (Liu, 2019)①. This trend is due to socioeconomic development, educational policy reform, and changing family attitudes. Firstly, societal evolution and national policy changes have led families to treat boys and girls equally, embracing the idea of girls pursuing higher education. Traditional male-dominated views have shifted toward gender equality (Li & Lin, 2022) ②. Secondly, urbanization and modernization in China, along with government policies aimed at improving educational resource equality, have boosted female enrollment.

---

① 刘文. (2019). 国际高等教育性别结构转变的脉络、条件与趋势——基于全球 190 个国家和地区的比较分析. 江苏高教, (11), 107-113.

② 李长洪 & 林文炼. (2022). 中国女性崛起:父母的观念转变与女性高等教育——来自"高校停招"的经验证据. 经济学报, (02), 317-343.

Certain female quotas in university admissions have further increased opportunities for women. Finally, as education becomes more widespread and the demand for intellectual labor rises, women's professional and social status has gained recognition, increasing their motivation for higher education and career development.

4. Profile of the Student-Respondents in Terms of Year Level

Among the 598 college student respondents, 166 (f=166, 27.8%) are freshmen, 172 (f=172, 28.8%) are sophomores, 149 (f=149, 24.9%) are juniors, and 111 (f=111, 18.6%) are seniors. In China, undergraduate programs typically last for four years, and this study's sample covers these four years fairly evenly, indicating a comprehensive sampling approach.

University courses typically consist of four progressive phases of learning: fundamental courses, fundamental professional courses, professional courses, and professional internships (Wang, 2018)①. Four years provides sufficient opportunities and experiences for students to excel in their future careers. Moreover, freshmen are in the period of psychological adaptation, sophomores in psychological confusion, juniors in psychological growth, and seniors in psychological maturity. College students need four years to progressively develop a healthy mental state, and eventually mature into independent, self-confident adults. All the factors mentioned above may leave an influence on the manifestation of ICC. Therefore, the four-year coverage of sampling is reasonable.

5. Profile of the Student-Respondents in Terms of Major

According to the *Catalog of Undergraduate Programs in Regular Higher Education Institutions in China* (2020 *Edition*) published by the MOE of PRC (MOE, 2020)②, there are twelve subject categories for undergraduate majors (excluding military science): four in natural sciences

---

① 王俊琳. (2018). 改革开放四十年中国高校教材建设研究：历程，进展和趋势. 黑龙江高教研究，(11)，16-22.

② 教育部. (2020). 普通高等学校本科专业目录(2020 年版). MOE. https://www.gov.cn/zhengce/zhengceku/2023-04/20/5752327/files/7256143e8b94465d9263f5fcfae1ecb1.pdf (science, engineering, medicine, agriculture) and eight in social sciences (literature, history, philosophy, economics, management, law, education, art). Given the comprehensive nature of the five universities involved, this study covers all twelve majors. For convenience, these majors are divided into two categories: Natural Sciences (e. g. , physics, chemistry, mathematics, which rely on mathematical and logical reasoning) and Social Sciences (e. g. , culture, language, history, which use methods like literature review, case studies, and observation). The distribution of students in this study includes 196 (32. 8%) from Natural Sciences and 402 (67. 2%) from Social Sciences. It's important to note that this classification is not a judgment of the value of different majors; all fields are respected and valued.

4. 2. 3 Level of ICC Manifested by the Student-Respondents

The four components of ICC are intercultural consciousness, intercultural knowledge, intercultural skills, and intercultural behavior. This description will cover the overall status of college students' ICC and each dimension individually. A 5-point Likert scale is used for its ability to offer more nuanced participant responses.

1. Overall Status Quo of College Students' ICC

Table 4-7 Descriptive Statistics on ICC

	N	Min.	Max.	Median	Mean	S. D.	Interpretation
Intercultural consciousness	598	1. 2	4. 7	4. 20	3. 922	0. 713	Satisfied
Intercultural knowledge	598	1. 4	4. 9	3. 90	3. 812	0. 728	Satisfied
Intercultural skills	598	1. 2	4. 7	3. 80	3. 619	0. 787	Satisfied
Intercultural behavior	598	1. 13	4. 88	3. 75	3. 610	0. 882	Satisfied
Total	598	1. 42	4. 63	3. 8421	3. 748	0. 596	Highly manifested

Note: S. D. = standard deviation. 1. 00 ~ 1. 80 Very Unsatisfied; 1. 81 ~ 2. 60 Unsatisfied; 2. 61~3. 40 Neutral; 3. 41~4. 20 Satisfied; 4. 21~5. 00 Very Satisfied.

This study performed statistical analysis based on the minimum value, maximum value, median value, mean value, and standard deviation of the ICC scale as a whole and each dimension listed in the preceding table. According to Table 4-7, the mean values of the collected sample data's overall scale and each dimension are all greater than 3. 41 points indicating high manifestation of ICC. The data can serve as a foundation for subsequent statistical analysis.

The ICC of college students is highly manifested overall and across all four dimensions ($M = 3.748$). Several factors contribute to this. First, national policies such as the "Belt and Road" initiative promote international cultural exchange and talent cultivation (Peng, Fu & Wu, 2020)①, creating a comprehensive and proactive educational openness. Second, foreign language education is compulsory in Chinese higher education, aiding integration into the international community and enhancing academic, business, and cultural exchanges. Additionally, with the flow of international students entering the "post-Western center" era (Buchanan, 2013)②, China has become a key destination for international students, with numbers growing from 11,500 in 1999 to 492,000 in 2018, making China the third largest study destination globally (Hu, 2021)③. This diverse learning environment allows students to interact with peers from various cultural backgrounds. Lastly, the Ministry of Education (MOE) of PRC actively promotes international exchange programs. Since 2012, China has collaborated with 181 countries, established Confucius Institutes in 159 countries, and signed mutual recognition agreements for academic qualifications with 58 countries (MOE of PRC, 2022)④. Universities also offer exchange programs, double degree programs, and international

---

① 彭仁忠，付容容 & 吴卫平.（2020）. 新时代背景下跨文化外语教学理论模型和实践模型研究. 外语界，（04），45-53.

② Buchanan, F. R. (2013). Higher education in emerging markets: A comparative commentary. *Development and Learning in Organizations*, 28(1), 12-15.

③ 胡雯.（2021）. 后疫情时代中国留学日趋多元——CCG 发布《中国留学发展报告（2020—2021）》蓝皮书. 中国对外贸易，（03），78-80.

④ 教育部.（2022-09-20）. 党的十八大以来教育国际合作与交流有关情况介绍. 中华人民共和国教育部政府门户网站. Retrieved June 6, 2023, from http://www. Moe. Gov. Cn/Fbh/Live/2022/54849/Sfcl/202209/T20220920_662968. html.

summer camps, enhancing students' ICC (Yu & Zhang, 2019) ①.

2. Level of ICC in Terms of Intercultural Consciousness

Intercultural consciousness refers to an individual's ability to recognize, understand, and appreciate cultural differences and similarities between people from different cultural backgrounds. It involves global perspective (CO1, CO2, CO3), intercultural communication awareness (CO4, CO5, CO6, CO7), and intercultural communication motivation (CO8, CO9, CO10).

Table 4-8 Descriptive Statistics on Intercultural Consciousness

	Indicators	Mean	S. D.	Interpretation
CO1	I realize that in the context of globalization, intercultural communication is the affirmation, respect and understanding of the cultural characteristics of different nations.	4. 15	1. 001	Satisfied
CO2	I realized that intercultural activity can help me understand and identify with my own culture, and cultivate myself to take the historical responsibility for the development of my own culture.	3. 89	0. 941	Satisfied
CO3	I realize that human beings coexist in a multi-cultural environment, and different cultural characteristics have the phenomenon of mutual penetration.	3. 82	0. 898	Satisfied
CO4	I realize that I can rationally analyze cultural differences in intercultural communication.	4. 07	0. 974	Satisfied
CO5	I realize that when communicating with foreigners, I should maintain an open and tolerant attitude and respect each other's culture.	3. 87	0. 984	Satisfied

① 于浩 & 张雪冰. (2019). 高校学生组织参与国际交流的路径探究——基于部分高校的实践调研. 中外企业家, (21), 204-205.

(Continued)

	Indicators	Mean	S. D.	Interpretation
CO6	I realize that the two cultures have different styles, different language use, and different cultures and languages have had an impact on society.	3. 92	0. 933	Satisfied
CO7	I realize that overcoming prejudice, eliminating stereotypes and maintaining cultural relativism can help achieve more effective intercultural communication.	3. 91	0. 926	Satisfied
CO8	I realize that the more I respect cultural differences, the more motivated I am to communicate across cultures.	3. 81	0. 945	Satisfied
CO9	I realize that the stronger the sense of global citizenship, the stronger the willingness to participate in intercultural communication.	3. 81	0. 971	Satisfied
CO10	I realize that maintaining a positive and lasting communication motivation can make intercultural communication more smoothy and efficient.	3. 96	0. 935	Satisfied
Total		3. 922	0. 713	Highly manifested

Note: CO = intercultural consciousness, S. D. = standard deviation. 1. 00～1. 80 Very Unsatisfied; 1. 81～2. 60 Unsatisfied; 2. 61～3. 40 Neutral; 3. 41～4. 20 Satisfied; 4. 21～5. 00 Very Satisfied.

The mean for each indicator on the intercultural consciousness dimension of the sample data collected is greater than 3. 41 points, indicating the student respondent highly manifest intercultural consciousness. CO1 received the highest average score of 4. 15, while CO8 and CO9 received the lowest average scores of 3. 80.

Table 4-8 reveals that students strongly demonstrate intercultural communication through affirmation, respect, and understanding of diverse cultural traits (M=4. 15). However, their cognition of mutual penetration

(M=3.82) shows a lower level of consciousness in intercultural practices, indicating inconsistency between their awareness and practical experience (Lasagabaster, 2017)①. This discrepancy may stem from limited opportunities for genuine intercultural experiences, hindering their understanding of how cultures interact (Romanowski, 2017)②. Cultural heritage and entrenched biases may also prevent students from fully appreciating cultural mutual penetration (Matusov & Marjanovic-Shane, 2017)③. Language barriers are another factor, impeding effective communication across cultures and limiting mutual understanding.

In terms of intercultural communication awareness, respondents feel capable of analyzing cultural differences (M=4.07). However, their openness and tolerance when interacting with foreigners (M=3.87) fall short of expectations, possibly influenced by prejudices or discomfort in cross-cultural interactions (Dudić, 2022)④.

Regarding motivation for intercultural communication, students agree that maintaining positive communication motivation enhances effectiveness (M=3.96). Yet, their motivation does not significantly increase with cultural respect or a sense of global citizenship (M=3.81), contrary to typical expectations (Nong, 2023)⑤. While global citizenship often fosters curiosity and openness to other cultures (Cotton et al., 2018)⑥, factors like shyness or

---

① Lasagabaster, D. (2017). Language learning motivation and language attitudes in multilingual Spain from an international perspective. *The Modern Language Journal*, 101(3), 583-596.

② Romanowski, P. (2017). *Intercultural communicative competence in English language teaching in Polish State Colleges*. Cambridge Scholars Publishing.

③ Matusov, E., & Marjanovic-Shane, A. (2017). Many faces of the concept of culture (and education). *Culture & Psychology*, 23(3), 309-336.

④ Dudić, A. (2022). Intercultural education and intercultural sensitivity of social work students: Experiences from Bosnia and Herzegovina, Serbia and Croatia. *Социална Работа*, 10(2), 1-25.

⑤ Nong, X. (2023). A study of the motivation of the Chinese college English learners. *Proceedings of the 2022 4th International Conference on Literature, Art and Human Development (ICLAHD 2022)* (pp. 596-605). Atlantis Press.

⑥ Cotton, D., Morrison, D., Magne, P., Payne, S., & Heffernan, T. (2018). Global citizenship and cross-cultural competency: Student and expert understandings of internationalization terminology. *Journal of Studies in International Education*, 23(3), 346-364.

lack of confidence may hinder students' willingness to engage in intercultural communication (Nijat et al., 2019)①.

3. Level of ICC in Terms of Intercultural Knowledge

Intercultural knowledge involves understanding various cultural practices, values, beliefs, and communication styles, essential for effective interaction across diverse cultural contexts. It encompasses six subcategories: linguistic knowledge, nonverbal knowledge, understanding of local cultures, familiarity with foreign cultures, awareness of cultural similarities and differences, and knowledge of communication strategies.

Table 4-9 Descriptive Statistics on Intercultural Knowledge

	Indicators	Mean	S. D.	Interpretation
KN1	I get the language knowledge such as pronunciation, vocabulary, grammar, discourse and pragmatic knowledge used in intercultural communication.	3.74	0.965	Satisfied
KN2	I understand the nonverbal knowledge used in intercultural communication, such as facial expressions, gestures, gestures, hugs and other body language.	3.79	0.928	Satisfied
KN3	I master my country's history, geography, socio political and cultural knowledge and values.	3.84	0.971	Satisfied
KN4	I know my own way of thinking, basic norms and behavioral knowledge.	3.9	0.939	Satisfied
KN5	I master the history, geography, social politics and cultural knowledge and values of other countries.	3.83	0.935	Satisfied

① Nijat, N., et al., (2019). Psychological factors that affect English speaking performance among Malaysian primary school pupils. *American International Journal of Education and Linguistics Research*, 2(2), 55-68.

(Continued)

	Indicators	Mean	S. D.	Interpretation
KN6	I know the way of thinking, basic norms and behavioral knowledge of other countries.	3. 83	0. 968	Satisfied
KN7	I have learned the comparative knowledge of significant differences between different cultures.	3. 82	0. 923	Satisfied
KN8	I understand the different strategies for treating high context culture and low context culture.	3. 77	0. 914	Satisfied
KN9	I know the achievement strategies for successful intercultural communication (reporting, asking for help, procrastination, etc.).	3. 79	0. 914	Satisfied
KN10	I know the avoidance strategies for successful intercultural communication (avoiding topics, avoiding language forms, etc.).	3. 82	0. 941	Satisfied
Total		3. 812	0. 728	Highly manifested

Note: KN=intercultural knowledge, S. D. =standard deviation. 1. 00～1. 80 Very Unsatisfied; 1. 81～2. 60 Unsatisfied; 2. 61～3. 40 Neutral; 3. 41～4. 20 Satisfied; 4. 21～5. 00 Very Satisfied.

The mean scores for each item in the intercultural knowledge dimension collected in this study were all above 3. 41, indicating the intercultural knowledge is highly manifested by the respondents . Among them, KN4 (M=3. 9) received the greatest score, whereas KN1 (M=3. 74) received the lowest.

Student respondents have learned English for at least 9 years in China, but they do not gain greatest satisfaction in language knowledge such as pronunciation, vocabulary, grammar, discourse, and pragmatic knowledge (M=3. 74). the reason behind it may that the majority of respondents are non-English majors who are less likely to, when compared with language majors, have a strong command of language for intercultural communication. They may have less exposure to diverse cultures and perspectives through their coursework, and other cultural immersion experiences, which can aid in the development of greater cultural sensitivity.

Nonverbal knowledge often convey meanings that words alone cannot, and they can carry a wide range of meanings (Paranduk & Karisi, 2020)①. With knowledge and instruction, students can readily comprehend nonverbal information. That why students present confidence in being aware of these differences in nonverbal communication ($M=3.79$). For example, the knowledge of a nod of the head can be obtained which may indicate agreement or understanding in some cultures, while in others it may indicate disagreement or even disrespect. Understanding nonverbal knowledge help individuals avoid misunderstandings, build trust, and establish positive relationships with people from different cultures (Benattabou, 2020)②.

Respondents commonly believe they understand their own way of reasoning, basic social norms, and behavioral knowledge ($M=3.9$). This can be based on personal experience, cultural upbringing, education, and other factors that shape one's worldview (Edwards & Edwards, 2017)③. Nevertheless, it is essential to acknowledge that the understanding of our own thoughts, norms, and behaviors is not always complete or accurate. In addition, the perception of our own behavior and norms may not always align with how others perceive us or the actual consequences of our actions.

KN3($M=3.84$) and KN4 ($M=3.9$) are presented as knowledge of the local culture, KN4($M=3.83$) and KN5($M=3.84$) for knowledge of the foreign culture, KN7 ($M=3.82$) for knowledge of similarities and differences

---

① Paranduk, R., & Karisi, Y. (2020). The effectiveness of non-verbal communication in teaching and learning English: A systematic review. *Journal of English Culture, Language, Literature and Education*, 8(2), 140-154.

② Benattabou, D. (2020). Helping EFL students avoid socio-pragmatic failure: Focus on nonverbal intercultural competence. *TESOL and Technology Studies*, 1(1), 23-41.

③ Edwards, F., & Edwards, R. J. (2017). A story of culture and teaching: The complexity of teacher identity formation. *The Curriculum Journal*, 28(2), 1-22.

between different cultures. It is quite clear that students have better understanding on knowledge of the local culture than that of the foreign culture, and knowledge of similarities and differences between different cultures is even lower($M=3.82$). Local cultural knowledge is often the cultural knowledge that individuals possess the most deeply and intimately. As for lower level of foreign cultural knowledge , there are a number of potential reasons. In some cases, an individual may have grown up in a relatively homogeneous community that did not expose them to diverse cultures. This can limit their understanding of other cultures and make it more difficult for them to learn about or engage with foreign cultures. Some students may have the tendency to view one's own culture as superior to other cultures. This ethnocentrism mindset can limit an individual's interest in learning about foreign cultures and can make it more difficult for them to appreciate cultural differences (Ting-Toomey & Dorjee, 2018)①. As with low levels of knowledge of similarities and differences between different cultures ($M=3.82$), the reason may be that limited exposure to different cultures limit an individual's understanding of cultural similarities and differences (Ott & Michailova, 2016)②. Stereotyping can make it more difficult for individuals to appreciate the similarities and differences between cultures, as they may be more focused on generalizations rather than individual differences (Allen, 2023)③. Additionally, If an individual does not speak the language of a culture, they may struggle to access information about cultural practices, values, and beliefs and ignore the knowledge of similarities and differences between different cultures.

The findings and interpretation support the study of Sun (2016)④ which

---

① Ting-Toomey, S., & Dorjee, T. (2018). *Communicating across cultures*. Guilford Publications.

② Ott, D. L., & Michailova, S. (2016). Cultural intelligence: A review and new research avenues. *International Journal of Management Reviews*, 20(1), 99-119.

③ Allen, B. J. (2023). *Difference matters: Communicating social identity (3rd Edition)*. Waveland Press.

④ 孙有中.(2016).外语教育与跨文化能力培养.中国外语,(3),1+17-22.

stressed that only through in-depth intercultural comparative research can students really develop their intercultural critical awareness, that is, understand the characteristics and causes of Chinese and foreign cultures, and be able to transcend the limitations of Chinese and foreign cultures and build a broader cultural and world outlook. Today, as a big country, China is playing an increasingly important role in the world. We urgently need a large number of new high-end foreign language talents, who are proficient in foreign languages and international rules, can vividly explain historical China and contemporary China to the world, and finally win the world's understanding of China.

4. Level of ICC in Terms of Intercultural Skills

Intercultural skills refer to the ability to effectively communicate and interact with people from different cultural backgrounds. The skills usually cover 4 subcategories as plurilingual skills, pluricultural skills, communication and cooperation skills as well adjustment and adaptation skills.

Table 4-10 Descriptive Statistics on Intercultural Skills

	Indicators	Mean	S. D.	Interpretation
SK1	I have mastered the skills of using foreign languages to communicate successfully with people from different social and cultural backgrounds and fields.	3. 62	0. 945	Satisfied
SK2	I have mastered the skills of nonverbal communication, such as facial expression, gesture and posture.	3. 6	0. 954	Satisfied
SK3	I have mastered the skills to understand and express meanings by combining specific contexts, using fabric knowledge.	3. 74	1. 115	Satisfied
SK4	I have mastered the skills to consider other countries' political, economic, religious and other events from different cultures and perspectives.	3. 63	1. 122	Satisfied

(Continued)

	Indicators	Mean	S. D.	Interpretation
SK5	I have mastered the skills to interpret cultural concepts and phenomena, and help resolve cultural conflicts.	3. 53	0. 978	Satisfied
SK6	I have mastered the skills of integrating language, culture and thinking from the perspective of holism.	3. 63	1. 05	Satisfied
SK7	I have mastered the cooperation skills of maintaining different cultures, actively breaking the silence and creating collaboration opportunities.	3. 61	1. 022	Satisfied
SK8	I have mastered the communication skills to effectively avoid offending the other party in terms of language and behavior in intercultural communication.	3. 55	1. 075	Satisfied
SK9	I have mastered the adaptive skills of adjusting my own behavior and handling the frustration encountered in intercultural communication.	3. 65	1. 088	Satisfied
SK10	I have mastered the adjustment skills of giving up, transforming and selectively absorbing language and cultural elements.	3. 64	1. 02	Satisfied
Total		3. 619	0. 787	Highly manifested

Note: SK = intercultural skills, S. D. = standard deviation. 1. 00～1. 80 Very Unsatisfied; 1. 81～2. 60 Unsatisfied; 2. 61～3. 40 Neutral; 3. 41～4. 20 Satisfied; 4. 21～5. 00 Very Satisfied.

The student respondents demonstrate high manifestation of intercultural skills, with average ratings for each item on this dimension exceeding 3. 41. Plurilingual skills (SK1: M=3. 62; SK2: M=3. 6; SK3: M=3. 74) and pluricultural skills (SK4: M=3. 63; SK5: M=3. 53; SK6: M=3. 63) are highlighted. Adjustment and adaptation skills (SK9: $M=3.65$; SK10: $M=3.64$) and communication and cooperation skills (SK7: $M=3.61$; SK8: $M=3.55$) are also noted. The highest-rated skill involves understanding and expressing meanings in specific contexts ($M=3.74$), while the lowest-rated involves interpreting cultural concepts and assisting in resolving cultural conflicts ($M=3.53$).

The preceding conclusions can be illustrated by the following facts. On the one hand, understanding and expressing meanings by using fabric knowledge requires a deep comprehension of the nuances and complexities of a particular culture (Liu & Shan, 2017)①. Interpreting cultural concepts and phenomena and resolving cultural conflicts, on the other hand, necessitate a higher level of ICC. This skill entails understanding and analyzing cultural patterns, beliefs, and values, as well as recognizing and resolving cultural differences and conflicts. It requires an in-depth knowledge of cultural dynamics, effective communication skills, and conflict resolution techniques. These skills may require extensive training and experience to acquire, and may be more difficult to acquire than fabric knowledge, which may explain the situation at hand.

The results indicate a higher manifestation of plurilingual skills with SK1 ($M=3.62$), SK2 ($M=3.6$), and SK3 ($M=3.74$) than pluricultural skills as SK4 ($M=3.63$), SK5 ($M=3.53$), and SK6 ($M=3.63$). Possible explanations include the following: To begin, the acquisition of language skills typically involves a greater degree of organization and standardization than the acquisition of cultural skills. Almost any language can be learned with the help of textbooks, grammatical guidelines, and vocabulary lists. Cultural skills learning may be less structured and tougher to define, making it more difficult

① 刘承宇 & 单菲菲. (2017). 大学英语课程的跨文化交际能力共核与差异——基于合法化语码理论的《大学英语教学指南》解读. 外语界, (04), 79-87.

to measure and evaluate (Galante & dela Cruz, 2021)①. Second, despite the existence of cultural differences, a shared language skill can aid in reducing misunderstandings and enhancing the overall quality of communication (Aichhorn & Puck, 2017)②, and respondents may pay more attention on plurilingual skills.

It is possible for students to demonstrate greater adjustment and adaptation skills (SK9, SK10) than communication & cooperation skills (SK7, SK8), given that adjusting to a new environment and adapting to new cultural norms are frequently the first challenges individuals face when moving to a new cultural context (Kim, 2017)③. When people first enter a new culture, they may experience culture shock and have difficulty adapting to their new surroundings. To manage with the stress and uncertainty of the new cultural context, it is necessary to develop robust adjustment & adaptation skills (Jackson, 2018)④. On the other hand, it may be more difficult to develop communication and cooperation skills because they require interacting with individuals from diverse cultural backgrounds and navigating cultural differences. ICC, which includes a comprehension of cultural values, beliefs, and practices, is necessary for effective communication and cooperation in a multicultural setting (Barrett, 2018)⑤.

5. Level of ICC in Terms of Intercultural Behavior

Intercultural behavior encompasses a wide range of behaviors, including intercultural experience (BE1, BE2, BE3), critical thinking training (BE4, BE5, BE6) and interactive practice (BE7, BE8).

---

① Galante, A., & dela Cruz, J. W. N. (2021). Plurilingual and pluricultural as the new normal: An examination of language use and identity in the multilingual city of Montreal. *Journal of Multilingual and Multicultural Development*, 1-16.

② Aichhorn, N., & Puck, J. (2017). Bridging the language gap in multinational companies: Language strategies and the notion of company-speak. *Journal of World Business*, 52(3), 386-403.

③ Kim, Y. Y. (2017). Cross-cultural adaptation. In J. Nussbaum (Ed.), *Oxford research encyclopedia of communication*. Oxford University Press.

④ Jackson, J. (2018). Intervening in the intercultural learning of L2 study abroad students: From research to practice. *Language Teaching*, 51(03), 1-18.

⑤ Barrett, M. (2018). How schools can promote the intercultural competence of young people. *European Psychologist*, 23(1), 93-104.

Table 4-11 Descriptive Statistics on Intercultural Behavior

	Indicators	Mean	S. D.	Interpretation
BE1	I have practical experience in updating language systems (such as vocabulary and reference) in intercultural communication.	3.81	1.093	Satisfied
BE2	I have the experience of successfully communicating with people from different cultural backgrounds and fields.	3.6	1.164	Satisfied
BE3	I have the experience of experiencing and updating cultural knowledge through intercultural activities.	3.57	0.991	Satisfied
BE4	I have the practice of accepting, comparing and evaluating different cultures.	3.59	1.09	Satisfied
BE5	I have the experience of conducting intercultural reflection and seeking appropriate ways to solve intercultural conflicts.	3.58	1.059	Satisfied
BE6	I have the experience of noticing the problems in my own language system, consciously analyzing language forms, and then producing corrected output.	3.51	1.064	Satisfied
BE7	I have the practice of regarding language and culture as a whole and negotiating with each other on meaning.	3.57	1.108	Satisfied
BE8	I have the practical experience of combining knowledge and customs in different fields to build and adjust my own cultural identity	3.65	1.089	Satisfied
Total		3.610	0.882	Highly manifested

Note: BE = intercultural behavior, S. D. = standard deviation. 1.00～1.80 Very Unsatisfied; 1.81～2.60 Unsatisfied; 2.61～3.40 Neutral; 3.41～4.20 Satisfied; 4.21～5.00 Very Satisfied.

According to Table 4-11, the sample data indicate that the average scores for each item on the intercultural behavior dimension are all greater than 3. 14, indicating intercultural behavior is highly manifested by the respondents, with the lowest score (M=3. 51) on BE6.

Students demonstrate a strong inclination towards updating their language systems in new cultural contexts (M= 3. 81), driven by several factors. Firstly, the motivation to enhance language skills in a new environment encourages students to actively seek opportunities for improvement. Secondly, the visible nature of language learning processes often makes students more aware of shortcomings in their new language system, leading to a heightened sensitivity to such issues. Lastly, the perceived importance of language proficiency for academic and social success in a new cultural setting motivates students to prioritize language skill enhancement. Conversely, students may overlook issues within their own language system (M=3. 53) if they do not perceive them as critical to their academic or interpersonal goals.

The level of critical thinking training, specifically BE4, BE5, and BE6, as reflected in the findings, is relatively low with mean scores of M=3. 59, M=3. 58, and M=3. 51 respectively. Many individuals may not fully grasp the importance of critical thinking training in developing intercultural communication skills (Yu & Van Maele, 2018)①. Without this awareness, they may not prioritize seeking opportunities for such training. Moreover, critical thinking training requires resources such as time, funding, and access to technology or materials for simulations. Some organizations or individuals may lack these resources or may not be aware of available support. Additionally, while critical thinking training can be beneficial for enhancing intercultural communication, it may not always be the most suitable or efficient approach for everyone. Alternative methods, such as direct exposure to diverse cultures or reflective practices, may be more effective for some individuals or situations.

---

① Yu, Q., & Van Maele, J. (2018). Fostering intercultural awareness in a Chinese English reading class. *Chinese Journal of Applied Linguistics*, 41(3), 357-375.

The findings align with Afshar and Movassagh (2017)①, who found a significant correlation between critical thinking scores and academic achievement in 76 undergraduate English majors from Iranian universities using the California Critical Thinking Skills Test. Similarly, Jin and Pu (2018)② discovered that critical thinking ability could predict academic performance, especially in language courses, based on a study of 1333 undergraduate freshmen at a foreign language college in Beijing. Barrett (2018)③ suggested various actions to promote ICC in young people, including study abroad, Internet-based intercultural contact, school-community links, and critical reflection on intercultural experiences using role plays, simulations, and analysis of texts, films, and plays. Lin and Shen (2020)④ conducted a survey at an international university in Hong Kong, indicating that informal intercultural contact, such as through interest group activities, roommates, or sports, positively impacts students' cultural quotient, thereby improving their ICC.

In addition, these findings are also backed with many studies such as empirical studies on the paths of intercultural contact among college students (Peng & Wu, 2016)⑤, the research on the motivational behavior of intercultural contact and English learning among college students (Xu, 2017)⑥, and the research on the media communication of intercultural contact (Xiao et al., 2018⑦).

---

① Afshar H. S., & Movassagh H. (2017). On the relationship among critical thinking, language learning strategy use and university achievement of Iranian English as a foreign language major. *The Language Learning Journal*, 45(3), 382-398.

② 金利民 & 濮实. (2018). 外语类院校本科生思辨能力对学业成绩预测力的研究. 外语界, (04), 44-50+93.

③ Barrett, M. (2018). How schools can promote the intercultural competence of young people. *European Psychologist*, 23(1), 93-104.

④ Lin, X., & Shen, G. Q. (2020). How formal and informal intercultural contacts in universities influence students' cultural intelligence? *Asia Pacific Education Review*, 21(6), 245-259.

⑤ 彭仁忠 & 吴卫平. (2016). 跨文化能力视域下的中国大学生跨文化接触路径研究. 外语界, (01), 70-78.

⑥ 徐智鑫. (2017). 跨文化接触和大学生英语学习动机行为的内在结构分析. 当代外语研究, (03), 59-64.

⑦ 肖珺, 石丽 & 方亚东. (2018). 在华留学生的跨文化媒介接触与中国形象感知. 中国媒体发展研究报告, (00), 104-125, 251-252.

4.2.4 Significant Difference Between the Profile and the Level of ICC

Student respondents show a high level of ICC across all four dimensions. To explore whether there is a significant difference in ICC based on demographics, independent samples t-tests will analyze differences in gender and major. For factors like age and year level, which have three or more groups, one-way ANOVA will be used.

1. Gender Differences in ICC

Among the 598 valid participants, there are 194 men and 404 women. Table 4-12 shows the mean and standard deviation of scores by gender for each ICC dimension. Females outperformed males in total ICC score and all components. Independent samples t-tests reveal significant differences, with females scoring higher than males in all dimensions except knowledge.

Table 4-12 Differential Analysis Result on Gender

	Gender	Mean	S. D.	t	*P*	Interpretation
CO	M	3.764	0.836	−3.447	0.001***	Significant
	F	3.998	0.633			
KN	M	3.734	0.764	−1.827	0.068	Insignificant
	F	3.850	0.709			
SK	M	3.518	0.856	−2.171	0.030*	Significant
	F	3.667	0.748			
BE	M	3.383	0.991	−4.118	0.000***	Significant
	F	3.719	0.804			
Total	M	3.611	0.686	−3.606	0.000***	Significant
	F	3.813	0.536			

Note: CO = intercultural consciousness, KN = intercultural knowledge, SK = intercultural skills, BE=intercultural behavior. * $P<0.05$, ** $P<0.01$, *** $P<0.005$

The conclusion is reached by comparing gender with the four dimensions and overall ICC using a t-test on independent samples. The results indicate that there are significant differences ($P<0.05$) between male and female respondents in, intercultural consciousness, intercultural skills, intercultural behavior and the overall ICC, with females scoring higher on average. Although there is no significant difference ($P>0.05$) in the intercultural knowledge.

A related study by Solhaug and Kristensen (2020)① explored gender differences in ICC using inclusive citizenship theory, gender socialization theory, and feminist standpoint theory with questionnaires from 895 students. Tompkins et al. (2017)② also found significant gender differences in ICC, especially related to study abroad experiences, while Gonzales (2017)③ confirmed significant differences in intercultural effectiveness between genders.

Typically, men are seen as more ambitious, competitive, and adventurous, while women are viewed as careful, emotionally sensitive, and detail-oriented. These traits affect ICC; women often excel in information integration and holistic thinking, enhancing their communication skills (Gur & Gur, 2017)④. Women also handle more domestic and social tasks, which improves attention to detail and language-based reasoning. Men, focusing more on leadership and competitiveness, may prioritize holistic and spatial thinking (Oláh et al., 2018)⑤. Women tend to express ideas and emotions better, using more diverse vocabulary, which aids in international communication (Meshkat & Nejati, 2007)⑥.

Research suggests women have higher empathy and social sensitivity, and are more open to diverse perspectives, active in listening, and emotional

---

① Solhaug, T., & Kristensen, N. N. (2020). Gender and intercultural competence: Analysis of intercultural competence among upper secondary school students in Denmark and Norway. *Educational Psychology*, 40(1), 120-140.

② Tompkins, A., Cook, T., Miller, E., & Lepeau, L. A. (2017). Gender influences on students' study abroad participation and intercultural competence. *Journal of Student Affairs Research and Practice*, 54(2), 204-216.

③ Gonzales, H. (2017). The intercultural effectiveness of university students. *Psychology*, 8(12). 2017-2030.

④ Gur, R. C., & Gur, R. E. (2017). Complementarity of sex differences in brain and behavior: From laterality to multimodal neuroimaging. *Journal of Neuroscience Research*, 95(1-2), 189-199.

⑤ Oláh, L. S., Kotowska, I. E., & Richter, R. (2018). The new roles of men and women and implications for families and societies. In G. Doblhammer, & J. Gumà (Eds.), *A demographic perspective on gender, family and health in Europe*. (pp. 41-64). Springer.

⑥ Meshkat, M., & Nejati, R. (2017). Does emotional intelligence depend on gender? A study on undergraduate English majors of three Iranian universities. *Sage Open*, 7(3), 215824401772579.

expression (Baez et al., 2017)①. However, these trends aren't universal, and individuals vary widely in their experiences and exposure to diverse cultures. Gender intersects with other identities like race, ethnicity, nationality, religion, and socioeconomic status, influencing intercultural consciousness. Hence, it's important to avoid stereotyping and instead use an intersectional approach to understand the complex identities individuals possess.

2. Age Differences in ICC

Table 4-13 Differential Analysis Result on Age

	Major	N	Mean	S. D.	f	*P*	Interpretation
CO	< 18 years	27	3.474	1.147	7.934	0.000***	Significant
	18~20 years	394	3.877	0.733			
	21~22 years	159	4.074	0.521			
	> 22 years	18	4.239	0.442			
KN	< 18 years	27	3.189	1.021	8.749	0.000***	Significant
	18~20 years	394	3.806	0.712			
	21~22 years	159	3.900	0.659			
	> 22 years	18	4.117	0.706			
SK	< 18 years	27	3.022	1.116	8.299	0.000***	Significant
	18~20 years	394	3.610	0.783			
	21~22 years	159	3.684	0.689			
	> 22 years	18	4.122	0.612			
BE	< 18 years	27	3.042	1.103	7.923	0.000***	Significant
	18~20 years	394	3.578	0.877			
	21~22 years	159	3.718	0.818			
	> 22 years	18	4.229	0.645			
Total	< 18 years	27	3.189	0.949	13.564	0.000***	Significant
	18~20 years	394	3.725	0.599			
	21~22 years	159	3.850	0.436			
	> 22 years	18	4.174	0.473			

Note: CO = intercultural consciousness, KN = intercultural knowledge, SK = intercultural skills, BE=intercultural behavior. * $P<0.05$, ** $P<0.01$, *** $P<0.005$

① Baez S., Flichtentrei D., Prats M., Mastandueno R., García A. M., Cetkovich M., & Ibáñez A. (2017). Men, women... who cares? A population-based study on sex differences and gender roles in empathy and moral cognition. *PLoS One*, 12(6), e0179336.

An ANOVA revealed statistically significant differences in ICC across age groups ($P<0.05$), with older individuals demonstrating higher ICC.

F-tests indicate significant differences in ICC and its dimensions between students of different ages. Several factors may explain this. First, as people age, they gain more life and work experiences, helping them better understand and integrate new information, respond to challenges, and solve problems, thus enhancing their ICC. Second, education and socialization processes continuously shape their thoughts, beliefs, and behaviors, increasing tolerance and acceptance (Hjerm et al., 2020)①. Third, older individuals may have more opportunities to travel, work, study, or interact with diverse cultural backgrounds, fostering a deeper understanding and appreciation of cultural differences. They may also reflect more on their own values and biases, developing a nuanced and empathetic approach to intercultural communication. Lastly, aging deepens their self-understanding and cognition of the world, allowing them to recognize its diversity and complexity more profoundly (Mellizo, 2017)②. Maturation also brings better emotional control and acceptance of different perspectives, enhancing self-awareness and emotional intelligence.

The study indicates that age directly affects college students' ICC: older students show greater openness, inclusivity, and adaptability due to their broader knowledge and stronger reasoning.

3. Year Level Differences in ICC

Comparing the year levels of respondents using one-way analysis of variance yielded statistically significant differences ($P<0.05$). There are 166 freshman, 172 sophomores, 149 juniors, and 111 seniors among the 598 valid respondents in this evaluation. Despite the fact that the number of students in

---

① Hjerm, M., Eger, M., Bohman, A., & Fors Connolly, F. (2020). A new approach to the study of tolerance: Conceptualizing and measuring acceptance, respect, and appreciation of difference. *Social Indicators Research*, 147 (3), 897-919.

② Mellizo, J. (2017). Exploring intercultural sensitivity in early adolescence: A mixed methods study. *Intercultural Education*, 28 (6), 571-590.

each grade is not completely symmetrical, this survey has revealed some intriguing phenomena. In terms of intercultural knowledge, senior students (M=4.113) scored higher than juniors (M=4.071), sophomores (M=3.688), and freshmen (M=3.509). However, juniors scored the highest in terms of intercultural consciousness (M=4.119), intercultural skills (M=3.791), and intercultural behavior (M=3.839).

Table 4-14 Differential Analysis Result on Year Level

	Year Level	N	Mean	S. D.	f	*P*	Interpretation
CO	Freshman	166	3.750	0.817	9.965	0.000***	Significant
	Sophomore	172	3.825	0.790			
	Junior	149	4.119	0.465			
	Senior	111	4.064	0.602			
KN	Freshman	166	3.509	0.809	26.901	0.000***	Significant
	Sophomore	172	3.688	0.744			
	Junior	149	4.071	0.549			
	Senior	111	4.113	0.534			
SK	Freshman	166	3.464	0.911	5.885	0.001***	Significant
	Sophomore	172	3.547	0.797			
	Junior	149	3.791	0.668			
	Senior	111	3.731	0.657			
BE	Freshman	166	3.426	0.974	7.188	0.000***	Significant
	Sophomore	172	3.519	0.899			
	Junior	149	3.839	0.770			
	Senior	111	3.722	0.773			
Total	Freshman	166	3.543	0.716	18.964	0.000***	Significant
	Sophomore	172	3.651	0.620			
	Junior	149	3.961	0.390			
	Senior	111	3.917	0.430			

Note: CO = intercultural consciousness, KN = intercultural knowledge, SK = intercultural skills, BE=intercultural behavior. * $P<0.05$, ** $P<0.01$, *** $P<0.005$

The findings are supported by Gao (2016)① and Sun (2020)②, who both found the higher the year level the higher the score of knowledge module. This is commonly accepted as a normal phenomenon. Firstly, as students' progress through their academic careers, they may become more motivated to excel and achieve academic success, which can drive them to perform better on knowledge assessments. Secondly, senior students have likely completed more coursework and participated in more practical experiences related to their field, and they may have developed stronger critical thinking competence through their coursework and practical experiences, which can help them to better analyze and solve complex problems.

However, why do college students not exhibit the same order in intercultural consciousness, intercultural skills, and intercultural behavior? Several explanations could be included. For one thing, senior students typically devote a considerable lot of time and energy to their graduation thesis, job hunting and internship, and their motivation of intercultural communication may decrease. The phenomenon of motivation decline is an important inducement to the degradation of ICC (Xu & Yang, 2023)③. Moreover, students may place a greater emphasis on learning and research in their particular subjects (Tan et al., 2019)④, which may result in a diminished focus on intercultural activities, hence impairing their ICC development. It is difficult for students to enhance their ICC when they do not devote adequate time and effort to this area.

---

① 高永晨. (2016). 中国大学生跨文化交际能力现状调查与分析. 外语与外语教学, (02), 71-78+146.

② 孙博. (2020). 海南高校外语专业学生跨文化能力调查研究. 当代教育理论与实践, (02), 149-156.

③ 徐锦芬 & 杨嘉琪. (2023). 国内外外语教育实证研究对比分析. 当代外语研究, (02), 113-123.

④ 谭姗燕, 冯春 & 崔巍. (2019). 英语口语教学中非英语专业大学生学习负动机影响因素研究. 中外企业家, (25), 195-196.

4. Major Differences in ICC

Table 4-15 Differential Analysis Result on Major

	Major	N	Mean	S. D.	t	*P*	Interpretation
CO	Social Science	402	4. 000	0. 639	3. 560	0. 000***	Significant
	Natural Science	196	3. 762	0. 823			
KN	Social Science	402	3. 867	0. 668	2. 448	0. 015*	Significant
	Natural Science	196	3. 701	0. 830			
SK	Social Science	402	3. 670	0. 719	2. 143	0. 033*	Significant
	Natural Science	196	3. 512	0. 903			
BE	Social Science	402	3. 638	0. 812	1. 020	0. 308	Insignificant
	Natural Science	196	3. 554	1. 011			
Total	Social Science	402	3. 802	0. 521	2. 900	0. 004***	Significant
	Natural Science	196	3. 636	0. 713			

Note: CO = intercultural consciousness, KN = intercultural knowledge, SK = intercultural skills, BE=intercultural behavior. * $P<0.05$, ** $P<0.01$, *** $P<0.005$

Significant difference is shown in Table 4-15. 598 individuals from all academic fields, excluding military science, participate in the survey. Their majors are classified into two categories for statistical purposes. 402 of the respondents are social sciences majors, representing 67. 2%, while 196 are natural science majors, representing 32. 8%. Table 4-15 displays statistically significant differences ($P<0.05$) in different majors, with participants from social science having higher average scores than those from natural science. This is supported by Gao (2016)①, who performed a survey across 16 universities and 10 provinces in China and discovered that humanities students have higher ICC levels than scientific students. The data also are shown in the following line graph. On the intercultural behavior dimension, however, there was no significant difference ($P>0.05$).

① 高永晨. (2016). 中国大学生跨文化交际能力现状调查与分析. 外语与外语教学, (02), 71-78+146.

Due to the nature of their coursework and the focus of their study, social science majors may have more opportunities to engage with other cultures and different points of view than natural science majors. Students might get a deeper understanding of the complexities of intercultural communication and interaction when they are required to investigate and analyze cultural and social differences in social science courses. In addition, social science programs frequently include chances for experiential learning including interactions with individuals from diverse cultural backgrounds, such as study abroad programs, community service projects, and internships in culturally diverse environments. Students can apply their understanding of intercultural communication and build intercultural skills such as effective communication, empathy, and cultural awareness through these activities (Yan, 2023)①. These encounters can provide chances for the development and practice of intercultural skills such as communication, empathy, and openness to different ideas.

4.2.5 Significant Relationship Between the Profile and the Level of ICC

When there is a connection between things while a direct causal relationship cannot be established, this type of relationship is called a correlation. In this study, the Pearson correlation is used to analyze the relationship between variables.

Table 4-16 Correlation Analysis Result (Simplified Format)

	Age	Gender	Year Level	Major
CO	0.188**	0.154**	0.196**	−0.157**
KN	0.161**	0.075	0.333**	−0.107**
SK	0.160**	0.089*	0.151**	−0.094*
BE	0.175**	0.178**	0.158**	−0.045
Total	0.221**	0.159**	0.271**	−0.131**

Note: CO = intercultural consciousness, KN = intercultural knowledge, SK = intercultural skills, BE=intercultural behavior. * $P<0.05$, ** $P<0.01$, *** $P<0.005$

① 严明. (2023). 新时代普通高校外语类一流本科专业建设的若干思考. 外语学刊, (01), 81-86.

Table 4-16 displays the correlation analysis results of the relationship between the four demographic variables of gender, age, grade level, and major and the ICC variables as intercultural consciousness, intercultural knowledge, intercultural skills, and intercultural behavior is examined. Apart for the non-significant correlations between gender and intercultural knowledge as well as major and intercultural behavior, the results indicate that there are substantial correlations between all other factors. The relationship between the overall ICC and year level was the largest among these variables ($r=0.271$), while the correlation between the overall ICC and major was the smallest ($r=-0.131$). This suggests that demographic variables influence ICC factors to some extent. In addition to investigating explicit factors such as consciousness, knowledge, skills, and behavior, ICC research must also consider demographic variables as implicit factors.

1. Relationship Between Age and the Level of ICC

A significant relationship is shown between age and ICC ($r=0.221$, $P<0.01$). Age has the largest association ($r=0.188$, $P<0.01$) with intercultural consciousness, followed by intercultural behavior ($r=0.175$, $P<0.01$) and intercultural knowledge and intercultural skills ($r=0.161$, $P<0.01$ and $r=0.160$, $P<0.01$ respectively). Age exhibits substantial relationships with all four of these dimensions, demonstrating that, to some extent, ICC increase as students' age increases.

This suggests that as students age, their intercultural consciousness, behavior, and skills will all increase. On the one hand, older students will have greater access to a broader range of knowledge and experience and values of various countries and cultures. This will help them comprehend and respect various cultures more effectively. On the other hand, as a four-year compulsory subject in Chinese institutions, English education allows students to steadily enhance their intercultural competence throughout the course of their studies. This also makes it easier for students to speak and connect with individuals from other nations and to have a deeper understanding of other cultures. In addition, as China's outreach to the outside world continues to expand, educational cooperation with other nations expands. Exchange programs such as visiting studies and study abroad (often in the third or fourth year) are being implemented successfully, giving college students with greater opportunity to converse and connect with individuals from diverse cultural backgrounds. This will assist students in comprehending and accepting cultural differences. Moreover, such exchanges can help students comprehend and appreciate the customs and values of different cultures, so increasing their ICC.

2. Relationship Between Gender and the Level of ICC

A significant relationship is shown between gender and ICC ($r=0.159$, $P<0.01$) The largest link ($r=0.178$, $P<0.01$) exists between gender and intercultural behavior, followed by intercultural consciousness ($r=0.154$, $P<0.01$), intercultural skills ($r=0.089$, $P<0.05$), and intercultural knowledge ($r=0.075$).

This finding is consistent with that of Schwarzenthal et al. (2017)① who found self-reported intercultural competence was unrelated to age in both immigrant and non-immigrant background adolescents' groups, whereas ICC, as measured by the situational judgment tests, increased with age. measured by the situational judgment tests, increased with age.

A study conducted by Herrera Granda et al. (2023)② also found out a positive relationship between older students and global citizenship and a low correlation between social awareness and younger students (aged 15 to 25 years).

The result of this study may also be supported by the study of Schwarzenthal et al. (2019)③ which showed that age is linked with ICC by

① Schwarzenthal, M., Juang, L. P., Schachner, M. K., van de Vijver, F. J. R., & Handrick, A. (2017). From tolerance to understanding: Exploring the development of intercultural competence in multiethnic contexts from early to late adolescence. *Journal of Community & Applied Social Psychology*, 27 (5), 388-399.

② Herrera Granda, A., Yepes, S. M., Montes Granada, W. F., & Alvarez Salazar, J. (2023). Students' self-perception of social, emotional, and intercultural competencies in a public higher education institution in Colombia. *Journal for Multicultural Education*, 17(1), 70-82.

③ Schwarzenthal, M., Juang, L., Schachner, Mk., & van de Vijver, Fj (2019). "When birds of a different feather flock together"—intercultural socialization in adolescents' friendships. *International Journal of Intercultural Relations*, 72, 61-75.

intercultural socialization.

Research indicates that women have an advantage over men when it comes to language acquisition (Hartshorne, et al., 2018)①. This provides female students with a higher advantage in mastering foreign languages, making it easier for them to communicate and interact with individuals of other cultures. Also, the cultural socialization and values that female individuals receive growing up make them more interpersonal, collaborative and listening, skills that are important for intercultural communication. Men, on the other hand, place a larger focus on competition, independence, and autonomy, traits that can impede intercultural communication.

3. Relationship Between Year Level and the Level of ICC

A significant relationship is shown between year level and ICC ($r=0.271$, $P<0.01$). Year level has significant correlations with all four dimensions of ICC, with intercultural knowledge having the highest correlation ($r=0.333$, $P<0.01$), followed by intercultural consciousness ($r=0.196$, $P<0.01$), and year level having nearly equal correlations with intercultural behavior and intercultural skills ($r=0.158$, $P<0.01$; and 0.151, $P<0.01$ respectively). In addition, year level has the highest association with ICC overall ($r=0.271$, $P<0.01$) when compared to age, gender, and major, indicating that year level has a significant impact on ICC.

The finding may be supported by the study conducted by Tuncel and Aricioglu (2018)② who determined that the more grade level rises, the more students' intercultural sensitivity perception level increases. Zhang and Zhou (2019)③ also found year level moderates the relationship between interventions and ICC development.

① Hartshorne, J. K., Tenenbaum, J. B., & Pinker, S. (2018). A critical period for second language acquisition: Evidence from 2/3 million English speakers. *Cognition*, 177, 263-277.

② Tuncel, I., & Aricioglu, A. (2018). The Factors affecting the intercultural sensitivity perception level of psychological counseling and guidance students. *International Education Studies*, 11 (3), 61-69.

③ Zhang, X., & Zhou, M. (2019). Interventions to promote learners' intercultural competence: A meta-analysis. *International Journal of Intercultural Relations*, 71, 31-47.

This is anchored to Avcılar and Gök (2022)[①] whose findings revealed that grade level is one of the background characteristics which are significant predictors of the intercultural effectiveness of university students. The others are parent's nationality, being and living in a foreign country, and having a close friend (s) from a different culture. Some research and policy recommendations are provided.

Raising year level provide college students a greater range of knowledge and experiences, social circles and activities. These engagements increase students' intercultural consciousness and behavior. Raising year level also entails exposure to additional intercultural educational resources and possibilities, such as international exchange programs, intercultural courses, etc. Students' multicultural consciousness and behavior will improve as a result of these opportunities and resources.

4. Relationship Between Major and the Level of ICC

A significant relationship is shown between major and ICC ($r=0.131$, $P<0.01$): Except for intercultural behavior ($r=-0.045$, $P=0.272$), major exhibited significant negative relationships with all ICC variables, with the largest correlation being with intercultural consciousness ($r=-0.157$, $P<0.01$), followed by intercultural knowledge ($r=-0.107$, $P<0.01$) and intercultural skills ($r=-0.094$, $P<0.05$). This means that major has an impact on the ICC.

Social science usually focuses more on humanities and social science fields, including history, culture, and language, which can help students better understand the differences and commonalities between cultures, and social science students may be more likely to acquire intercultural experiences and knowledge. In addition, social science education typically focuses more on the development of interpersonal and communication skills, which can also aid improve ICC. In contrast, natural science education focuses more on the study of science and technology and may place less emphasis on intercultural

① Avcılar, A., & Gök, E. (2022). Intercultural effectiveness of international and domestic university students: A case of Turkey. *Journal of International Students*, 12(2), 531-549.

knowledge and skills.

4.2.6 Challenges Encountered to Become Intercultural Competent

Table 4-17 Descriptive Statistical Analysis of Intercultural Challenges

Items	N	Percent	Percentage of cases	Rank
Q54 linguistic knowledge	168	5.60%	28.10%	4
Q54 cultural knowledge of foreign countries	137	4.50%	22.90%	11
Q54 global perspectives	127	4.20%	21.20%	16
Q54 cultural integration skills	102	3.40%	17.10%	18
Q54 nonverbal knowledge	149	4.90%	24.90%	7
Q54 communication motivation	133	4.40%	22.20%	13
Q54 cultural understanding skills	89	2.90%	14.90%	20
Q54 strategy knowledge	157	5.20%	26.30%	6
Q54 opportunities for intercultural contact	229	7.60%	38.30%	3
Q54 cultural knowledge of the native country	137	4.50%	22.90%	10
Q54 adjustment and adaptation skills	139	4.60%	23.20%	9
Q54 opportunities for meaning negotiation	99	3.30%	16.60%	19
Q54 critical thinking ability	283	9.40%	47.30%	1
Q54 cultural differences comparison	255	8.50%	42.60%	2
Q54 cultural heritage awareness	141	4.70%	23.60%	8
Q54 language knowledge application skills	112	3.70%	18.70%	17
Q54 opportunities to regulate identity	167	5.50%	27.90%	5
Q54 awareness of cultural equality	130	4.30%	21.70%	14
Q54 adapt & adjust skills	128	4.20%	21.40%	15
Q54 communication & cooperation skills	135	4.50%	22.60%	12
Total	3017	100.00%	504.50%	

A multiple response set analysis in SPSS 21 of the question "What are the greatest challenges encountered to become interculturally competent?" revealed that "Critical thinking ability" was the most frequently chosen option with 283 selections (47.3%), followed by "cultural differences comparison" with 255 selections (42.6%), and "opportunities for intercultural contact" with 229 selections (38.3%).

1. Critical Thinking Ability

Critical thinking is a primary goal in higher education and a crucial indicator of talent competitiveness in the global context. Prestigious universities like Oxford and Cambridge use critical thinking as a criterion for talent selection (Afshar & Movassagh, 2014)①. Enhancing critical thinking through foreign language education is a key focus in China's education reform (Sun, 2015)②.

Historically, critical thinking has been misunderstood as mere criticism, leading to a limited understanding of students' cognitive abilities (Ruan, 2020)③. However, critical thinking is a higher-level cognitive process driven by rationality and openness. The "Delphi Report" by the American Philosophical Association outlines that critical thinking comprises cognitive skills (interpretation, analysis, evaluation, reasoning, explanation, self-regulation) and emotional traits (curiosity, truth-seeking, fairness, openness, confidence, honesty, perseverance) (Facione, 1990)④. These dimensions are interconnected and essential for making well-founded judgments and knowledge development (Wen & Sun, 2015)⑤. Language and thought are interdependent for thinking is a brain function, and language is the tool for expressing thoughts.

In China, foreign language education has historically lacked focus on

---

① Afshar, H. S., & Movassagh, H. (2014). On the relationship among critical thinking, language learning strategy use and university achievement of Iranian English as a foreign language major. *The Language Learning Journal*, 45(3), 382-398.

② 孙有中. (2015). 外语教育与思辨能力培养. 中国外语, (2), 1+23.

③ 阮全友. (2020). 新时代高校外语教育中师生思辨素养共同发展的现实路径. 外语界, (05), 38-46.

④ Facione, P. A. (1990). *Critical thinking: A statement of expert consensus for purposes of educational assessment and instruction* (*Research Report*). The California Academic Press.

⑤ 文秋芳 & 孙旻. (2015). 评述高校外语教学中思辨力培养存在的问题. 外语教学理论与实践, (3), 6-12+94.

critical thinking, leading to an "absence of critical thinking" among English learners. This issue is often attributed to East Asian "compliance culture," characterized by rote learning and a perceived lack of critical thinking (Floyd, 2011)①. However, Chinese learners' passivity in expressing ideas in foreign languages is more related to language-switching difficulties than cultural traits (Chan & Rao, 2010②; Cortazzi et al., 2011③; Floyd, 2011④).

Traditional foreign language education in China emphasizes language skills over critical thinking, focusing on sentence structure imitation and bilingual conversion rather than integrating language acquisition with humanistic education. Consequently, there is insufficient emphasis on analytical, synthetic, and problem-solving skills in real-world contexts (Ren, 2013)⑤. Although critical thinking ability is part of talent training objectives, implementation often remains at the basic level of memory and understanding.

To address these gaps, foreign language education reform must prioritize developing students' objective and rational judgment abilities based on standards (Wen et al., 2019)⑥. Despite improvements in language skills, the ability to apply, analyze, evaluate, and create remains underdeveloped, necessitating continued focus on enhancing critical thinking in foreign language teaching.

2. Cultural Differences Comparison

Language and culture are essential in language teaching, yet traditional English teaching often focuses mainly on language knowledge, theory, and

---

① Floyd, C. (2011). Critical thinking in a second language. *Higher Education Research & Development*, 30(3), 289-302.

② Chan, C. K. K., & Rao, N. (2010). *Revisiting the Chinese learner: Changing contexts, changing Education*. Springer. Comparative Education Research Centre.

③ Cortazzi, M. Pilcher, N., & Jin, L. (2011). Language choices and "blind shadows": Investigating interviews with Chinese participants. *Qualitative Research*, 11(5), 505-535.

④ Floyd, C. (2011). Critical thinking in a second language. *Higher Education Research & Development*, 30(3), 289-302.

⑤ 任文. (2013). 再论外语专业学生的思辨能力：“缺席”还是“在场”? 兼论将思辨能力培养纳入外语专业教育过程——以英语演讲课为例. 中国外语, (1), 10-17.

⑥ 文秋芳，王建卿，赵彩然，刘艳萍 & 王海妹. (2009). 构建我国外语类大学生思辨能力量具的理论框架. 外语界, (01), 37-43.

application, neglecting cultural aspects. This leads to students struggling with intercultural communication due to a lack of understanding of the cultural context behind the language. As this study found, comparing cultural differences is a significant challenge in enhancing ICC.

The emphasis on introducing target language culture has led to concerns about "losing the native culture" among learners. Scholars now stress the importance of cultivating students' ICC, which involves understanding both Western and Chinese cultures (Zhou & Zhan, 2016)①. Although ICC is a main goal of foreign language education in China, teaching often prioritizes target language culture. Effective intercultural communication requires understanding one's own culture first (Gao, 1994)②. Thus, learning about both cultures is crucial.

Cultivating talents with good ICC is essential, and enhancing Chinese cultural literacy is a basic requirement (Zhou & Xue, 2019)③. Foreign language education should not only teach the target language and its culture but also use the language to spread Chinese culture. Successful intercultural communication involves sharing thoughts and feelings between people from different cultural backgrounds, rather than a one-way cultural infusion (Liu & Liao, 2015)④.

However, in practice, there is often insufficient focus on dual cultural education, leading to poor ICC manifestation among learners. "Local cultural aphasia" is a significant issue, where learners struggle to describe Chinese cultural aspects in English and lack profound cultural literacy.

The core question of education in China is what kind of people to cultivate and for what purpose. Foreign language education must address "local cultural aphasia" by teaching students about both Chinese and global cultures,

---

① 周学恒 & 战菊. (2016). 从《要求》到《指南》:解读《大学英语教学指南中的课程设置. 中国外语, (1), 13-18.

② 高一虹. (1994). 生产性双语现象考察. 外语教学与研究, (01), 59-64.

③ 周雪婷 & 薛菽莉. (2019). 高校中国文化素养培养策略研究. 湖南社会科学, (01), 153-158.

④ 刘荣 & 廖思湄. (2015). 跨文化交际. 重庆大学出版社.

enabling them to represent China internationally (Xiao & Huang, 2020)①. Improving ICC for foreign language learners, both domestically and abroad, is urgent to achieve this goal.

3. Opportunities for Intercultural Contact

The pathway to developing ICC is diverse, but the basic principle is to immerse students in the cultural context of the target language, as language reflects a way of thinking. Chinese college students have limited experience studying and living in English-speaking countries, which contributes to their low ICC. This study's findings on the biggest challenge to ICC align with this observation.

The concept of "inter/cross-cultural contact" originates from Allport's intergroup contact theory or contact hypothesis. Allport (1954)② posited that effective intergroup contact can reduce prejudice and promote communication and understanding between groups. Clément (1980)③ first applied this theory to second language acquisition, highlighting that the quality and quantity of intergroup contact motivate language learning. Other scholars have since explored the positive impacts of intergroup contact on second language learning (Tip et al., 2019)④, noting that pleasant contact experiences enhance learners' confidence, attitudes, and motivation (Macintyre & Vincze, 2017⑤; Shao, Pekrun & Nicholson, 2019⑥). Such contact can also influence language learners' identities and promote cultural integration (Bhatia & Priya,

---

① 肖琼 & 黄国文. (2020). 关于外语课程思政建设的思考. 中国外语, 5(1), 1+10-14.

② Allport, G. (1954). *The nature of prejudice*. Doubleday.

③ Clément, R. (1980). Ethnicity, contact and communicative competence in a second language. In Giles, H., Robinson, W. P., & Smith, P. M. (Ed.), *Language*, (pp. 147-154). Pergamon.

④ Tip, L. K., Brown, R., Morrice, L., Collyer, M., & Easterbrook, M. J. (2019). Improving refugee well-being with better language skills and more intergroup contact. *Social Psychological and Personality Science*, 10(2).

⑤ Macintyre, P. D., & Vincze, L. (2017). Positive and negative emotions underlie motivation for L2 learning. *Studies in Second Language Learning and Teaching*, 7(1), 61-88.

⑥ Shao, K., Pekrun, R., & Nicholson, L. J. (2019). Emotions in classroom language learning: What can we learn from achievement emotion research? *System*, 86, 102-121.

2018[①]; Schotte et al., 2018[②]).

There are two main approaches to inter/cross-cultural contact for second language learners: direct contact (verbal or written interactions) and indirect contact (interpersonal contact and cultural product contact through media such as books, internet, TV, movies) (Kormos & Csizér, 2007)[③]. Studies (Peng & Wu, 2016[④]; Xu, 2017[⑤]; Guang & Gao, 2021[⑥]; Xiao et al., 2018[⑦]) show that Chinese college students primarily achieve intercultural contact through indirect means. This indicates that current approaches to intercultural contact are limited, and ICC needs further improvement. This paper explores how to use available resources and technology to cultivate ICC by immersing students in the language context and thinking style of the target language culture.

4.3 Summary

This chapter conducts a questionnaire around the current situation of ICC among college students, with the aim to determine Chinese college students' ICC among selected universities in Changsha, Hunan province of China. The descriptive-correlational research was design was used to determine the level of ICC and its relationship with the students' demographic profile while

---

① Bhatia, S., & Priya, K. R. (2018). Decolonizing culture: Euro-American psychology and the shaping of neoliberal selves in India. *Theory & Psychology*, 28(5), 645-668.

② Schotte, K., Stanat, P., & Edele, A. (2018). Is integration always most adaptive? The role of cultural identity in academic achievement and in psychological adaptation of immigrant students in Germany. *Journal of Youth and Adolescence*, 47, 16-37.

③ Kormos, J., & Csizér, K. (2007). An interview study of inter-cultural contact and its role in language learning in a foreign language environment. *System*, 35(2), 241-258.

④ 彭仁忠 & 吴卫平. (2016). 跨文化能力视域下的中国大学生跨文化接触路径研究. 外语界, (1), 70-78.

⑤ 徐智鑫. (2017). 跨文化接触和大学生英语学习动机行为的内在结构分析. 当代外语研究, (03), 59-64.

⑥ 官翠玲 & 高山. (2021). 媒介接触对中医药跨文化传播的影响——基于中医药院校留学生中医药文化认同的实证分析. 湖北大学学报(哲学社会科学版), (02), 164-171.

⑦ 肖珺, 石丽 & 方亚东. (2018). 在华留学生的跨文化媒介接触与中国形象感知. 中国媒体发展研究报告, (00), 104-125, 251-252.

descriptive research was designed to provide a snapshot of the current situation. This study employs a 5-Likert scale and data reveal that ICC is highly manifested by the respondents in both overall ICC and its four dimensions as intercultural consciousness, intercultural knowledge, intercultural skills and intercultural behavior. For the test of significant difference on the level of ICC when grouped to age, gender, year level and major, significant difference is found in both overall ICC and it four dimensions. In the correlation analysis between the demographic profile and the level of ICC, it is shown that there is a significant relationship. The multiple response set analysis is performed to show that critical thinking ability, cultural differences comparison and opportunities for intercultural contact are the top three challenges encountered by the student respondents to become intercultural competent.

Chapter 5
Theoretical Model and Practical Model of ICC Cultivation in Foreign Language Education

Guide 2020 formulated by MOE of the PRC defines the nature and purpose of university foreign language courses as both "instrumental" and "humanistic." The instrumental aspect pertains to the practical and specialized nature of foreign languages, while the humanistic aspect emphasizes the cultural dimension, particularly in the context of intercultural communication. Zhang (2012)① highlighted that foreign language education encompasses dual objectives: linguistic and literary goals, as well as social and humanistic goals. In today's globalized world, the social and humanistic dimension of foreign language education specifically focuses on intercultural education, aiming to cultivate individuals with intercultural awareness, knowledge, and skills, enabling them to engage in harmonious interactions, effective communication, and equitable collaboration with individuals from diverse cultural backgrounds. The goals of foreign language education have evolved from solely developing language skills such as listening, speaking, reading, writing, and translation to nurturing qualities of international leaders, equipping students with an international perspective and ICC, and promoting a positive image of China (Wang, 2016)②.

However, the current state of cultivating ICC in foreign language

① 张红玲.(2012).以跨文化教育为导向的外语教学：历史，现状与未来.外语界，(02)，2-7.
② 王守仁.(2016).《大学英语教学指南》要点解读.外语界，(03)，2-10.

teaching in China is concerning (Gu, 2017)[①]. In terms of understanding, many teachers possess a vague understanding of ICC, often confusing it with communication skills or equating it to knowledge of cultural customs, traditions, and history. In terms of pedagogical practice, teachers frequently lack a systematic framework for developing ICC, leading to unclear objectives and limited cultural instruction only when time permits. Attention is often skewed towards the perspectives of mainstream foreign countries or fragmented cultural knowledge. Intercultural teaching in university foreign language education has long been marginalized, occupying a secondary, subsidiary, and dispensable role, failing to meet the increasing demand for talent in the rapidly evolving field of intercultural communication. This indicates the absence of a universally accepted model for cultivating ICC in foreign language education. Therefore, it is imperative to propose a model for fostering ICC among college students that aligns with the educational objectives and context of Chinese universities, encompassing both theoretical and practical aspects.

5.1 Concept of Constructing ICC Cultivation Models in Foreign Language Education

Globalization is an irreversible trend that has brought nations closer and increased their interconnectedness and communication. In this context, the demand for intercultural communication has become increasingly prominent, as cultural differences can impact people's interactions, collaborations, and even lead to conflicts. In the international stage of contemporary China, the country's status and influence are becoming more significant. As the world's second-largest economy, China has emerged as a crucial driving force in the global economy, with growing influence and discourse power in politics,

① 顾晓乐. (2017). 外语教学中跨文化交际能力培养之理论和实践模型. 外语界, (01), 79-88.

culture, technology, and other fields. The rise in China's international status and influence requires its people to better understand and adapt to cultural differences, actively engaging in international cooperation and communication. Therefore, the need for intercultural communication in contemporary China has become more urgent.

To address this demand, the ICC cultivation model should concentrate on nurturing students' ICC, empowering them to adapt to diverse cultural environments, comprehend and appreciate other cultures, and foster positive intercultural relationships. Cultivating ICC encompasses more than just language skills; it also involves developing cultural knowledge, social customs, and values. Therefore, the ICC cultivation model should be comprehensive, systematic, adaptable, and practical, addressing the holistic development of ICC across these four dimensions.

5.1.1 Integrated Objectives

In today's globalized and informatized world, intercultural communication has become one of the essential goals of foreign language education. China's foreign language education aims to cultivate talents with ICC, which is also a necessity for adapting to China's opening-up to the outside world and disseminating China's voice in the new era. Integrating foreign language proficiency and ICC organically is an indispensable means of cultivating ICC.

Firstly, enhancing ICC is one of the objectives of foreign language education. Foreign language education is not merely a process of learning a foreign language; it is also an experience of intercultural exchange. Learning a foreign language requires not only mastering the basic knowledge and skills of the language but also understanding the backgrounds, values, customs, and social systems of different countries and cultures. Therefore, while improving foreign language proficiency, it is also necessary to emphasize the cultivation of ICC. Foreign language proficiency and ICC are interdependent, and neither can be omitted.

In addition, in terms of China's international communication, enhancing both foreign language proficiency and ICC is equally important. Chinese culture and language are gradually stepping onto the world stage, with an increasing number of people paying attention to and learning Mandarin and Chinese culture. In this context, foreign language education should not only focus on students' foreign language proficiency but also transmit Chinese culture and values to people worldwide. By organically integrating foreign language proficiency and ICC, we can improve our understanding of the cultural backgrounds of foreign countries, enhance cultural understanding and communication skills, convey China's values and development achievements, and promote exchanges and cooperation between China and other countries. Therefore, in the process of China's international communication, enhancing both foreign language proficiency and ICC is equally crucial to better introduce Chinese culture and disseminate China's voice to foreigners.

In summary, foreign language education is not merely a process of learning a foreign language; it is also a process of recognizing intercultural communication. By organically integrating foreign language proficiency and ICC, we can better understand the cultural backgrounds of foreign countries, enhance cultural understanding and communication skills, and introduce Chinese culture and values to the world.

5.1.2 Systematic Implementation

ICC cultivation should be approached as a cohesive and interconnected system, especially in today's globalized context. In China, adopting a holistic perspective on ICC is crucial, integrating its various aspects throughout all stages of foreign language teaching. This integration ensures that language instruction encompasses not just linguistic proficiency but also cultural understanding and communicative skills (Mackey & Gass, 2021)①.

---

① Mackey, A., & Gass, S. M. (2021). *Second language research: Methodology and design*. Routledge.

Curriculum design plays a pivotal role by structuring courses that complement each other horizontally and vertically, integrating disciplinary knowledge with intercultural thinking. Utilizing modern tools like multimedia and online resources enhances students' communicative abilities and cultural awareness. Teacher development is equally important, requiring educators to possess high proficiency in language and cultural knowledge, supported by ongoing training and exchange programs. Students benefit greatly from engaging in exchange activities, internships, and practical projects, which foster practical ICC skills beyond the classroom. These experiences allow students to immerse themselves in diverse cultural contexts, improving their adaptability and respect for cultural differences. Additionally, independent study through various media enhances learning efficiency and motivation. To assess students' ICC effectively, a comprehensive evaluation system should be established, complemented by participation in international examinations and competitions. This collaborative effort across different stages of education ensures alignment in syllabi, educational philosophies, and curriculum design. Integration of educational technology, extracurricular activities, and international exchanges further enhances the synergistic approach to ICC development.

In conclusion, fostering ICC requires a coordinated effort among stakeholders, integrating classroom learning with practical experiences and independent study. This approach not only enhances students' cultural awareness and communicative competence but also prepares them to effectively navigate intercultural interactions in a globalized world.

5.1.3 Diversified Approaches

In response to China's increasing global prominence, enhancing ICC through innovative and diverse teaching approaches is crucial. Diversifying classroom instruction is paramount, integrating contextual learning, real-life language use, and culturally rich materials. Methods like role-playing, presentations, and case studies facilitate effective language acquisition and cultural understanding. Incorporating information technology enhances interactive learning experiences, allowing students to practice language skills authentically across different contexts.

Practical teaching approaches should also diversify to broaden students' international perspectives. Establishing international education platforms and organizing exchanges, internships, and volunteer programs provide firsthand exposure to foreign cultures, customs, and industries. These experiences deepen students' ICC by immersing them in diverse cultural environments. On-campus cultural activities further enrich students' ICC through festivals, competitions, language corners, and international forums.

Engaging in inter-school international cooperation and exchanges expands opportunities for intercultural experiences and practice, contributing to faculty and curriculum internationalization. By integrating these approaches, students develop robust ICC, equipping them to navigate global challenges confidently and emerge as globally-minded leaders.

5.1.4 Dynamic Process

Our brain operates as an adaptable system, allowing us to embrace new ideas and experiences, thereby enhancing our ICC. However, static knowledge alone is insufficient for effective communication (Wang & Qin, 2011)①. ICC requires continuous practice and exploration to meet ever-changing communication needs.

Foreign language education must evolve in alignment with long-term national development goals and the concept of lifelong learning (Wang & Wu, 2019)②. It should integrate language learning with evolving societal demands

① 王玉萍 & 秦建华. (2011). "跨文化交际学"课程中大学生创造力培养的实证研究. 外语教学, (3), 57-61.

② 王嘉铭 & 武建鑫. (2019). 论外语教育的学科化发展：应然性与实然性分析. 外语界, (01), 53-60.

and global contexts. As globalization progresses, ICC—intercultural consciousness, knowledge, skills, and behaviors—must continuously adapt to diverse contexts and communication goals (Baker, 2012)[①]. Communication dynamics vary with external changes, necessitating flexible adjustments in teaching methods to meet evolving student and societal needs. Therefore, foreign language teaching must continually refine its methods to effectively serve students and society.

5.2 Principles of Constructing ICC Cultivation Models in Foreign Language Education

The principles guiding ICC model construction in foreign language education are crucial for designing effective educational plans. These principles include integrating practical skills and humanities, aligning language and cultural teachings, and highlighting both local and foreign cultures.

5.2.1 Integration of Instrumentality and Humanities

Foreign languages are not merely tools for communication but also profound carriers of culture and humanity, reflecting the essence of human civilization. In the realm of foreign language education, it is crucial to balance instrumentality and humanities to foster a holistic educational approach.

From a humanities perspective, foreign languages serve as conduits for cultural understanding and personal development. They enable individuals to engage deeply with different cultures, fostering empathy and a nuanced appreciation of cultural diversity. Through language learning, students not only acquire linguistic skills but also cultivate critical thinking and analytical abilities. This process enriches their cultural literacy and enhances their

① Baker, W. (2012). From cultural awareness to intercultural awareness: Culture in ELT. *ELT Journal*, 66(1), 62-70.

capacity for innovation, equipping them to navigate global challenges competently.

Conversely, from an instrumental viewpoint, proficiency in foreign languages is essential in today's interconnected world. It facilitates international communication, academic pursuits, career opportunities, and societal integration. The pragmatic value of language proficiency cannot be overstated, particularly in a society driven by economic imperatives and global competitiveness. However, while acknowledging these practical benefits, it is imperative not to overlook the humanistic dimensions of language education.

Education should transcend mere skill acquisition; it should nurture the human spirit and cultivate a deep understanding of cultural nuances embedded in languages (Feng, 2022)①. Language and culture are intricately intertwined, and foreign language education should emphasize both instrumentality and humanism to foster students' cultural awareness and ICC (Van Rooy, 2019)②.

Furthermore, T. S. Eliot's critique underscores the importance of balancing skills with cultural values in education. A balanced approach not only prepares individuals for personal and professional success but also fosters societal progress and cohesion. In today's globalized era, where cultures converge and interact on a daily basis, foreign language education plays a pivotal role in shaping individuals who can effectively navigate and contribute to multicultural societies.

Foreign language teaching should not solely emphasize language skills but also focus on understanding the cultural nuances embedded in foreign languages. It should cultivate learners' ICC and international understanding. The 21st century is an era of globalization and the coexistence of diverse

---

① 冯建军. (2022). 在自我与他者之间:重塑陌生人社会的道德关系. 武汉科技大学学报(社会科学版), (06), 596-602+576.

② Van Rooy, B. (2019). Reconsidering Kachru's work on Englishes in their multilingual ecologies. *World Englishes*, 38(1-2), 280-293.

cultures. As modern society's citizens, we should learn to interact with individuals from various social backgrounds, cultural contexts, and political systems. Foreign languages serve as vehicles of globalization, and one of the primary objectives of foreign language learning is to comprehend foreign cultures and societies, grasp the distinctions between the global and Chinese-Western cultures, broaden our horizons, and foster personal growth within a multicultural society. Therefore, in the process of intercultural teaching, it is essential to emphasize the integration of instrumentality and humanism, employing methodologies such as guiding students with humanistic awareness.

5.2.2 Parallelism of Language Teaching and Cultural Teaching

Language and culture are inseparable and mutually influential. As emphasized by Kenneth Chastain in the 1970s, the instruction of foreign languages should incorporate cultural education. This is supported by two reasons: firstly, effective communication with speakers of another language depends not only on language skills but also on understanding the cultural customs and expectations. Secondly, fostering intercultural understanding is a fundamental objective of modern education (Zhang & Lv, 2013) ①. Without delving into the cultural depth of a foreign language, all learning efforts would be in vain. Culture encompasses a collective mindset, behavioral patterns, and way of life. It represents the spiritual richness and embodiment of a nation's unique civilization. On the other hand, language plays a vital role as a component of culture, with national languages closely aligned with their respective cultures. Traditional cultures, lifestyles, national psychology, religious beliefs, and even specific modes of thinking all rely on language for formation, accumulation, development, and transmission. In a sense, language serves as the carrier of culture. For instance, in the Chinese language, words such as "礼" (li) and "义" (yi) profoundly reflect the values

① 张红霞 & 吕林海. (2013). 杜威教育哲学在全球化时代的发展. 教育发展研究, (17), 64-70.

embedded in traditional Chinese culture. Merely acquiring grammatical structures and vocabulary in the Chinese language without understanding the cultural connotations would lead to a limited understanding of Chinese.

Language and culture are intertwined facets that mutually enrich understanding and communication in foreign language education. To comprehend a language deeply, one must first grasp its cultural underpinnings. Language serves not only as a means of communication but also as a reflection of cultural values, norms, and historical contexts. Without a solid foundation in cultural literacy, language comprehension remains superficial and incomplete. Conversely, cultural understanding enhances language learning by providing insights into the nuances of expressions, idioms, and social etiquette embedded within the language. In today's globalized world, where intercultural communication is increasingly vital, individuals must continuously develop their language skills and cultural competencies. Effective intercultural communication hinges on robust language proficiency and a nuanced understanding of cultural contexts. Currently, foreign language education in universities often emphasizes the instrumental aspects of language at the expense of cultural education. This approach leads to a focus on grammar, vocabulary, and exam-oriented exercises, neglecting the contextual discourse and oral communication skills essential for genuine language proficiency. To address this imbalance, it is crucial to integrate and prioritize cultural education within language teaching.

Firstly, language teaching and cultural teaching are mutually dependent and complementary. The meanings, values, and social customs conveyed through a language are closely intertwined with the culture it originates from. Thus, to genuinely comprehend a culture, one must first understand its language. Similarly, to truly master a language, one must also grasp the cultural context it is rooted in. Disregarding cultural education in language teaching leads to tedious and uninspiring instruction, while cultural education without language teaching becomes fruitless. Understanding a culture necessitates understanding its language, and understanding language entails understanding the associated culture. Neglecting cultural education results in monotonous language teaching lacking engagement. Students only acquire basic language knowledge, lacking advanced language proficiency and hindering effective intercultural communication. Cultural education, built upon language teaching and serving as a "feedback" and validation mechanism, can promote language instruction, reinforce language fundamentals, and enhance communicative abilities. By expanding the depth and breadth of language teaching, cultural education effectively improves the quality of language instruction. Moreover, cultural education facilitates language teaching, consolidating language fundamentals and enhancing communicative abilities. Simultaneously, language teaching can reciprocally promote cultural education, enabling students to better comprehend and apply the cultural implications and meanings embedded in the language they study. Cultural education expands the scope of language instruction, leading to more profound and extensive language teaching, ultimately raising its quality. Therefore, it is only by integrating cultural education into language teaching, deepening students' understanding and awareness of the language they study, that their language proficiency and ICC can be effectively enhanced. Thus, while teaching language, it is vital to prioritize the cultivation of cultural literacy, facilitating comprehension and application of the cultural connotations and meanings inherent in the language learned. Coordinating language teaching and cultural teaching is essential for genuine development of ICC.

Secondly, language teaching and cultural teaching should be harmonized and synchronized. In the process of second language learning, students often develop a "self-imposed boundary" that creates a barrier between the target language culture and their own culture, limiting their language learning and ICC. The purpose of learning the target culture is to surpass this boundary and expand their cultural perspective, overcoming the obstacles that arise from encountering different cultures. This enables learners to empathize with native speakers of the target language, think and solve problems from their perspective, and attain a genuine sense of empathy and a new self-identity. The goal is to eliminate cultural barriers and enhance students' ICC (Li & Ke, 2021)①. In the process of second language learning, students need to acquire not only language knowledge but also an understanding of the background, values, and social customs of the target language culture. Only through this can they better comprehend the meaning and usage of the target language, improving their language proficiency. Cultural learning also allows students to recognize the similarities and differences between their own culture and the target language culture, expanding their horizons, boosting cultural confidence, and improving their ICC. The coordination of language teaching and cultural teaching promotes the integration of language acquisition and cultural acquisition mechanisms, making it easier for students to understand and grasp both the language and cultural knowledge of the target language. Simultaneously, this prevents the occurrence of superficial language learning that focuses solely on language and detached cultural teaching that lacks real-life applications.

Thirdly, language teaching and cultural teaching are mutually compatible and inseparable. The fusion of language and culture indicates that regardless of the language teaching method employed, cultural education naturally follows. In fact, integrating language teaching with cultural teaching is an inevitable trend in foreign language education. As early as the 1960s, the theory of intercultural communication emerged, asserting that foreign language teaching must integrate cultural elements with language learning to enhance ICC. Teaching intercultural communication skills involves not only imparting language knowledge and skills but also cultivating students' cultural awareness and ICC, enabling them to adapt to the communicative demands of

---

① 李成飞 & 柯应根. (2021). 地方高校英语专业学生跨文化能力发展困境与对策. 巢湖学院学报, (5), 145-151.

different cultural environments. In recent years, with the rapid development of globalization and information technology, the importance of ICC has become increasingly prominent. Companies and organizations increasingly seek talent with ICC, prompting foreign language education to emphasize the cultivation of students' ICC and keep pace with the times. Therefore, the notion that language teaching and cultural teaching are mutually compatible and inseparable is widely accepted and applied. Only by integrating language teaching and cultural teaching can foreign language education achieve its highest goal, enabling students to truly acquire ICC throughout their educational journey.

5.2.3 Emphasizing on Both Local Culture and Foreign Language Culture

President Xi Jinping stated in his 2023 New Year's address that Today's China is closely connected to the world. This statement highlights the connection and interaction between China and the world, emphasizing China's significance to the world and the world's demand for China. With the deepening of globalization, the ties between China and the world are becoming increasingly close, and foreign language communication is also becoming more important.

China plays a significant role in global foreign language learning, with a vast number of learners and professionals. Mastering foreign languages goes beyond practical skills; it enriches our understanding of diverse worldviews, beliefs, and values. In today's information age, foreign language proficiency grants access to a wealth of global knowledge, enhancing cultural literacy (Ou, 2019)①. China aims to promote its rich cultural heritage through foreign language communication, showcasing its history, culture, and societal aspects to the world. This exchange also allows China to contribute ideas globally, fostering mutual understanding and international cooperation. However, the

---

① 欧婧. (2019). 他国化和中国文化“走出去”的策略. 大理大学学报, (7), 102-108.

influx of Western cultural influences, like fast food and media, has impacted Chinese society, sometimes overshadowing traditional values and cultural identity among Chinese youth. This shift has raised concerns about maintaining a balance between foreign language education and preserving Chinese cultural heritage (Wang, 2022)①. Achieving reciprocity and mutual respect in cultural exchange is crucial to leveraging foreign language learning as a catalyst for global peace and development.

(1) It is advisable to recognize the importance of learning the Chinese language and embracing Chinese civilization. While the study of foreign languages and other cultures is also crucial, we must not underestimate the significance of our mother tongue. The mother tongue is the language we learn first, and it accompanies us throughout our lives. It serves as the fundamental tool for expressing and communicating our thoughts. First and foremost, learning our mother tongue enables us to have a better understanding and command of it. It is the language we are most familiar with and the one we acquire initially. By studying our mother tongue, we can enhance our proficiency in expressing ourselves and develop a sense of language and aesthetic awareness. Secondly, our mother tongue culture forms our roots and serves as the source of our cultural confidence and national pride. Each nation possesses its own unique culture, and our mother tongue culture embodies this distinctiveness. Through the study of our mother tongue culture, we gain a deeper understanding and appreciation of our own cultural heritage, fostering cultural confidence and national pride. In the context of globalization, to effectively engage with the world, we must showcase our culture with confidence and pride (Ren, 2019)②. Lastly, the study of our mother tongue culture facilitates intercultural communication. Cultural differences exist

---

① 王银泉. (2022). 外语教育国家意识与外语学科跨学科融合发展. 当代外语研究, (01), 27-46.

② 任丽梅. (2019). 传统文化创造性转化和创新性发展研究初探. 观察与思考, (05), 54-62.

among various societies, and our mother tongue culture represents our own distinct culture. By delving into our mother tongue culture, we not only gain a better understanding of our own culture but also develop an appreciation for other cultures. Recognizing the differences and similarities between our own culture and others is pivotal in intercultural communication. This intercultural consciousness and communication skills are cultivated through the study of our mother tongue culture.

(2) Integrating "Chinese characteristics" into language expression is expected. Foreign languages have evolved with various regional variants over time. Although these variants possess certain characteristics and differences due to language environment, cultural background, and language habits, it does not diminish their application and value in international communication. Conversely, for Chinese individuals, mastering language expression with "Chinese characteristics" holds immense strategic and immediate practical significance (Si, 2021)①. Firstly, proficiently expressing ourselves with Chinese characteristics allows us to convey our opinions and perspectives accurately and vividly. It facilitates a better interpretation of the concepts of "Chinese speed," "Chinese spirit," and "Chinese power," thereby enhancing communication effectiveness. Secondly, incorporating language expression with "Chinese characteristics" strengthens our cultural confidence. In the context of globalization, western culture and language exert a growing influence, which can sometimes lead to a sense of inferiority among Chinese individuals in language communication. By integrating language expression with "Chinese characteristics," we can express our viewpoints with greater confidence and possess the necessary assurance to understand and learn from other cultures. Lastly, incorporating language expression with "Chinese characteristics" contributes to the promotion of Chinese culture and values. As

① 司显柱.(2021).中国特色对外话语体系的构建:回顾与前瞻.当代外语研究,(04),103-112+129.

China's international stature continues to rise, there is an increasing interest and curiosity among foreigners regarding Chinese culture and values. By incorporating language expression with "Chinese characteristics," we can vividly and comprehensively introduce China's history, culture, and social system, enabling the world to gain a deeper understanding of China and fostering intercultural communication and comprehension. Of course, to ensure acceptability, it is important to adhere to the language norms and expression methods of foreign languages, considering both ourselves and others, thus increasing trust among users (Jiang, 2022)①. In the event of cultural conflicts, efforts should be made to explain the cultural background and significance behind them, with the aim of achieving mutual understanding and promoting international communication and cooperation.

In the age of globalization, striking a balance between foreign language education and the preservation of Chinese traditional culture is crucial. While learning foreign languages enhances our understanding of Western culture and global engagement, we must prioritize safeguarding and promoting our own rich cultural heritage. Our culture is a national treasure, deeply rooted in history and traditions, and essential for our identity and pride. Foreign languages facilitate bilateral cultural exchange, fostering ICC and global understanding. This prepares individuals to succeed and adapt in a diverse global society.

5.3 Objectives of Constructing ICC Cultivation Models in Foreign Language Education

In foreign language teaching, establishing clear objectives is crucial for effective planning and organization. Education revolves around determining

① 姜智芹.(2022).中国当代文学海外传播研究的若干关键性议题——评"中国当代文学海外传播研究丛书".中国比较文学,(04),210-214.

the type of individuals to nurture. This focus on defining cultivation objectives is at the core of educational essence. Understanding this essence requires a deep consideration of historical and current practices, addressing educational issues in alignment with national and party development goals, and formulating appropriate policies to ensure comprehensive educational development.

5.3.1 Integrating Instrumentality and Humanism to Uphold the Essence of Education in Cultivating Individuals and Talent

Education is a dynamic social and historical activity that evolves alongside human society's development and progress. Its essence lies in cultivating individuals, a universal and intrinsic pursuit that distinguishes it from other endeavors. This holistic approach encompasses moral, intellectual, physical, and aesthetic dimensions, reflecting the dialectical relationship between universal educational goals and society-specific needs. Throughout history, diverse ideologies and theories have shaped education, emphasizing the importance of nurturing individuals crucial for social progress. This includes cultivating knowledge, preserving cultural heritage, ensuring national continuity, and contributing to institutional functioning. Therefore, foreign language education should align with national aspirations, urgencies, and needs, playing a pivotal role in cultivating talent for the Party and the nation.

The instrumental and humanistic aspects of foreign language teaching originate from the inherent nature of language itself. The study of language's humanistic nature has not gained mainstream recognition in linguistics, mainly because the closest equivalent term found in Western literature is "culture" (Cai, 2017)①. Language serves not only as a tool for expressing thoughts, emotions, and transmitting culture but also as a means for achieving various

① 蔡基刚. (2017). 从语言属性看外语教学的工具性和人文性. 东北师大学报(哲学社会科学版), (02), 1-6.

functional purposes. Cook (2007)① underscores that learning a foreign language entails both external goals like information exchange and internal goals related to personal development. These objectives highlight the instrumental nature of language learning. Conversely, the humanistic aspect of foreign language teaching involves broadening students' perspectives and exposing them to different cultures through the study of both their native language and foreign languages. This intertwines linguistic learning with humanistic education, where the study of specific terminology can unveil cultural insights. Therefore, while foreign language education emphasizes linguistic acquisition and academic knowledge exchange, it also encompasses humanistic values, thereby enhancing ICC.

Guide 2020 outlines clear objectives for university foreign language courses, aiming to enhance students' language proficiency, intercultural communication awareness, and autonomous learning abilities. These goals also include improving cultural literacy and enabling effective language use in academic, social, and professional contexts. This shift marks a departure from previous approaches focused on knowledge memorization rather than practical application, emphasizing reading over listening, speaking, and writing skills. The establishment of these new objectives elevates foreign language education standards, prioritizing ICC through intercultural teaching. This approach is crucial as it cultivates students' ability to communicate appropriately within specific cultural contexts, understanding the cultural nuances embedded in language use. Thus, foreign language education integrates both instrumental and humanistic aspects, recognizing language as both a tool for communication and a carrier of cultural essence.

In our current era, the instrumental and humanistic aspects of language are not contradictory but unified. Instrumentality forms the foundation and

---

① Cook, V. J. (2007). The goal of ELF: Reproducing native speakers or promoting multi-competence among second language users? In Cummins, J. & Davison, C. (Eds), *International handbook of English language teaching*. (pp. 237-248). Springer.

means of humanism, while humanism serves as the carrier and essence of instrumentality. The evolving guidelines for university foreign language teaching emphasize an increasing focus on humanistic care within language courses. This acknowledges that language education encompasses both practical skills and cultural understanding, enhancing students' linguistic abilities while fostering their ICC. The cultivation of ICC has become the primary objective of foreign language education, responding to global trends in politics, economy, and culture (Cui, 2021)①. This shift underscores the role of foreign language education in talent development, skill enhancement, and communication facilitation. It recognizes language's dual nature as both a tool for communication and a repository of cultural and ideological values (He, 2019)②.

The integration of foreign language education in China, harmonizing Chinese and foreign elements, and aligning with the present and the future is a significant challenge for foreign language professionals. China needs a substantial number of professionals who are well-versed in Party and state policies, understand the national conditions of China, possess a global perspective, demonstrate proficient foreign language skills, comprehend international rules, and are skilled in international negotiations to actively engage in global governance. We must fully leverage our advantages, incorporate the responsibility of cultural dissemination into foreign language education, integrate outstanding Chinese culture and core socialist values into the foreign language curriculum, effectively attract international students and foreign language professionals, actively promote China's ideas, and showcase its developmental achievements. Our focus should be on effectively conveying the narrative of China in the new era, promoting exchanges and mutual learning, and fostering people-to-people connectivity. We must keep pace with the times, enhance our personal qualities, root ourselves in Chinese culture, practice core socialist values, effectively bridge the gap between Chinese and Western cultures, and cultivate students' international perspectives,

---

① 崔启亮.(2021).语言服务行业的本地化专业建设.北京第二外国语学院学报,(01),12-24.

② 何莲珍.(2019).新时代大学外语教育的历史使命.外语界,(01),8-12.

patriotism, and critical thinking skills.

5.3.2 Parallelizing Language and Culture to Eliminate the Influence of "Chinese Cultural Aphasia"

Learning a language is synonymous with learning its culture. In essence, foreign language teaching involves the exchange and fusion of Eastern and Western cultures. It introduces foreign languages and cultures into the pre-existing Chinese language and cultural background of students, equipping them with dual capabilities. Given that students already possess a well-established Chinese cultural background, the cultural transfer of the Chinese language inevitably intertwines with foreign language learning. Thus, creating a "cultural language atmosphere" in foreign language teaching has become a crucial topic for reform. This approach emphasizes not only skills development but also enhances students' understanding of the objective cultural background, communicative environment, and differences in thinking patterns associated with the language. By doing so, students can effectively navigate practical language communication, avoiding inappropriate or awkward situations.

During the learning process, the phenomenon known as transfer occurs when prior knowledge influences the learning of new knowledge. Positive transfer refers to the transfer that facilitates the learning of new knowledge, while negative transfer hinders the learning process. According to behaviorist psychology, negative transfer in foreign language learning is often caused by learners' native language habits. In this study, cultural transfer is discussed as the cultural interference resulting from cultural differences. It is characterized by individuals unconsciously guiding their speech, behavior, and thoughts based on their own cultural norms and values, using them as criteria to judge others' speech, behavior, and thoughts (Liu et al., 2020) ①.

Cultural transfer primarily manifests as inappropriate language use, leading to communication difficulties, misunderstandings, and even conflicts

① 刘妍，马晓英，刘坚，魏锐，马利红，徐冠兴... & 甘秋玲.(2020).文化理解与传承素养：21世纪核心素养5C模型之一.华东师范大学学报(教育科学版),(02),29-44.

during intercultural communication or foreign language learning. Therefore, it is crucial to address this type of transfer and gradually enhance learners' cultural literacy. Students should diligently study the cultural knowledge of foreign language countries, improve their cultural sensitivity, and gradually eliminate the impact of cultural transfer on foreign language learning and usage.

In intercultural foreign language teaching, efforts should be made to anticipate instances of cultural transfer during the learning process. By analyzing and comparing the English and Chinese languages, it is possible to reduce negative cultural transfer from Chinese culture and effectively utilize positive transfer from the native language to promote positive cultural transfer of Chinese culture. This approach ultimately enhances the ICC of college students.

5.3.3 Striking Balance Between Indigenous and Foreign Cultures to Enhance Cultural Identity

China's initiatives like the Belt and Road Initiative and the concept of building a community with a shared future have expanded opportunities for foreign language education in Chinese universities. Embracing this mission, Chinese foreign language education should prioritize enhancing students' understanding of Chinese culture, fostering patriotism and national identity, and empowering them to promote Chinese culture globally through foreign languages. Professor Yang Dan from Beijing Foreign Studies University emphasizes the importance of embodying Chinese culture authentically, cautioning against neglecting cultural essence while focusing solely on mastering foreign languages (Xinhua News Agency, 2021) ①.

Since the new era, education's central question revolves around the types of individuals to cultivate, how to cultivate them, and for whom to cultivate them. In foreign language teaching, the issue of cultural aphasia extends

---

① 新华社客户端. (2021-09-22). 为什么说这所大学是"共和国外交官摇篮"——专访北京外国语大学校长杨丹. 新浪网. Retrieved June 20, 2023, from https://k.sina.com.cn/article_1882481753_7034645902000uegd.html.

beyond pedagogical concerns to the fundamental purpose of education—shaping individuals capable of understanding China's rich history and global cultures while effectively promoting Chinese culture internationally (Xiao & Huang, 2020)①.

Kramsch, as cited by Byram (2020) ②, challenges the notion of assimilation in foreign language education, advocating instead for cultural teaching that fosters intercultural awareness and competence through dialogue rather than mere acceptance or accumulation of cultures. As early as 1999, Liu Runqing③ emphasized the importance of giving equal weight to learners' native culture and Western culture in cultural education within foreign language teaching. Scarino (2009)④ stressed that in language learning, students should not only learn their own language and culture but also the language-related culture of the language they are studying. Nguyen (2011)⑤ argued that the goal of learning a second language should be to become a competent second language user while maintaining one's own cultural identity. Therefore, the purpose of cultural teaching in foreign language education is not to assimilate learners into the target language culture (i. e., reductionist learning) or simply accumulate the two cultures in learners (i. e., additive learning). Instead, it aims to create an interaction between learners' native culture and the second culture, enabling them to possess cultural creativity.

Developing strong ICC is crucial in today's globalized world, with Chinese cultural literacy playing a pivotal role in enhancing these skills (Zhou & Xue, 2019)⑥. Foreign language education thus aims not only to impart language

---

① 肖琼 & 黄国文.(2020).关于外语课程思政建设的思考.中国外语,(05),1+10-14.

② Byram, M. (2020). *Teaching and assessing intercultural communicative competence: Revisited*. Multilingual Matters.

③ 刘润清.(1999).论大学外语教学.外语教学与研究出版社.

④ Scarino A. (2009). Assessing intercultural capability in learning languages: Some issues and considerations. *Language Teaching*, 42(1), 67-80.

⑤ Nguyen, T. M. (2011). Learning to communicate in a globalized world: To what extent do school textbooks facilitate the development of intercultural pragmatic competence? *RELC Journal*, 42(1), 17-30.

⑥ 周雪婷 & 薛菽莉.(2019).高校中国文化素养培养策略研究.湖南社会科学,(01),153-158.

proficiency and cultural understanding but also to empower students to use foreign languages as vehicles for promoting Chinese culture internationally. In intercultural communication, it's essential to acknowledge the diverse nature of cultures and avoid reducing cultural comparison to a unilateral transmission of one culture onto another (Zhao, 2012)①. Effective intercultural communication hinges on genuine exchanges among individuals from different cultural backgrounds.

Cultural identity, refers to the positive affirmation of one's own culture through long-term immersion in a national community. It involves a sense of belonging to one's culture, including social values, religious beliefs, customs, traditions, language, and art. Intercultural communication refers to interactions between individuals of different linguistic and cultural backgrounds, facilitating mutual understanding and cooperation in an increasingly interconnected world (Lv & Yu, 2021)②. Language serves as a crucial medium for transmitting culture, embodying its symbols and values. Effective intercultural communication requires a balanced integration of both target language culture and local culture within foreign language education. This approach addresses the "cultural deficit" issue in teaching by emphasizing storytelling and developing curricula that encompass both cultures.

In the new era, China actively promotes cultural self-confidence by highlighting Chinese culture and amplifying the Chinese voice, thereby enhancing the country's soft power and cultural influence. Cultural identity aids Chinese individuals in better understanding and conveying their own culture, further improving China's international image and cultural self-assurance. It promotes exchanges and cooperation between China and other countries, strengthens the country's image and cultural self-confidence, alleviates intercultural conflicts, and elevates the ability and influence of Chinese culture in external communication.

---

① 赵军. (2012). 跨文化交际：认知差异与文化语言习得. 北京大学出版社.

② 吕丽盼 & 俞理明. (2021). 双向文化教学——论外语教学跨文化交际能力培养. 中国外语, (04), 62-67.

5.4 Components of the ICC Cultivation Model in Foreign Language Education

The cultivation of ICC in higher education foreign language teaching encompasses specific content that is a subset rather than an exact representation of the ICC framework. Two main reasons contribute to this distinction. Firstly, ICC involves a wide range of abilities, including psychological and cognitive aspects, which students develop through active engagement and reflection in their social environments (Fantini, 2020)①. While universities play a role in this development, real intercultural communication primarily occurs outside academic settings. Secondly, foreign language teaching aims to enhance ICC, but it cannot achieve this alone. ICC draws on disciplines such as linguistics, sociology, and cultural studies, requiring collaboration across these fields for comprehensive development (Zhang, 2007②; Few et al., 2021③).

Based on empirical research integrating theoretical insights and current analysis of ICC, researchers emphasize the importance of cultivating balanced development in higher education foreign language teaching to enhance students' consciousness, knowledge, skills, and behaviors. This approach aims to tackle discourse challenges like "inarticulateness," "inefficient message conveyance," and "lack of message credibility." Each aspect of ICC deserves equal attention, focusing on both explicit and implicit dimensions within intercultural communicative competence. Researchers have outlined specific content for ICC cultivation in Chinese higher education, defining a model that includes internal components related to teaching processes—

---

① Fantini, A. E. (2020). Reconceptualizing intercultural communicative competence: A multinational perspective. *Research in Comparative and International Education*, 15(1), 52-61.

② 张红玲. (2007). 跨文化外语教学. 上海外语教育出版社.

③ Few, R., Spear, D., Singh, C., Tebboth, M. G., Davies, J. E., & Thompson-Hall, M. C. (2021). Culture as a mediator of climate change adaptation: Neither static nor unidirectional. *Wiley Interdisciplinary Reviews: Climate Change*, 12(1), e687.

curriculum design, course structure, teaching materials, methods, faculty, and assessments—and external components involving activities like language exposure and practice outside the classroom to foster students' ICC.

5.4.1 Internal Components

Effective language teaching encompasses various aspects, including language theory, teaching principles, instructional methods and techniques, curriculum design, and the utilization of teaching materials. Consequently, effective language teaching is the outcome of the interplay between different components. The curriculum design and teaching syllabus are central to internal components of education. They set the direction and goals of instruction, directly influencing student outcomes. Teaching materials provide cultural insights from diverse regions, helping students understand cultural differences and similarities. Instructional methods facilitate ICC development practically. Faculty quality impacts teaching excellence, providing crucial resources and support. Assessment enhances motivation and overall teaching quality. Effective ICC training requires focus on teaching philosophy, learning objectives, instructional models, materials, methods, and extracurricular guidance (Zheng, 2009)①.

Curriculum design should align closely with China's global communication needs, focusing on goals, systematic planning, international perspectives, and practical application. Priority should be given to developing ICC to meet global demands. Courses should be integrated to provide comprehensive knowledge and skills. Alongside traditional language courses, universities should introduce mandatory intercultural communication courses to familiarize students with cultural differences and connections, enhancing their ICC. Optional courses on foreign language cultures, comparative Chinese and

---

① 郑晓红.（2009）.论文化价值取向在大学英语教材中的呈现——以《大学英语综合教程》（全新版）为例.外语界，（2），86-91.

Western studies, and ICC should also be offered to deepen cultural understanding and improve communication across diverse backgrounds. Practical language skills can be honed through initiatives like simulated United Nations programs, providing students with real-world language and communication experience that meets China's international communication needs.

Instructional methods and techniques should be adapted to course specifics, content, and instructional technology, taking into account students' needs, proficiency levels, and preferences. Employing a flexible range of approaches is crucial to meet China's international communication needs effectively. These may include classroom lectures, interactive discussions, group collaborations, case studies, role-playing, and gamified teaching methods, all aimed at stimulating student engagement and improving learning outcomes. Integration of modern technological tools like online classrooms, e-learning platforms, and multimedia teaching can expose students to diverse cultural information, further enhancing their ICC and aligning with China's international communication goals.

The development, selection, and use of foreign language teaching materials should align with China's international communication goals and prioritize ICC cultivation. These materials should cover diverse content from both Chinese and Western cultural backgrounds, including social phenomena and historical events. This approach helps students gain deep insights into communication differences across cultures, thereby enhancing their ICC. Teachers and students should be encouraged to independently select and create teaching materials that meet China's practical international communication needs. The use of these materials should be responsive to students' requirements, employing a variety of adaptable teaching methods to effectively improve both language skills and ICC. This approach contributes positively to the advancement of foreign language education in China.

The development and composition of faculty should be attuned to ICC cultivation. Teachers bear substantial educational responsibilities and play a crucial role in shaping students' ICC. Their awareness of cultivating ICC, mastery of effective teaching methods for international students in China, and ability to adapt teaching to individual needs and resource constraints significantly impact ICC effectiveness.

In testing and evaluation, assessments should be comprehensive and varied. Apart from traditional "summative assessments" like final exams, it's essential to introduce "formative assessments" and consider "situated assessments" that incorporate diverse, authentic evaluation contexts. Moving beyond reliance on single exam papers for grades is vital. Formative assessments should gauge students from multiple perspectives—such as learning attitudes, approaches, effort levels, and stage-based progress—focusing on their developmental journey. Relying solely on exams assesses learning outcomes but overlooks attitudes and methods. Formative assessments enable a thorough evaluation of student growth, identifying and addressing issues in attitudes and methods, thus aiding targeted teaching and problem-solving. Additionally, authentic situational assessments, like real-life demonstrations of learning and evaluations of ICC in genuine cross-cultural or intercultural interactions, are valuable. The core goal is to assess students' ability to navigate specific communication contexts. Ultimately, establishing an evaluation system that integrates "summative," "formative," and "situated" assessments is crucial, evaluating not only explicit knowledge and skills but also implicit awareness, emotions, and other aspects of the learning process.

5.4.2 External Components

The development of ICC extends beyond the classroom to encompass external components such as language exposure and practice. These elements provide valuable opportunities for students to engage in intercultural communication, fostering a deeper understanding of cultural differences and similarities. They allow students to apply and refine their intercultural skills learned in class. In Chapter 6, specific studies on these external components will be conducted. Overall, there's a symbiotic relationship between internal and external components: internal components lay the foundation for ICC by providing knowledge and theoretical support, while external components enable practical application and reinforce learning. Further exploration of these components will continue in the next chapter's investigation of the ICC cultivation model.

5.5 Theoretical Model of ICC Cultivation in Foreign Language Education

ICC cultivation should not be limited to improving second language acquisition (SLA), but should also focus on internationalization and localization, emphasizing cultural dynamism and diversity. This approach aims to cultivate learners' "productive" construction of cultural identity and go beyond culture instead of going across culture (Gao, 2002)①. Based on a comprehensive consideration of foreign language education theories and ICC theories together with China's foreign language learning environment, this study has constructed a theoretical model together with a practical model of ICC in foreign language education. This set of models are applicable to the cultivation of ICC in foreign language education within Chinese universities.

5.5.1 Interpretation of the Theoretical Model

Figure 5-1 illustrates the theoretical model of ICC in foreign language education, structured into three layers: the platform layer, the forming layer, and the competence layer.

---

① 高一虹.(2002).跨文化交际能力的培养:"跨越"与"超越".外语与外语教学,(10),27-31.

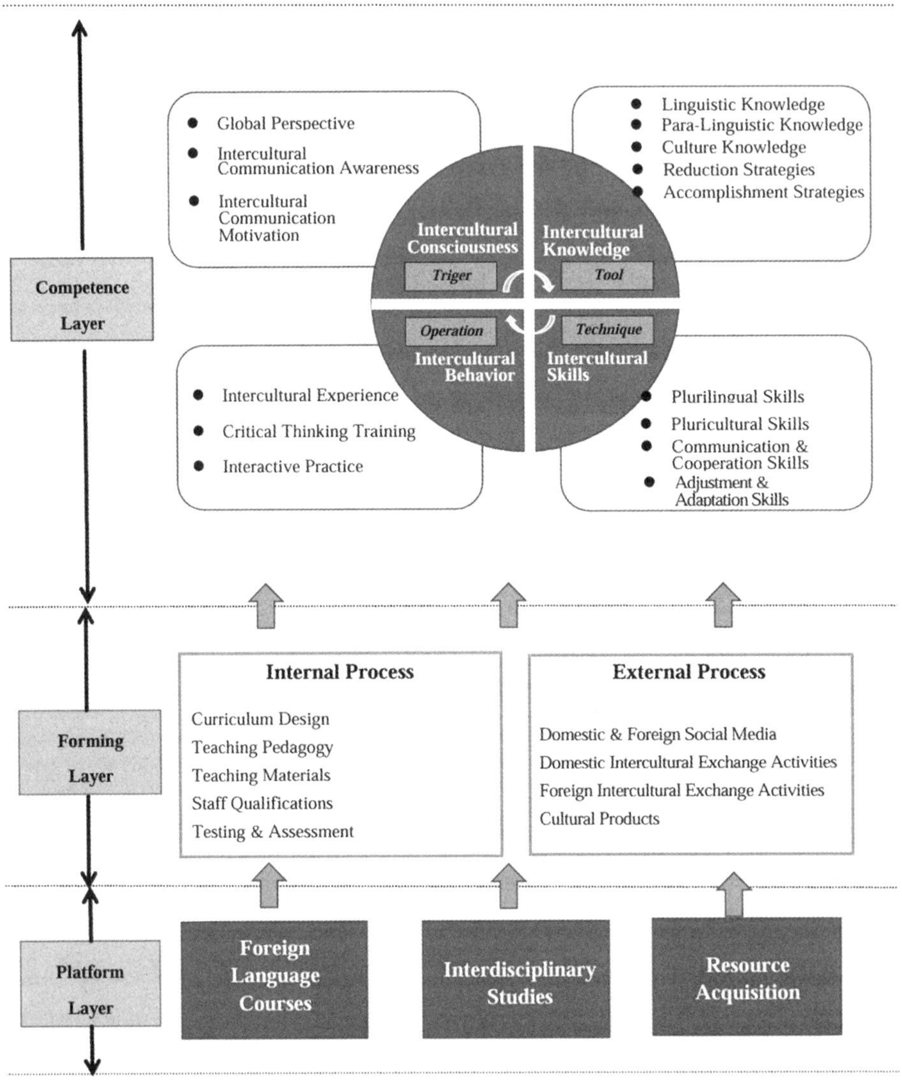

Figure 5-1 Theoretical Model of ICC Cultivation in Foreign Language Education

1. The Platform Layer

The platform layer is essential for cultivating ICC in foreign language education, providing a comprehensive learning environment for students' holistic development. It includes three key components: foreign language courses, interdisciplinary studies, and resource acquisition.

Primarily, foreign language courses stand as widely acknowledged bastions for ICC education. Foreign language courses are one of the most effective fields for implementing ICC teaching (Zhang, 2012)①. The profound integration of information technology and education has revolutionized the landscape of foreign language education. Leveraging the convenience, diversity, and intuitive nature of online resources, online courses, virtual classrooms, and learning management systems (LMS) provide accessible learning that is "open to everyone, anytime, anywhere", enhancing intercultural experiences and improving foreign language education effectiveness. For example, on the Chinese university MOOC platform UMOOCS②, innovative and enriched ways of cultivating ICC include Dalian Foreign Language University's *Intercultural Communication*, Zhejiang Normal University's *Intercultural Communication*, Tianjin Foreign Studies University's *World Cross-Cultural Communication*, Zhengzhou University's *Cultural Differences and Intercultural Communication*, and Beijing Foreign Studies University's *Intercultural Critical Thinking in English Teaching: Ideas and Methods*.

Furthermore, the interdisciplinary amalgamation not only broadens students' intellectual horizons but also elevates their overall scholarly acumen. Facilitated through interactive online and offline platforms, learning communities foster peer-to-peer and student-teacher communication and collaboration. By participating in such communities, students are afforded opportunities to share intercultural learning experiences and resources, fostering a conducive scholarly environment. Engaging in these learning communities allows students to apply theoretical knowledge in practical settings, thereby further refining their intercultural communicative proficiency.

---

① 张红玲. (2012). 以跨文化教育为导向的外语教学：历史，现状与未来. 外语界，(02)，2-7.

② UMOOCS (moocs. unipus. cn) is a MOOC platform for foreign language courses offered by Chinese universities, and it is the exclusive online course platform for foreign languages in Chinese universities. UMOOCS brings together high-quality courses from domestic and foreign universities. Each university can introduce high-quality resources from the alliance to develop its own quality courses, achieving cross-school course sharing and credit recognition.

Resource acquisition provides students with digital libraries, online databases, and Open Educational Resources (OER), supporting self-directed learning and academic growth. These resources enable students to engage in personalized learning and expand their ICC. Empowered to autonomously select learning resources commensurate with their interests and needs, students engage in personalized learning journeys. The rich and diverse array of resources proffer students an expansive intellectual playground, facilitating their comprehensive augmentation of ICC.

2. The Forming Layer

The forming layer comprises internal processes and external processes. This division ensures a holistic approach to ICC cultivation, encompassing theoretical knowledge and practical experiences systematically.

Internally, educational institutions and teachers handle aspects like curriculum design, teaching pedagogy, teaching materials, staff qualifications, and testing. A well-designed curriculum exposes students to a wide range of cultural knowledge, ensuring they gain insights and respect for various cultures. Effective teaching methods encourage engagement in intercultural interactions, enhancing students' communication and problem-solving skills. Carefully selected teaching materials provide perspectives on diverse cultural values, fostering cultural sensitivity and respect. Qualified educators with expertise in intercultural education mentor students, guiding their personal growth. Finally, robust assessment mechanisms evaluate students' ICC, offering feedback and opportunities for improvement, ensuring continuous refinement of their skills and understanding.

Externally, students engage with diverse cultures through various activities beyond the classroom. These include interactions on domestic and foreign social media platforms, participation in intercultural exchange events, and exposure to cultural products. Social media allows students to connect with individuals from different cultural backgrounds, gaining insights into distinct perspectives. Intercultural exchange events, such as academic programs and visits, provide hands-on opportunities for intercultural communication and collaboration. Exposure to cultural products like art, literature, film, and music broadens their cultural horizons, deepens their understanding of diversity, and fosters cultural sensitivity and global perspectives. This multifaceted approach, combining theoretical knowledge with practical experiences, enriches students' intercultural awareness, communication skills, and respect for diversity.

3. The Competence Layer

The competence layer includes four dimensions of ICC: intercultural consciousness, intercultural knowledge, intercultural skills, and intercultural behavior. The conscious-competence model (as cited by Cannon et al., 2010)① illustrates four stages of learning: unconscious incompetence, conscious incompetence, conscious competence, and unconscious competence. In the first stage, individuals are unaware of what they don't know; consciousness serves as the internal motivation to overcome this stage. In stage 2, individuals recognize their lack of knowledge; gaining knowledge becomes essential. In stage 3, individuals become aware that they can now perform; skills provide the technical support for applying this knowledge. In the final stage, individuals can perform without conscious effort; behavior represents the automatic integration of consciousness, knowledge, and skills, reinforcing unconscious competence.

"Unconscious incompetence" is the first stage of conscious-competence model, in which consciousness means intercultural consciousness and competence refers to intercultural communication. Intercultural consciousness is the internal driving force of intercultural activities and serves as a trigger of ICC, including global perspective, intercultural communication awareness, and intercultural communication motivation. A) Global perspective refers to communicators' awareness that in the context of globalization and diversity,

① Cannon, H., Feinstein, A., & Feinstein, D. (2010). Managing complexity: Applying the conscious-competence model to experiential learning. *Developments in Business Simulation and Experiential Learning*, 37, 172-182.

all humanity is a connected and interdependent whole, which allows for a deep understanding of the status of their own culture and the historical responsibility of cultural development, and a rational analysis of the differences in cultural characteristics, and an understanding of the mutual infiltration of core cultural characteristics of both sides (Yuan, 2022)①. B) Intercultural communication awareness is a psychological attribute that refers to communicators' conscious attention and reflection on language and language use in order to gain an understanding of the workings of language (Bolitho et al., 2003)②. C) Intercultural communication motivation refers to the positive psychological factors that communicators hold towards communication partners and the culture of another country in specific communication situations, including an open-minded attitude, a willingness to communicate, an identity adaptation willingness, and a realistic attention awareness.

Intercultural Knowledge is an experience system formed in the human brain in a learning way, which is an instrumental element in "conscious incompetence" stage of promoting ICC. It encompasses linguistic knowledge, para-linguistic knowledge, cultural knowledge, reduction strategies, and achievement strategies. A) Linguistic knowledge, comprising phonetics, vocabulary, grammar, discourse, and pragmatic knowledge, forms the cornerstone of verbal communication proficiency across cultures. B) Para-linguistic knowledge encompasses nonverbal communication cues like facial expressions, gestures, and other nonverbal forms, facilitating nuanced understanding in intercultural exchanges. C) Cultural knowledge extends beyond one's own cultural context to encompass understanding of foreign customs, religious beliefs, history, geography, worldview, values, thought patterns, and behavioral norms, fostering a comprehensive intercultural perspective. D) Reduction strategies include topic avoidance and linguistic

① 袁靖.(2022).非英语专业学生跨文化交际能力量表的构建[博士学位论文,黑龙江大学].

② Bolitho, R., Carter, R., Hughes, R., Ivanic, R., Masuhara, H., & Tomlinson, B. (2003). Ten questions about language awareness. *ELT Journal*, 57(3), 251-259.

form avoidance. E) Achievement strategies include paraphrasing, seeking help, delaying, and nonverbal strategies, among others.

The "conscious competence" stage is of intercultural skills. Depend on existing knowledge, skills are automatic action systems formed and consolidated by individuals through operation and training. They are the technical support of this stage. Intercultural skills are dependent on existing knowledge and are automatic action systems formed and consolidated through practice and training, mastered through operational methods and serve as the technique in ICC, which include plurilingual skills, pluricultural skills, communication and cooperation skills, and adjustment and adaptation skills. Plurilingual skills include the application of language and sublanguage knowledge in the knowledge dimension, as well as the application of communication strategies. Critically absorb multilingual, multimodal, and multisymbol resources in the language database, flexibly adjust the way and timing of language use, and ensure the smooth progress of intercultural communication (García & Li, 2014①; Canagarajah, 2018②). A) Pluricultural skills include cultural understanding and cultural integration skills. Cultural understanding skills include discovering and comparing cultural similarities and differences, interpreting cultural concepts and phenomena, and summarizing and synthesizing cultural perspectives. B) Cultural integration skills involve integrating rich cultural resources and language resources in a dynamic communicative context, blending language and communication content, language and culture, and language and thinking from a holistic perspective. C) Communication and cooperation skills involve actively seizing opportunities, proactively solving problems through language skills, intervening proactively, carrying out effective dialogue, evaluating inherent connections, and supporting others' expressions. D) Adjustment and adaptation

---

① García, O., & W. Li. (2014). *Translanguaging: Language, bilingualism and education*. Palgrave Macmillan.

② Canagarajah, S. (2018). Translingual practice as spatial repertoires: Expanding the paradigm beyond structuralist orientations. *Applied Linguistics*, (39), 31-54.

skills refer to the process of active restructuring of oneself in intercultural communication, abandoning inappropriate language and cultural elements, transforming the nature of language and cultural elements, or selectively absorbing foreign language and cultural elements (Niu & Zhang, 2020)①.

The stage of "unconscious competence" is the status of anatman realm beyond the threshold of transcendence with intercultural behavior. Intercultural behavior is the practice in this stage, including language experience, speculative training and interactive practice. Intercultural behavior is a practical element of ICC, which includes intercultural experience, critical thinking training, and interactive practice. A) Intercultural experience refers to firsthand experience with another language, including classroom education, extracurricular activities, studying abroad, travel, immigration, online communication, and other forms. B) Critical thinking training is the process of expanding and enriching one's language use by accepting heterogeneous cultures, respecting them, comparing different cultures, and evaluating them on the basis of understanding diverse cultures. C) Interactive practice is a social practice that respects cultural subjectivity and is a process of interacting with various cultural subjects to generate meaning.

In the three-layer theoretical model of ICC in foreign language education, the platform layer is at the bottom and serves as the foundation of ICC cultivation. The forming layer is an important link between the platform level and the competence level, enabling students to develop goals that move from mastering basic foreign language skills such as listening, speaking, reading, and writing to integrating language skills and ICC at a higher level. The competence level is the core of the model which is composed of four factors in conscious-competence model, namely, consciousness, knowledge, skills and behavior. Consciousness, as the trigger, is the internal power of ICC in the stage of "unconscious incompetence"; Knowledge serves as a tool to reserve foundation for effective and appropriate intercultural activities in "conscious

---

① 牛家儒 & 张晓明. (2020). 新时期民族传统文化传承与发展的几点思考. 社会科学家, (11), 142-145.

incompetence" stage; Skills are techniques with which intercultural movement system is consolidated through operation training at the stage of "conscious competence"; Behavior is a practical element, a concrete application of the automatic combination of consciousness, knowledge and skills in the "unconscious competence" stage, and a sign of the improvement of ICC. These four conceptual factors reconstructed in this study emphasize the important value of the competence ladder,

5.5.2 Characteristics of the Theoretical Model

The model is timely, comprehensive, and systematic, addressing the developmental needs of Chinese university students' ICC and the current state of foreign language education. It emphasizes the integration of experiential, speculative, and interactive learning with foreign language courses for cultivating intercultural competence with several key characteristics:

Firstly, it shows the organic connection between language, culture, and communication. Byram's (1997)① ICC model includes knowledge, skills, attitudes, and critical thinking but does not explicitly link them with language proficiency, making it challenging to integrate ICC with foreign language teaching in practice. The new model integrates language, communication strategies, and culture into the dimensions of consciousness, knowledge, skills, and behavior, reflecting their interdependence in ICC.

Secondly, the model emphasizes global awareness and cultural equality in intercultural foreign language education. It goes beyond adding intercultural elements to communicative competence by advocating for intercultural citizenship, recognizing learners' intercultural identities, and emphasizing cooperation, negotiation, and adjustment in communication.

Thirdly, the model combines globalization and localization. The consciousness element includes global awareness, cultural awareness, and cultural relativism, promoting respect for all cultures. The knowledge

① Byram, M. (1997). *Teaching and assessing intercultural communicative competence*. Multilingual Matters.

dimension covers one's own and other cultures, stressing the importance of understanding both. The skills dimension involves using this knowledge to express and understand both one's own and other cultures in communication.

In summary, this model integrates the development needs of Chinese college students' ICC with the current state of foreign language education, highlighting the essential relationship between cultural comparison, critical thinking, intercultural experiences, and foreign language courses in cultivating ICC.

5.6 Practical Model of ICC Cultivation in Foreign Language Classroom

This study builds on a theoretical model of three levels in intercultural foreign language teaching and introduces a practical model for classroom implementation. The practical model consists of four levels: teaching objective, teaching process, teaching activity, and teaching assessment, as shown in Figure 5-2.

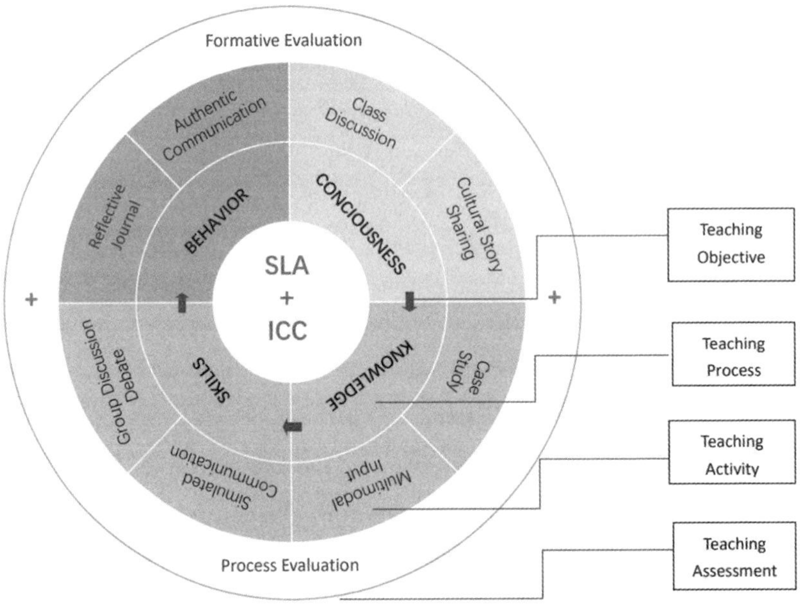

Figure 5-2 Practical Model of ICC in Foreign Language Classroom

5.6.1 Interpretation of the Practical Model

The core of the practical model is the teaching objective, and the other three levels revolve around the teaching objective and serve it.

The teaching objective is divided into two major abilities: intercultural communication competence (ICC) and second language ability (SLA), which takes into account both the humanistic and instrumental aspects of foreign language teaching. On the one hand, foreign language teaching develops students' language ability, standardizes oral and written language expression, and enables students to use language accurately and effectively; on the other hand, it cultivates students' ICC, enabling them to treat individuals with different social and cultural identities equally, and engage with them in effective and appropriate interactions (Byram et al. 2002)①.

The teaching process is a structured, multistage development pathway that maps the four core dimensions of the ICC framework: intercultural consciousness, intercultural knowledge, intercultural skills, and intercultural behavior. It aligns with the conscious-competence model in ICC cultivation. A) The cultivation of intercultural consciousness serves as the starting point of the entire teaching process and forms the cornerstone of the ICC framework. This stage focuses on guiding students to adopt an open, inclusive, and fair perspective towards intercultural interactions. By fostering global perspective and intercultural communication awareness, students begin to examine their own and others' cultures from new perspectives, thereby stimulating their motivation for intercultural communication. This corresponds to the "unconscious incompetence" stage, where awakening intercultural consciousness drives students to move forward. B) Teachers help students actively develop intercultural knowledge. Through interactive learning, students not only understand the cultural background, thinking

---

① Byram, M., Gribkova, B., & Starkey, H. (2002). *Developing the intercultural dimension in language teaching: A practical introduction for teachers*. Council of Europe.

patterns, information coding, and decoding methods behind communication phenomena, but also learn to compare, discover, analyze, and interpret cultural differences. At the same time, they also learn reduction strategies and achievement strategies, such as topic avoidance, paraphrasing, and seeking help, to adapt to the communication needs in different cultural contexts. In this stage, students become aware of their deficiencies in intercultural communication (i. e. , the "conscious incompetence" stage), and knowledge becomes the basic reserve for them to engage in effective and appropriate intercultural activities. Therefore, by learning intercultural knowledge, students fill these gaps and enhance their ICC. C) Teachers design communication tasks or projects to simulate real-life intercultural communication environments, allowing students to negotiate communication meanings and enhance various skills through practical application. Through activities such as role-playing, students can translate their acquired knowledge into practical actions, honing their abilities in language application, multilingual communication, teamwork, adjustment, and adaptation. At this stage, students realize that they possess the ability to engage in intercultural communication (i. e. , the "conscious competence" stage), with skills serving as technical support, helping them externalize their inner communication desires into outward behaviors. D) After each communication activity, students engage in critical reflection, evaluating their performance in terms of consciousness, knowledge, and skills, identifying shortcomings, and seeking improvements. Through continuous reflection and reinforcement, students' ICC is gradually enhanced through sustained intercultural experiences, critical thinking training, and interactive practice. This step aligns with the "unconscious competence" stage, where students reach an advanced stage, capable of engaging in intercultural communication effortlessly and naturally. These four stages are not isolated; rather, they infiltrate and reinforce each other. Their intimate connection underscores the continuity and coherence between the ICC framework and the ICC cultivation model. This process aligns with the laws of students' cognitive development and offers students robust support in building and refining their ICC.

The practice model emphasizes the role of evaluation in teaching, combining formative and process evaluation. A) Formative evaluation focuses on the development of students' ICC at each stage, especially during simulated communication activities. Tools like reflective journals, learning portfolios, and teacher observations provide ongoing feedback. For instance, in the consciousness stage, reflective journals help students document their evolving perspectives. In the knowledge stage, learning portfolios track students' understanding of cultural differences. B) Process evaluation assesses the overall teaching results, typically through final exams or self-evaluation questionnaires. This measures how well students have internalized intercultural knowledge and skills. For example, in the skills stage, students' performance in role-playing activities is evaluated. In the behavior stage, self-evaluation questionnaires and reflective journals allow students to assess their progress. Commonly accepted ICC evaluation methods among intercultural teachers and researchers, such as case analysis, interviews, observations, and self-evaluation questionnaires, ensure a thorough and multifaceted assessment of students' competencies (Deardorff 2006)①. Combining formative and process evaluations ensures teaching activities align with objectives, supporting students as they progress through the ICC framework. This comprehensive strategy supports the continuous enhancement of their ICC.

Based on the study findings, foreign language education should be tailored to demographic disparities like age, gender, and year level. This includes personalized teaching plans to meet diverse student needs and enhance teaching effectiveness.

For younger students, emphasizing the importance of intercultural communication through topics related to university life and social skills can aid in their adjustment to university. Older students can benefit from focusing on

---

① Deardorff, D. K. (2006). Identification and assessment of intercultural competence as a student outcome of internationalization. *Journal of Studies in International Education*, 10(3), 241-266.

skills like nonverbal communication, conflict resolution, and cultural adaptation, along with fostering cultural self-awareness and relativism. Topics on social responsibility and global citizenship can help students understand their societal roles.

Freshmen could receive enlightenment education to grasp the value of international dialogue and develop intercultural awareness. Sophomores may benefit from deeper explanations of intercultural communication knowledge to understand cultural differences and connections. Juniors could explore specialized intercultural courses relevant to their professional fields, such as healthcare relationships or marketing. Seniors could focus on applied intercultural education and interview skills to enhance career prospects.

Male students may be encouraged to participate more in intercultural activities like field trips and exchange programs, emphasizing cultural sensitivity and multicultural expression to understand emotional differences across cultures.

In social sciences, incorporating subjects like intercultural communication, international relations, world history, and linguistics through case studies, readings, lectures, and discussions can deepen students' understanding of cultural diversity. Natural sciences can integrate multicultural scientific outcomes, intercultural medicine, and psychology, employing methods like experiments, simulations, and model-building to enhance intercultural research skills.

5.6.2 Characteristics of the Practical Model

The practical model seamlessly integrates ICC with teaching processes and activities, offering a thorough reflection of foreign language classroom instruction. It effectively connects theoretical ICC cultivation with practical implementation.

Firstly, the practice model integrates ICC theory with constructivist learning theory, encompassing all ICC elements while emphasizing context, collaboration, conversation, and meaning construction. Its four-ring structure effectively blends ICC cultivation, teaching activities, and evaluation, reflecting the practical process of foreign language teaching comprehensively and authentically.

Moreover, the model provides practical guidance for foreign language teaching by focusing on classroom instruction. It addresses both macro-level teaching goals and micro-level teaching activities, strategies, and evaluation. The interplay among teaching goals, process, and activities progressively advances instruction. Evaluation primarily assesses student outcomes relative to teaching goals, offering flexibility in choosing appropriate assessment tools for different teaching stages and guiding teaching practices.

Furthermore, the model promotes innovation in higher education by expanding teaching goals beyond traditional language skills. It emphasizes integrating ICC development with foreign language skills training, encouraging students to construct knowledge in specific contexts, connect language with culture, and engage in reflective learning processes. This approach supports students' autonomy and initiative in learning.

5.7 Summary

The cultivation of ICC in China has both strengths and weaknesses across different levels. National documents and guidelines have emphasized the importance of developing internationally competent individuals and integrating intercultural communication into the curriculum. However, the cultivation process lacks a systematic approach, clear standards, and guiding content. This study has devised a model for fostering ICC in foreign language education at Chinese universities. This model can be summarized as follows: adherence to three principles and objectives, focus on three levels, emphasis on four content aspects, and recognition of the collaborative efforts among various teaching phases. Building upon this foundation, this study establishes both a theoretical model for cultivating ICC and a practical model for foreign language classroom instruction.

The principles of ICC cultivation entail the integration of instrumental and humanistic goals, parallelism teaching of language and culture, and equal emphasis on local and foreign cultures. These principles contribute to the sustainable development of ICC.

ICC cultivation in China is in alignment with the educational policies of the Communist Party of China and encompasses three core objectives: integrating instrumentality and humanism to uphold the essence of education in cultivating individuals and talent, parallelizing language and culture to eliminate the impact of "Chinese cultural aphasia," and striking a balance between indigenous culture and foreign culture to enhance cultural identity. These objectives are closely aligned with the principles of ICC cultivation.

The goal of cultivating ICC is to comprehensively enhance students' consciousness, knowledge, skills, and behaviors in intercultural communication. This enables them to effectively and appropriately communicate across cultures, addressing China's challenges in international communication, such as the inability to articulate reasoning, ineffective dissemination, and lack of credibility.

The cultivation of ICC entails corresponding requirements for both the internal and external aspects of foreign language education. Internally, this includes curriculum guidelines, course design, teaching materials, methods and techniques, faculty, assessment and evaluation. Externally, it encompasses activities like language exposure and language practice.

ICC cultivation should not solely focus on improving second language acquisition (SLA), but also emphasize internationalization, localization, cultural vitality, and diversity. This study integrates theories of foreign language education, ICC, and the Chinese foreign language learning environment to construct both a theoretical model and a practical model for ICC cultivation in foreign language education. The theoretical model comprises three layers: the platform layer, forming layer, and competence layer. The competence layer follows the conscious-competence model and reflects the competence development from intercultural consciousness, knowledge, and skills to behavior. The practical model for foreign language classroom instruction encompasses four levels: teaching objectives, teaching process, teaching activities, and teaching assessment. This model provides a comprehensive and authentic reflection of the foreign language educational process, bridging the gap between the theoretical model of ICC cultivation and its practical implementation.

To further explore the cultivation of ICC in foreign language education at Chinese universities, the next chapter will delve into the specific application of the ICC model in foreign language teaching.

Chapter 6
Application of the ICC Models

This chapter explores the practical application of the ICC cultivation model in foreign language teaching at Chinese universities. While previous chapters detailed the practical model for course instruction, this chapter focuses on the internal and external factors within the formative layer of the theoretical model. These factors include the curriculum, teaching faculty, and modern information technology. The aim is to integrate ICC cultivation into foreign language teaching. However, due to time and scope limitations, this study does not extensively cover internal aspects such as curriculum design, course structure, and testing.

6.1 Cultivating ICC in Foreign Language Education

In this globalized and digitalized era, the construction of an academic discourse system in foreign language and literature is crucial, especially given China's pursuit of the "Two Centenary Goals." Historical experiences underscore the importance of foreign language strategy and ICC in national security and development (Xu, 2018)①. As China's influence grows and its people engage more extensively in global activities, including travel, work, and global affairs, the ability to effectively tell China's stories and perspectives internationally hinges significantly on ICC. This competence not only enhances soft power but also indicates a nation's global influence. Strengthening

① 徐英. (2021). 我国外语战略建设：现状与展望. 北京第二外国语学院学报，(04)，45-57.

university-level foreign language teaching reforms and enhancing talent development are essential to cultivate professionals with strong international competitiveness. However, challenges in planning and implementing foreign language education in China must be carefully studied and addressed with strategic solutions to avoid hindering economic development and jeopardizing national comprehensive strength and global competitiveness.

6.1.1 Current State of Foreign Language Classroom Teaching

From an international perspective, there is still room for improvement in cultivating ICC in foreign language classroom teaching. These issues primarily involve the gap between theory and practice, the need for enhanced cultural teaching, and the lack of comprehensive ICC development. Firstly, there exists a disconnect between theory and practice in ICC research within language education (Sercu, 2010)①. While theoretical advancements are rapid, teaching methods often remain traditional and do not fully integrate theoretical insights. According to Rose and Galloway (2019)②, foreign language teaching focuses heavily on "learning to communicate" through language acquisition, sidelining broader communicative competencies. Secondly, cultural teaching in classrooms is often overshadowed by language instruction (Kim, 2020)③. Despite cultural topics being included in curriculum standards, their actual implementation during instruction is inadequate (Bennett & Salonen, 2007)④. Language teachers prioritize teaching grammar and vocabulary over cultural aspects, resulting in limited

---

① Sercu, L. (2010). 2. Assessing intercultural competence: More questions than answers. In A. Paran & L. Sercu (Ed.), *Testing the untestable in language education* (pp. 17-34). Multilingual Matters.

② Rose, H., & Galloway, N. (2019). *Global Englishes for language teaching*. Cambridge University Press.

③ Kim, D. (2020). Learning language, learning culture: Teaching language to the whole student. *ECNU Review of Education*, 3(3), 519-541.

④ Bennett, J. M., & Salonen, R. (2007). Intercultural communication and the new American campus. *Change: The Magazine of Higher Learning*, 39(2), 46-50.

development of students' intercultural skills and understanding. Moreover, the overall ICC cultivation is insufficiently integrated into foreign language teaching. Teachers tend to see themselves primarily as language instructors rather than educators of ICC (Sercu, 2006)①. While classroom foreign language teaching incorporates ICC-related knowledge and skills, attitudes and values are only sporadically addressed and often excluded from teachers' instructional goals and plans.

Examining foreign language teaching in China reveals significant challenges. Traditional approaches often prioritize task-oriented learning over real-world relevance, cultural depth, and values. Shu (2020)② notes a trend where some universities reduce credits and class hours for foreign language courses, diminishing their cultural educational impact. Many teachers focus heavily on teaching vocabulary and grammar for exams, neglecting broader cultural content. This leads to monotonous classroom instruction and inadequate exposure to Western culture. Students' emphasis on memorization for exams often results in passive language skills and difficulties in practical communication, failing to meet the goals of social communication and international competence required in today's global context.

6.1.2 New Requirements for Cultivating ICC in Foreign Language Classrooms

Enhancing ICC is vital for China's global strategy. To effectively share China's story and voice, talents must strengthen their language proficiency, critical thinking, and cultural confidence. These abilities are essential for presenting a genuine and multidimensional image of China in international interactions and cooperation.

1. Clearing the Objectives as "SLA+ICC"

The revised *Guide 2020* emphasizes the mission of cultivating students'

---

① Sercu, L. (2006). The foreign language and intercultural competence teacher: The acquisition of a new professional identity. *Intercultural Education*, 17(1), 55-72.

② 束定芳.(2020).大学英语教学与国际化人才培养.外国语,(05),8-20.

intercultural consciousness and improving their foreign language application abilities, particularly their ICC (Xiang, 2020)[①]. Foreign language education should integrate SLA (second language acquisition) with ICC. This comprehensive approach guides students to explore cultural origins through language, blending language skills with intercultural competence. Evaluating talent development should focus on improved language abilities, cultural awareness, and emotional resonance, promoting overall ICC enhancement.

SLA forms the foundation for ICC, essential for bridging cultural divides. Effective intercultural communication requires strong bilingual or multilingual proficiency coupled with understanding cultural semantics, thought patterns, and values inherent in language. This enables clear and authentic expression, facilitating mutual comprehension and acceptance. However, possessing high language conversion ability alone does not fully meet the requirements of intercultural communication. Developing language application thinking extends communication beyond language to cultural exchange, demanding deep intercultural knowledge. This includes understanding national conditions, cultures, international relations, and diverse customs. Moreover, individuals should be able to comprehend the impact of diverse cultural backgrounds on individual thinking and behavior. It is crucial to integrate multidisciplinary and multicultural knowledge, embrace and understand diverse cultures, consciously overcome the thinking patterns and inertia of one's native culture, and approach intercultural communication from the perspectives of universal values and humanistic care. By considering the target culture's language usage habits, one can bridge the gap between different cultural backgrounds and achieve genuine understanding and acceptance.

Intercultural communication talents represent China's stories and voice globally. They need a global perspective, patriotism, and a mission to promote Chinese culture while appreciating other civilizations. They should

---

① 向明友. (2020). 顺应新形势，推动大学英语课程体系建设——《大学英语教学指南》课程设置评注. 外语界，(04)，28-34.

maintain a firm political stance, a progressive spirit, political sensitivity, discernment, a clear mind, and always prioritize national interests and the national image. During critical moments, they should proactively seize the initiative and possess discourse power through their ICC, thereby safeguarding the image of the Party and the country.

2. Reflecting the Complexity of Intercultural Communication

With globalization accelerating, foreign language teaching has gained increasing importance in contemporary society. It goes beyond language skills, involving understanding diverse cultures, traditions, and values. Intercultural communication complexity is crucial in foreign language classrooms. Languages act as bridges between cultures, reflecting varied cultural values, traditions, and customs. Despite being lingua francas, foreign languages aren't standardized; they represent diverse cultural nuances. This diversity poses challenges like language variations, cultural differences, etiquette, and customs. For instance, American English, British English, and Australian English differ in pronunciation, vocabulary, grammar, and usage. Moreover, foreign languages serve as a global means of communication for individuals from different countries and regions, each with their distinct cultural backgrounds and contexts. Polite language and forms of address, for example, hold significant importance in certain countries, while others may have a more relaxed approach. Therefore, engaging in intercultural communication using foreign languages necessitates learners to adopt a multicultural perspective and actively shape a credible, likable, and respectable image of China through the principle of "empathy." Furthermore, the complexity of the target language user group requires learners to understand and accept language variations. Just as variations occur in the widespread dissemination and diffusion of ideas, languages also undergo such changes. In the era of globalization, the growing number of foreign language users, cultural heterogeneity, and geographic dispersion have led to a plethora of language variations and hybrids, resulting in what can be called "new languages." These variations can be observed in vocabulary, pronunciation, grammar, and usage (Ivanova & Merkulova, 2021)①. Within multilingual and multicultural societies, foreign languages have given rise to new language forms and standards influenced by local contexts. For example, the term "lorry" commonly used in British English is replaced by "truck" in American English. "Flat" is used to refer to an apartment in British English, while "apartment" is preferred in American English. The word "schedule" is pronounced as [ˈʃɛdjuːl] in British English, whereas it is pronounced as [ˈskedʒuːl] in American English, and so on. Therefore, foreign language learners need to maintain an open mindset, embrace language branches and derivatives, respect and understand their differences, and actively avoid misunderstandings and conflicts in intercultural communication.

3. Enhancing Authentic Language Contexts in Foreign Language Classrooms

Developing ICC in foreign language education requires a practical and comprehensive approach. Creating classroom environments that promote ICC and simulate international exchanges is essential. Immersive learning models like case studies, scenario reconstruction, speculative activities, and simulated exercises are effective. These activities involve students in experiencing, perceiving, understanding, and practicing intercultural communication, enhancing their ability to switch between languages fluently. They also encourage intercultural speculation, introspection, logical reasoning, and critical questioning, helping students transcend native language and cultural biases. By considering shared human values and the language customs of target countries, effective communication and innovative discourse can be fostered.

Stern identified four necessary conditions for language proficiency development: contact with native speakers of the target language, an

---

① Ivanova, N. K., & Merkulova, N. E. (2021). New English words for describing the international English as a current world language reality. *Research in Language*, 19(1), 77-94.

immersive language environment, genuine opportunities for language use, and learner participation (Piccardo & North, 2019)[1]. However, integrating form, meaning, and pragmatics in foreign language teaching in China poses challenges due to the lack of conducive language environments and opportunities for intercultural communication in daily life. Without such environments, students often struggle to find motivation for language learning. To address this, teachers in daily classroom instruction should create an atmosphere conducive to intercultural communication. They should provide practical interaction opportunities and expose students to authentic communication processes in the target language (Meniado, 2019)[2]. Active involvement in language use within the classroom allows students to test, consolidate, and refine their language knowledge through practical application, making foreign languages more useful and interesting to them. There are various approaches to constructing intercultural communication contexts in foreign language classrooms: A) Introduce intercultural communication themes and topics: Teachers can spark students' interest and engagement by introducing themes and topics related to cultural differences, customs, etiquette, values, and more. B) Incorporate authentic language materials: Teachers can utilize authentic language materials, such as movies, TV programs, advertisements, news reports, and other sources, to help students gain a better understanding of communication styles and language characteristics across different cultures. C) Organize intercultural communication activities: Teachers can arrange activities such as role-playing, debates, cultural exhibitions, interviews, and more, to provide students with opportunities to use the language in authentic communicative environments. This fosters the development of their communicative skills and cultural

---

① Piccardo, E., & North, B. (2019). *The action-oriented approach: A dynamic vision of language education*. Multilingual Matters.

② Meniado, J. C. (2019). Second language acquisition: The case of Filipino migrant workers. *Advances in Language and Literary Studies*, 10(1), 47-57.

consciousness. D) Facilitate reflection and discussion: Teachers should encourage students to reflect on and discuss intercultural communication, prompting them to contemplate communication styles and meanings in diverse cultural contexts. This cultivates students' intercultural consciousness and thinking abilities. E) Utilize modern teaching technologies: Leveraging local area networks, teachers can facilitate interactive exercises between teachers and students or among students themselves. Online technologies can be employed to assist students in synchronous or asynchronous intercultural communication with individuals from abroad. In-depth exploration of the methods and approaches involving modern information technology to construct intercultural contexts will be covered in the fifth section of this chapter.

4. Inspiring Students' Sense of Mission

In the past, our focus was on learning foreign languages and exploring Western culture and technology. Today, our goals have shifted. We aim to master foreign languages, showcase Chinese culture on the global stage, and move beyond admiration to actively demonstrate China's beauty to the world. Foreign languages are no longer just a tool to understand the world; they are a means for the world to understand us. As foreign language education evolves, its mission has transformed significantly. In the 21st century, propelled by China's economic growth, technological advancements, and global influence, China has transitioned from a learner to a prominent global player. Foreign language education acts as a crucial "bridge" and "link" in China's international engagement, nurturing talented individuals, fostering exchanges with other nations, and promoting China's active role in global governance reform and development (Wu, 2019)①.

A language embodies its cultural traditions and ways of thinking. Learning different languages not only meets our communication needs but also enriches our understanding of diverse lifestyles, thought patterns, and

---

① 吴岩.(2019).新使命 大格局 新文科 大外语.外语教育研究前沿,(02),3-7+90.

cultural traditions worldwide. It helps us appreciate cultural diversity, grasp different ways of thinking, and foster an objective worldview. From a national perspective, foreign language education enhances a country's engagement in international affairs and competitions, strengthens its ability to communicate globally, amplifies China's voice, and shares its stories. It also contributes to national security. Thus, foreign language education has evolved from a standalone discipline to a field that promotes intercultural communication. In the new era, Chinese foreign language teachers integrate Chinese perspectives and capabilities into intercultural dialogue. This mission prepares students to thrive in future society, drive social progress, achieve personal fulfillment, and tackle global challenges. Moreover, it supports China's active participation in global affairs and competitions, bolstering international communication and outreach efforts.

Cultivating students' sense of mission in intercultural communication enhances their language skills, global perspectives, and cultural literacy. Given the current challenges in China's external dissemination, this cultivation is crucial. True intercultural communication involves not only absorbing Western influences but also spreading Eastern culture to the West. We must value the bidirectional exchange of cultures and effectively share our own culture with the world. First, guide students to understand the challenges posed by cultural differences and communication barriers. Through case studies and cultural interpretation, help them grasp the differences in communication styles between China and other countries. Encourage them to express their own opinions to foster their ICC. Second, address China's insufficient prominence and influence in external dissemination. Students should recognize their responsibility to promote Chinese culture and image as cultural representatives of China. Classroom activities, such as simulations and role-plays, can help students experience this responsibility while honing their language skills and expanding their global perspectives. Finally, acknowledge the multiple constraints and challenges China faces in external dissemination, including political, historical, and social factors. Guide students to understand the background and current situation of China's external dissemination, the challenges it encounters, and its role and position on the international stage.

6.1.3 Classroom Teaching Conjugating SLA and ICC

Cultivating ICC seamlessly integrates language, thoughts, and culture. Language serves as both a carrier and integral part of culture. In foreign language education, the focus extends beyond imparting language knowledge to fostering students' ability to communicate and engage in intercultural interactions using the target language.

The incorporation of target culture teaching has progressively become the mainstream approach in foreign language education. Initially, scholars primarily concentrated on reinforcing the introduction of the target culture in foreign language teaching, emphasizing that "a genuine grasp of social skills is impossible without an understanding of the culture of the target country" (Hu, 1992)①. Furthermore, the cultivation of ICC necessitates an understanding of the culture associated with the language being learned. Learning a language inherently entails acquiring knowledge about the culture it represents (Zhang, 1997)②. However, as early as the inception of intercultural communication studies in China, He (1986)③ proposed that a prerequisite for studying intercultural communication is "to know oneself, to understand one's own culture first. Only by knowing oneself can one comprehend others and achieve a profound understanding of their culture." Since the 1990s, scholars have recognized that the introduction of native culture, which plays a pivotal role, is often overlooked in foreign language teaching. They suggest that "the ability to appreciate both the target culture

① 胡文仲. (1992). 文化教学与文化研究. 外语教学与研究, (01), 3-9+80.
② 张连仲. (1997). 英语教学中语言与文化的关系. 课程. 教材. 教法, (05), 21-23.
③ 何道宽. (1986). 文化在外语教学中的地位. 外国语文, (01), 96-116.

and native culture mutually reinforces each other, allowing learners to fully unlock their potential" (Gao, 1994)①. Native culture serves as a tool for comparison and contrast with the target culture, fostering students' enthusiasm for learning the foreign language and its associated culture. Scholars have also emphasized from the perspective of ideological education that cultural introduction in foreign language teaching should adopt a "cultural equality perspective and language equality perspective" (Zhang, 1997)② to avoid the unbalanced misconception that the target culture is superior to the native culture, which could undermine the value of the native culture. In 2000, Professor Cong's article, "*Aphasia of Chinese Culture*": *The defect of English teaching in China*, published in the Guangming Daily, brought attention to the issue of the lack of native culture in foreign language teaching in China, introducing the concept of the "aphasia" of Chinese culture for the first time (Cong, 2000)③. Scholars have called for the cultivation of students' ICC, emphasizing the need for students to not only understand Western culture and values but also actively promote outstanding traditional Chinese culture (Zhou & Zhan, 2016)④. In 2020, the MOE of the PRC issued the *Guide 2020* which expanded the description of the humanities aspect of college foreign language courses, stating that college foreign language courses can cultivate students' understanding and interpretation of Chinese culture and contribute to the international dissemination of Chinese culture (Xiang, 2020)⑤. Therefore, learning a foreign language encompasses not only acquiring authentic language skills and understanding the cultural traditions of foreign language-speaking countries but also entails the responsibility of utilizing the foreign language as a medium to communicate Chinese culture to

---

① 高一虹.(1994).生产性双语现象考察.外语教学与研究,(01),59-64.

② 张连仲.(1997).英语教学中语言与文化的关系.课程.教材.教法,(05),21-23.

③ 从丛.(2000)."中国文化失语":我国英语教学的缺陷.光明日报,10(19),1.

④ 周学恒 & 战菊.(2016).从《要求》到《指南》:解读《 大学英语教学指南》中的课程设置.中国外语,(1),13-18.

⑤ 向明友.(2020).顺应新形势,推动大学英语课程体系建设——《大学英语教学指南》课程设置评注.外语界,(04),28-34.

non-Chinese-speaking friends abroad.

Since the advent of the new era, education must address the question: "What kind of individuals to cultivate, how to cultivate them, and for whom to cultivate them." This is especially relevant in foreign language teaching, where the goal extends beyond pedagogy to nurturing well-rounded individuals. Chinese university students should not only learn about Chinese history and culture but also understand global cultures and civilizations. They need the ability to communicate China's voice internationally, fulfilling their roles in cultural exchange and conflict resolution, thereby contributing to their country (Xiao & Huang, 2020) ①. This approach corrects the neglect of native culture in ICC development and aims to produce individuals capable of thriving in both domestic and international contexts. In language teaching, it is crucial to expose students to both standard and varied usages of the target language, fostering acceptance of these variations. Language variations are closely tied to the speaker's context, so instruction should include both standard discourses and the social language embedded within them. Cultivating students' multicultural awareness is also essential, encouraging a multicultural perspective on cultural and linguistic issues (Kim, 2021)②. Cultural teaching should not limit students to a single cultural viewpoint but empower them to explore their own ethnic culture and diverse global cultures. The curriculum should include knowledge of the target language culture and multicultural knowledge of their own and other countries. This approach fosters identification with both national and global cultures, enhancing intercultural communication skills through comparison and reflection (Song, 2010)③. Students should understand that language semantics and pragmatics change with different communication partners, and they should adapt their

---

① 肖琼 & 黄国文. (2020). 关于外语课程思政建设的思考. 中国外语, 5(1), 1+10-14.

② Kim, M. S. (2021). Towards new conceptions of multicultural identity in intercultural communication. *Empedocles: European Journal for the Philosophy of Communication*, 12(2), 183-202.

③ 宋梅砚. (2010). 语言文化教学与"文化体验"研究. 河南大学学报(社会科学版), 50(4), 142-147.

communication methods and thinking patterns accordingly in real-life intercultural interactions.

The objectives of cultivating ICC should shift from merely enhancing language skills to improving language transformation and application abilities. This shift requires a systematic approach, ensuring balanced development and synchronous improvement in students' consciousness, knowledge, skills, and behaviors related to intercultural communication. Upholding the principles of SLA in foreign language education is crucial. Classroom teaching should also enable students to compare their own culture with others, approaching cultural differences and conflicts dialectically. They should differentiate and interpret cultural differences scientifically and neutrally, maintaining an objective stance while engaging in theoretical and discursive innovation. This approach allows for resolving conflicts effectively and safeguarding national interests and image.

6.2 Extracurricular Activities in Foreign Language Education

Authentic intercultural communication occurs beyond the classroom, in the social environment. Enhancing ICC involves developing comprehensive skills. While classroom simulations and role-playing are effective, they cannot fully replicate genuine communication scenarios. Exposing students to diverse cultural backgrounds outside the classroom deepens their understanding and respect for different cultures. This exposure also provides insights into global trends, enhancing their international perspectives. Thus, both classroom learning and external activities offer valuable opportunities for cultural immersion, intercultural communication knowledge, and ICC development.

6.2.1 Current State of Extracurricular Activities

The development of students' ICC relies on immersion in the cultural context of the target language, recognizing language acquisition as partly a cognitive habit. A survey by Peng & Wu (2016)① among 600 Chinese undergraduate students identified six primary avenues for intercultural encounters: domestic and foreign social media, domestic and foreign intercultural exchange activities, cultural products, and coursework. These avenues, except cultural products, involve direct encounters and are crucial for extracurricular intercultural exposure.

1. Domestic Social Media

Domestic social platforms like QQ, MSN, WeChat, Weibo, and email facilitate communication between language learners and native speakers of the target language through text, voice, and video interactions. Luo and Gao (2022)② demonstrated the effectiveness of using digital technology in a Chinese—American telecollaborative exchange via WeChat, highlighting its role in enhancing ICC. These online platforms provide learners with rich sensory experiences and active participation opportunities, thereby increasing exposure to authentic language input. Moreover, they improve the authenticity and effectiveness of language materials, leading to significant enhancements in learners' language intuition and reflective abilities.

2. Foreign Social Media

Learners use platforms like Facebook, Twitter, Instagram, LinkedIn, TikTok, Snapchat, WhatsApp, and YouTube to communicate in the target language through text, voice messages, and video chats. Studies, such as those by McLain (2019)③, indicate that engagement with these platforms enhances college students' ICC. Interacting on foreign social media exposes learners to authentic language contexts and dynamic interactions with native speakers, deepening their understanding of language nuances and cultural

---

① 彭仁忠 & 吴卫平. (2016). 跨文化能力视域下的中国大学生跨文化接触路径研究. 外语界, (01), 70-78.

② Luo, H., & Gao, P. (2022). Intercultural learning through Chinese-American telecollaboration: Results of a song sharing project. *Computer Assisted Language Learning*, 37(2), 1-29.

③ McLain, T. R. (2019). Social media treasure hunt—practical lessons using Twitter in the English classroom. *Teaching English with Technology*, 19(2), 88-100.

meanings. These interactions also prompt more feedback from native speakers, aiding in effective language and cultural assimilation.

3. Domestic Intercultural Exchange Activities

Domestic intercultural exchange activities primarily involve participating in various meaningful celebrations of foreign festivals, such as Thanksgiving, as well as cultural exchange days, international study fairs, and cultural lectures. By engaging in these activities, learners can enhance their awareness and understanding of different cultures, improve their cultural sensitivity and communication skills, expand their social circles, and bolster their cultural confidence, thereby enhancing their ICC.

4. Foreign Intercultural Exchange Activities

Foreign intercultural exchange activities encompass participating in paid internships abroad, attending international academic conferences, university exchange programs, summer camps, and international volunteer activities. These activities provide foreign language learners with more in-depth and comprehensive intercultural communication experiences. They not only enhance their language proficiency and cultural understanding but also improve their communication skills and cultivate cultural adaptability. Consequently, they play a significant role in enhancing ICC.

5. Cultural Products

Cultural products serve as an indirect means of intercultural exposure, encompassing online language courses, physical and electronic books, and reading newspapers and magazines to gain insights into the culture of target language-speaking countries. Jiang et al. (2023)① conducted a study using survey data on intercultural encounters among undergraduate students in Anhui Province, referencing the questionnaire developed by Peng & Wu (2018)②. The study revealed limited direct intercultural exposure among

① 姜培培，鲍秀梅 & 曾必好.(2023)安徽高校大学生跨文化接触与跨文化能力相关性研究. 蚌埠学院学报，12(1)，105-109.

② 彭仁忠 & 吴卫平.(2018). 中国大学生跨文化接触情况调查研究. 外语学刊，(05)，87-93.

students, with infrequent encounters noted. It also found that domestic and foreign intercultural exchange activities showed strong correlations with students' foreign cultural knowledge ($r=0.56$ and $r=0.49$, respectively). This highlights how engaging in authentic cultural exchanges through such activities enhances students' understanding and knowledge of foreign cultures within specific cultural contexts.

6.2.2 New Requirements of Extracurricular Activities for Cultivating ICC

Extracurricular activities are crucial for fostering students' ICC. Teachers must guide students beyond classrooms into diverse practical experiences to enhance their ICC proficiency.

Firstly, it is crucial to emphasize the social functions of language to effectively address the demands of intercultural communication. Communicative competence should integrate linguistic forms, meanings, and cultural applications. Learners' motivations range from basic survival to social and professional needs. Language serves cohesive functions for information exchange and social interaction. Therefore, Chinese foreign language education must adopt a communicative approach that emphasizes language's role in achieving communicative goals (Prihartini & Buska, 2020)①. China recognizes the escalating significance of nurturing ICC to facilitate amicable exchanges and collaborations with other nations. Through the cultivation of ICC within foreign language education, students can better comprehend and adapt to social environments within diverse cultural contexts, enhance their abilities and confidence in intercultural communication, and effectively facilitate mutual understanding and collaboration on the international stage.

Secondly, in intercultural communication, language serves as a medium, while culture assumes a significant role. Cultural experiences constitute an

① Prihartini, Y., & Buska, W. (2020). Lecturers' speech acts in Arabic language learning interactions at UIN Sulthan Thaha Saifuddin Jambi. *AL-TA LIM*, 27(1), 41-57.

integral component of language and cultural learning, with interactive cultural activities within communication and foreign language contexts being indispensable for the cultivation of ICC (Sunendar et al., 2021)①. These experiences enable students to engage naturally in intercultural communication. Developing intercultural consciousness helps understand cultural differences, preventing conflicts and misunderstandings. It also enhances appreciation of one's own culture, boosting confidence and adaptability in intercultural exchanges (Luo, 2019) ②. China confronts substantial challenges in intercultural communication due to the substantial disparities between traditional Chinese culture and Western modern culture. In light of this, it becomes imperative for China to intensify the cultivation of cultural self-consciousness by nurturing an understanding of and respect for other cultures, thereby augmenting intercultural communication and external dissemination.

Thirdly, efforts should be made to enhance practical skills development and improve ICC. Enhancing practical skills and improving ICC in foreign language education involves refining cognitive abilities and focusing on socio-cultural contexts (Blumenthal, 2014)③. Language acquisition is intertwined with social interaction and functional application, enriching pragmatic knowledge (Xu et al., 2022)④. Acknowledging both explicit and implicit knowledge is crucial in language learning; reinforcing language output practice helps transform explicit knowledge into implicit and declarative knowledge into procedural, enhancing language automatism. The development of ICC progresses hinges on expanding knowledge, nurturing communicative

---

① Sunendar, D., Darmawangsa, D., & Sukmayadi, V. (2021). Thriving in Indonesian Academia: French students' intercultural communication competence in studying abroad. *Journal of Intercultural Communication*, 21(1), 80-91.

② 罗选民. (2019). 翻译与跨文化传播中的文化自觉. 外语电化教学, (04), 3.

③ Blumenthal, L. F. (2014). *Self-efficacy in low-level English language learners* [Doctoral dissertation, Portland State University].

④ 徐亚妮, 杨连瑞 & 杨向梅. (2022). 国外课堂二语习得研究动态(2010—2019). 北京第二外国语学院学报, (01), 25-41+80.

awareness, and refining skills, while placing a significant focus on practical experience and interactive learning. Attaining native-like proficiency in communication entails more than just classroom instruction; it necessitates learners actively pursuing diverse, authentic communication opportunities. Therefore, foreign language education ought to reinforce the cultivation of practical abilities via a myriad of experiential activities, enabling students to apply their language skills and ICC in real-world intercultural communication, thereby ultimately bolstering their communicative acumen and adaptive capacities.

6.2.3 Approaches to Extracurricular Activities in Foreign Language Learning

Extracurricular activities in foreign language learning should seamlessly integrate with classroom teaching to enhance students' cultural knowledge, intercultural communication awareness, and communication skills. These activities serve as extensions of classroom learning, stimulating student interest and motivation in language and culture while fostering autonomous learning. By providing practical experiences in intercultural communication, extracurricular activities aim to develop and enhance ICC, addressing the current deficit of intercultural communication contexts in China.

1. Domestic and Foreign Social Media

In the media-driven landscape, platforms like WeChat, Xiaohongshu, Facebook, and Instagram offer extensive opportunities for intercultural interactions among the public. Intercultural communication has become crucial for individuals, groups, and grassroots organizations to express themselves and enhance their communicative influence (Zhou & Zhong, 2020)①. Influential intercultural communicators characterized by inclusiveness, diversity, ubiquity, and autonomy are shaping the new era. The diverse

① 周翔 & 仲建琴. (2020). 智能化背景下"中国故事"叙事模式创新研究. 新闻大学, (09), 79+94-122.

discourse of heterogeneity enhances the vitality and fluidity of intercultural exchanges, enriching cultural communication on a broader social scale. Contemporary university students, as representatives of their era, bear the responsibility to showcase and promote Chinese culture globally with ambition, confidence, and resilience.

In the current context, leveraging social media for intercultural learning and communication practices is increasingly essential. Social media platforms offer efficient, convenient, and widespread channels that facilitate flexible and diverse intercultural interactions, transcending the limitations of time and space. Learners can access abundant opportunities and resources, such as relevant materials, intercultural communication videos, and interactions with overseas friends, enriching their understanding and experience of intercultural communication. Given China's rich history and cultural complexities in international interactions, emphasizing intercultural learning and communication practices becomes crucial to addressing cultural conflicts and communication barriers. Social media's diverse practice environment supports cultural exchange and understanding, allowing learners to access languages, customs, and historical backgrounds from various regions. This fosters mutual understanding and respect, supported by empirical research indicating significant progress in ICC development through online exchanges (Schuetze, 2008)①. Proficiency in asking questions, sharing personal experiences, providing examples, discovering supplementary materials, and engaging in online dialogue contribute to their success. China's cultural outreach strategy has evolved from a monologue-style of "understanding others through oneself" in the 19th National Congress to a dialogical-style of "empathizing with others" in the 20th National Congress. Consequently, cultivating ICC should focus on implementing the "glocalization" strategy in cultural exchanges and mutual learning. This strategy aims for reciprocal understanding, promoting

① Schuetze, U. (2008). Exchanging second language messages online: Developing an intercultural communicative competence? *Foreign Language Annals*, 41(4), 660-673.

China as "reliable, admirable, and respectable" internationally. Social media enhances practical international communication by enabling real-time interactions, facilitating better understanding of counterparts' intentions and cultural backgrounds, thus reducing potential misunderstandings and barriers. Moreover, social media amplifies the dissemination of Chinese culture globally while facilitating Chinese understanding of foreign cultures. This mutual exchange enhances global friendship, trust, and provides broader opportunities for China's globalization efforts. Finally, engaging in intercultural communication through social media enriches individuals' cultural literacy and global perspectives, fostering cultural self-confidence and a broader outlook on global challenges and diversity.

Consequently, it is imperative for foreign language education to optimize the utilization of media resources. This involves actively engaging in cultural dissemination globally, moving beyond traditional one-way communication models to embrace interactive approaches. Emphasis should be placed on enhancing communication with individuals from diverse countries, promoting Chinese culture and values, fostering mutual understanding, encouraging people-to-people connections, facilitating cultural exchanges, and ultimately enhancing China's international influence and image.

2. Domestic Intercultural Communication Activities

The implementation of domestic intercultural communication activities allows individuals to gain a deeper understanding of the characteristics and charm of different cultures, enhance respect and understanding towards other cultures, and improve their ICC. These activities provide platforms for students to engage authentically with diverse cultural backgrounds. For instance, participating in international study abroad fairs enable students to learn about opportunities and communicate with international peers, improving their intercultural communication. Similarly, engaging in foreign festivals allows individuals to experience and understand different traditions firsthand, promoting practical intercultural communication experiences. These activities also help address China's external communication challenges by showcasing its culture globally, fostering international friendships, and reducing misunderstandings. Organizing cultural lectures and international events further enhances understanding among participants, paving the way for broader international cooperation. Such initiatives empower students to creatively promote intercultural exchange, such as through organizing foreign culture weeks and leveraging media to attract participation and promote Chinese culture effectively.

China, renowned for its rich cultural heritage, seeks to enhance its international image and promote Chinese culture globally. To achieve this, schools can organize a variety of engaging and educational activities. These may include language corners, foreign language song contests, speech and debate competitions, intercultural business simulations, and model United Nations conferences. These activities not only cultivate students' intercultural awareness but also improve their practical skills in intercultural communication. Additionally, schools can host events like Foreign Language Day, Culture Week, lectures on language and culture topics, exhibitions of foreign language classics, music appreciation sessions, and analyses of foreign newspapers and literature. These initiatives help students build intercultural knowledge, enhance their cultural literacy, broaden their global perspectives, and strengthen their ability to engage with the international community. Moreover, inviting foreign teachers and international guests to interact with students regularly provides authentic language exchanges and cultural experiences. This interaction breaks down cultural barriers, promotes bilateral cultural exchange, and enhances China's international influence and image. Finally, to maximize the impact of cultural and communicative activities, foreign language teachers should encourage students to actively explore and apply their language and cultural knowledge beyond the classroom. Students should actively participate in cultural and language activities on campus, while cultivating empathy to avoid ethnocentrism when *engaging in communication with foreigners* (Souza, 2019)[①]. These activities can also increase students' international perspectives and cultural literacy, strengthen their focus and understanding of international affairs, thereby enhancing China's discourse power and influence in international communication.

3. Foreign Intercultural Communication Activities

Participating in foreign intercultural communication activities deepens understanding of other cultures, cultivates intercultural sensitivity, and reduces misunderstandings and biases in international interactions. Face-to-face communication in a foreign language enhances second language acquisition (SLA) by promoting effective communication techniques, such as perspective-taking and cultural awareness, thereby improving ICC. These experiences broaden individuals' global perspectives, enabling them to better understand international affairs and trends, which enhances their international competitiveness and contributes significantly to China's external communication efforts.

Universities can harness international cooperation platforms to expand students' exposure to foreign cultures and language learning in target countries, addressing China's external communication challenges effectively. Key forms of foreign intercultural activities include short-term training, study abroad programs, inter-school visits, student exchanges, and hosting international students. Firstly, universities can organize short-term study abroad programs, language camps, and inter-school visits. These initiatives allow students to apply classroom knowledge practically, enhancing their ICC and acquiring new perspectives on both foreign and national cultures. Secondly, study abroad and student exchange programs are pivotal for language acquisition and cultural immersion. Immersion in target country

---

① Souza, M. L. (2019). Decolonising postcolonial thinking: Ethnocentrism and sociocentrism as transideological and multiscalar phenomena. *ACME: An International E-Journal for Critical Geographies*, 18(1), 1-24.

environments significantly accelerates language learning and fosters ICC development. According to Lee and Song (2019)①, students participating in study abroad programs exhibit enhanced ICC, greater cultural openness, and a more global perspective compared to those remaining domestically. These experiences cultivate ICC, approachability, and openness. Therefore, leveraging international exchange platforms enables Chinese universities to meet students' needs for studying and experiencing life in target language countries, thereby enhancing their ICC, addressing communication challenges, and bolstering China's global competitiveness and influence.

4. Cultural Products

Cultural products encompass various offerings like online courses, books, newspapers, and magazines, fulfilling cultural needs and enhancing ICC for China's external communication challenges. Firstly, cultural products enable understanding and engagement with diverse cultural backgrounds, including values, customs, and social systems. Engaging with such materials aids language acquisition and enhances language expression skills, crucial for effective intercultural communication. Secondly, these products provide timely updates on cultural developments, keeping individuals informed about global trends. This knowledge helps navigate cultural differences, fostering sensitivity in intercultural interactions. Thirdly, cultural products promote mutual understanding through broadening perspectives and deepening respect for diverse cultures. Online courses facilitate language learning and promote Chinese cultural exchange globally. By accessing international media and cultural expressions like movies and music, individuals gain insights into global cultures, enhancing their appreciation for diversity and improving China's external communication.

---

① Lee, J., & Song, J. (2019). Developing intercultural competence through study abroad, telecollaboration, and on-campus language study. *Language Learning & Technology*, 23(3), 178-198.

6.3 Foreign Language Teaching Faculty

Faculty members are crucial educational assets, central to improving teaching quality and driving educational reforms. In academic settings, they act as mentors and knowledge facilitators, shaping students' learning outcomes and future growth through their expertise, teaching experience, beliefs, and personal influence. ICC involves interpersonal cross-cultural communication skills and promoting Chinese culture globally. Thus, fostering ICC in university foreign language teaching requires aligning faculty concepts, qualities, development, and structure with ICC cultivation goals.

6.3.1 Current State of Foreign Language Teaching Faculty

Sercu's (2006)① seminal study on ICC in foreign language education surveyed teachers from six countries (Belgium, Bulgaria, Greece, Mexico, Poland, Sweden). It found that while many teachers are progressing towards becoming "foreign language and intercultural teachers," they often lack the full knowledge, skills, and attitudes required for this role. Most teachers are categorized as either focusing on developing foreign language communication skills or integrating culture to enhance student motivation. Despite recognizing ICC's importance and advocating for its cultivation to improve language learning outcomes, teachers themselves often have limited intercultural knowledge. Bennett and Salonen (2007)② have noted challenges in teaching culture and ICC within diverse American campuses, where culture, despite being part of curriculum standards, may receive insufficient emphasis during teaching.

Moreover, many foreign language teachers have not fully integrated core

---

① Sercu, L. (2006). The foreign language and intercultural competence teacher: The acquisition of a new professional identity. *Intercultural Education*, 17(1), 55-72.

② Bennett, J. M., & Salonen, R. (2007). Intercultural communication and the new American campus. *Change: The Magazine of Higher Learning*, 39(2), 46-50.

elements of the target language culture into ICC development. Their efforts often focus on introducing aspects such as holidays, customs, and etiquette from Western countries in foreign language education. Some teachers feel unequipped to teach courses related to effective intercultural communication, language and culture, and communication skills. They may struggle to find a starting point, particularly in promoting Chinese civilization. The dissemination of Chinese civilization is limited by the barriers of "tradition", flowing into the surface of "symbols" and ending in the presentation of "differences" (Wan, 2022)①. The dissemination of Chinese civilization tends to emphasize traditional aspects, overlooking modernization and internationalization processes in contemporary China. Teachers commonly use traditional culture, such as festivals, calligraphy, painting, and knots, as entry points to introduce China, reflected in textbooks that predominantly feature traditional themes. However, some media representations reduce China's diverse culture to stereotypical symbols like dragons, koi fish, lotus flowers, bats, and peaches, failing to convey their deeper cultural meanings. Emphasizing the cultural core through meaningful contrasts rather than mere differences could foster better understanding without creating unnecessary misunderstandings and further distancing cultures. Exploring the significance of the cultural core through contrasting differences would be more meaningful than using differences solely for attention-grabbing purposes.

6.3.2 New Requirements for Foreign Language Teaching Faculty in Cultivating ICC

The professional framework for foreign language teachers is complex and dynamic, encompassing interconnected dimensions (Dai, 2008)②. Foreign language teachers must possess diverse qualities, including ICC, to effectively

---

① 万赫达.(2022).实现跨文化传播的"双向奔赴"——国际中文教师跨文化传播的实践取向研究.神州学人,(12),48-51.

② 戴炜栋.(2008).高校外语专业教育发展报告(1978—2008).上海外语教育出版社.

promote Chinese culture and engage with the global community. Teaching foreign languages aims to foster students' ICC and second language acquisition (SLA), involving the transmission of language knowledge, skill development, and ICC cultivation. This places significant demands on teachers' professional competence and teaching abilities (Wang, 2011)①. In addition to selecting teaching materials, conducting effective classroom instruction, guiding student learning and practice, assessing ICC, and utilizing modern technology, teachers should emphasize three crucial aspects to demonstrate proficiency in intercultural foreign language teaching and adapt to the evolving promotion of Chinese civilization.

1. Integrating Contemporary Wisdom to Redefine Chinese Culture

In his 2014 speech at the UNESCO headquarters in Paris, President Xi Jinping emphasized the importance of promoting cultural spirits that transcend time, surpass national boundaries, possess timeless charm, and embody contemporary values. He stressed the need to breathe life into artifacts stored in museums, legacies displayed across the land, and words written in ancient books (Xi, 2014)②. Rather than simply presenting antiquities, we should showcase the transformation of both material and spiritual culture through contemporary expressions, such as the Spring Festival travel rush, high-speed railways, and transoceanic bridges. Scholars like Li and Ding (2017)③ have also advocated for abandoning the traditional mindset of prioritizing the past over the present. They suggest starting from language teaching and the dissemination of Chinese culture, with a focus on meeting the needs of foreign students in understanding contemporary China's national conditions and culture. This approach involves strengthening contemporary awareness,

---

① 王守仁. (2011). 关于高校大学英语教学的几点思考. 外语教学理论与实践, (01), 1-5.

② 习近平. (2014-03-28). 习近平在联合国教科文组织总部的演讲. 中央政府门户网站. Retrieved June 6, 2023, from https://www.gov.cn/govweb/xinwen/2014-03/28/content_2648480.htm.

③ 李泉 & 丁秋怀. (2017). 中国文化教学与传播：当代视角与内涵. 语言文字应用, (01), 117-124.

expanding perspectives, and enhancing the introduction and interpretation of contemporary China and its culture. Some scholars once pointed out that since traditional culture is not the cultural identity of modern China, making it the "main course" of Chinese culture "going global" in intercultural communication will certainly become rootless wood and sourceless water (Wan, 2022)①. Although this argument may seem extreme, it prompts us to reflect on intercultural communication. As noted by the American sinologist Levenson, traditional Chinese values that are reaffirmed by modern individuals will continue to hold value according to their respective standards, including values that even those unfamiliar with tradition acknowledge. Therefore, in the context of China's evolving communication landscape, foreign language teachers need to embrace contemporary wisdom, actively explore new modes of expression, integrate contemporary perspectives, and vividly interpret the essence and charm of Chinese civilization. They should delve deep into uncovering and showcasing the quintessence of Chinese culture, guiding students in promoting Chinese culture to the world.

2. Exploring Cultural Connotations to Enhance Cultural Confidence

Chinese culture's profound connotations require foreign language teachers to deeply understand its historical and cultural aspects. Exploring its origins and development enables teachers to offer students a nuanced interpretation, fostering appreciation for its uniqueness and nurturing cultural confidence. Cultural confidence refers to the resolute belief held by a nation or ethnic group in the value and significance of its own culture. This belief not only facilitates the enduring preservation and innovation of cultural heritage, but also allows for adaptation to societal progress. Additionally, it empowers cultures to maintain robust vitality and comparative advantages in their interactions with other cultures. Establishing cultural confidence serves as an inexhaustible source and driving force behind the enhancement of a nation's

① 万赫达.(2022).实现跨文化传播的"双向奔赴"——国际中文教师跨文化传播的实践取向研究.神州学人,(12),48-51.

soft power (Han, 2019)①. It enhances national cohesion, identity, and pride, bolstering a nation's soft power and resilience against external cultural influences. Importantly, cultural confidence encourages openness to foreign cultures, integrating them with native elements to renew cultural expressions and prevent stagnation. When teaching cultural symbols, teachers should emphasize exploring deeper layers of meaning to deepen students' understanding of their cultural heritage and cultivate their cultural confidence. For example, in discussing heroes, teachers should move beyond textbook narratives to examine China's historical context and compare Eastern and Western perspectives on heroism. This approach encourages critical thinking, fosters intercultural awareness, and promotes respect for diverse cultural viewpoints. By employing such pedagogical strategies, foreign language teachers can facilitate the cultivation of critical thinking skills and foster intercultural awareness among students. Ultimately, this cultivates a sense of confidence in their own culture while instilling respect for other cultures.

3. Leveraging Cultural Commonalities to Enhance the Appeal of Chinese Culture

In the pursuit of fostering ICC among foreign students, it is crucial for foreign language teachers to highlight the commonalities and similarities between Chinese and foreign cultures. This emphasis facilitates a deeper understanding and appreciation of each culture. Political scientist Huntington argues that the coexistence of civilizations necessitates the exploration of shared ground among the majority of civilizations (Hui, 2022)②. To maintain peace in a multicultural world, people from different civilizations should seek and expand shared values, systems, and practices with other civilizations. While the ultimate goal of communication is universally shared among cultures, the approaches to achieving this goal may vary due to cultural

---

① 韩文乾. (2019). 习近平关于坚定文化自信重要论述的四个维度. 思想理论教育导刊, (11), 4-8.

② 惠春琳. (2022). 文明交流互鉴的理论逻辑与实践启示. 山东大学学报(哲学社会科学版), (02), 97-107.

differences. Ideas with cultural commonalities should serve as the "entry point" for intercultural communication (Li & Li, 2016)①. Commonalities outweigh differences, and commonalities form the foundation for intercultural communication and exchange. The purpose of intercultural communication is not to establish individual cultural subjectivity, but to foster mutual understanding among cultural subjects based on others' perspectives. It is precisely because of the existence of differences that cultures can reference and learn from one another, gain a deeper understanding of themselves through comparison, and self-reflect through the lens of others. This process leads to creative forces that drive innovation and change. Therefore, teachers should recognize that in the process of fostering ICC, the presence of differences cannot be overlooked, and it should not be assumed that these differences are insurmountable. Instead, efforts should be made to bridge the gaps, promote the dissemination of Chinese culture, enhance its influence, delve into its spiritual core, actively seek cultural consensus and shared values among all humanity, strive to establish international discourse power commensurate with our comprehensive national strength and international standing, deepen exchanges and mutual learning among civilizations, and promote a better global presence of Chinese culture.

6.3.3 Pathways for Teacher Development

In the field of foreign language education in China, research on intercultural communication emerged in the early 1990s and has made significant progress to date. However, the existing literature primarily consists of speculative articles on Western-based theories of intercultural communication and studies focusing on students, with limited research on teachers. While existing literature emphasizes the importance of incorporating intercultural teaching, there is a scarcity of research on how teachers can

---

① 李宝贵 & 李辉. (2016). "一带一路"沿线国家孔子学院发展现状，问题及对策研究——以白俄罗斯孔子学院为个案. 辽宁师范大学学报(社会科学版), (06), 110-120.

enhance students' ICC (Liu & Shang, 2017)①. Therefore, it is essential to explore the development pathways for foreign language teachers in alignment with national development strategies.

1. Strengthening Teacher Beliefs

Teacher beliefs encompass perspectives and convictions about education, teaching, students, and their role, shaped by personal experiences, knowledge, values, and cultural background. These beliefs significantly influence instructional decisions and behaviors, guiding pedagogical practices and impacting educational reform and professional development (Safa & Tofighi, 2021)②. To enhance students' intercultural awareness and communication skills, teachers must update their beliefs. The role of teachers is emphasized on inspiring young minds with ideals and beliefs through their words and actions. Educational reform often meets resistance due to teachers' lack of innovative awareness, misalignment with their values, increased workload, and concerns about personal interests (Carless, 2012)③. Integrating foreign language teaching and ICC cultivation faces challenges, including teachers' insufficient ICC knowledge and reluctance to engage in cultural teaching due to student resistance or exaggerated admiration for foreign languages. Addressing these challenges requires understanding and reshaping teacher attitudes. Effective foreign language education hinges on exploring and aligning teacher beliefs with the imperative of cultivating ICC comprehensively.

Foreign language teachers undergo three transformative processes in their beliefs. Firstly, ideological construction is paramount, as ideology influences

---

① 刘熠 & 商国印. (2017). 世界英语背景下高校英语教师对跨文化教学的信念研究. 北京第二外国语学院学报, (05), 87-97+126.

② Safa, M. A., & Tofighi, S. (2021). Intercultural communicative competence beliefs and practices of Iranian pre-service and in-service EFL teachers. *Innovation in Language Learning and Teaching*, 16(2), 164-175.

③ Carless, D. (2012). Innovation in language teaching and learning. In Chapelle, C. A. (Eds)., *The encyclopedia of applied linguistics*. Blackwell Publishing Ltd.

social values and public opinion (Zhang, 2022)①. Teachers must effectively convey Chinese stories, promote the Chinese voice, interpret Chinese characteristics, and bolster China's international discourse power. Emphasizing ideological construction addresses cultural gaps and establishes a robust ideological foundation. Secondly, teachers must align with talent cultivation objectives in foreign language education, fostering strong cultural confidence. Curriculum should integrate foreign language cultural materials with targeted language instruction, promoting comprehensive cultural exchange and critical thinking (Hao, 2019)②. This approach moves beyond one-sided cultural dissemination, enhancing ICC, cultural consciousness, and global perspectives. Lastly, foreign language teachers should possess a clear understanding of their roles, tasks, and the required qualities in intercultural foreign language teaching. Liu and Yue (2020)③ argue that university foreign language teachers need to update their perspectives on talent cultivation, teacher capabilities, teaching philosophies, and instructional pathways while firmly establishing the goal of holistic education. Education practitioners must adhere to moral principles and integrate morality into their personal conduct, learning, and teaching to better fulfill their responsibilities as guides and mentors in students' healthy growth (Xi, 2014)④. Teachers' moral integrity and educational abilities are crucial for guiding students' growth and fostering respect and trust in learning (Wen, 2021)⑤. Foreign language teachers facilitate students' familiarity with the target language culture by providing them with general cultural background knowledge. Additionally, they prepare learners for future intercultural needs by teaching social and sociolinguistic skills, helping them overcome biases and prejudices towards other cultures,

---

① 张志丹. (2022). 百年大党理论创新的成功密码. 理论探讨, (01), 11-19.

② 郝运慧. (2019). 牢固树立外语教育中的文化自信. 光明日报, 10(21), 02.

③ 刘正光 & 岳曼曼. (2020). 转变理念、重构内容,落实外语课程思政. 外国语(上海外国语大学学报), (05), 21-29.

④ 习近平. (2014-05-05). 习近平在北京大学师生座谈会上的讲话. 中央政府门户网站. Retrieved June 18, 2023, from https://www.gov.cn/xinwen/2014-05/05/content_2671258.htm.

⑤ 文秋芳. (2021). 大学外语课程思政的内涵和实施框架. 中国外语, (02), 47-52.

and promoting empathy, openness, and respect for others.

2. Conducting Action Research for Foreign Language Teachers

The emergence of "action research" in the field of education can be traced back to the early 1980s. Teacher action research follows a cyclical process encompassing planning, implementation, observation and analysis, and reflection. McNiff (2013)① outlined five specific steps in action research: A) Teachers identify teaching problems through their awareness and perception of the teaching process. B) They propose targeted solutions to address these issues. C) They develop and implement teaching plans to tackle the identified problem. D) They collect and analyze data to assess the effectiveness of teaching actions. E) Based on analysis and evaluation, they redefine teaching problems for subsequent research cycles.

Foreign language teachers can utilize action research to develop effective strategies for fostering students' ICC in their teaching practice. Initially, teachers can assess students' ICC levels and dimensions through methods such as questionnaires and interviews conducted outside the classroom. This assessment informs the formulation of teaching objectives, design of classroom activities, and development of evaluation strategies for cultural teaching. In classroom practice, teachers can employ pedagogical approaches like situational teaching, task-based teaching, and case-based teaching. They should integrate collaborative and autonomous learning methods, creating communicative contexts within thematic units to enhance students' ICC. Activities such as speeches, presentations, debates, simulated business conferences, and case analyses promote interactive communication and student engagement. Throughout the course, teachers should collect and analyze relevant data, reflect on teaching practices, adjust lesson plans, and refine teaching techniques to enhance effectiveness. Qualitative methods like induction and description can be employed to analyze interview results with students on teaching objectives, methods, content, and outcomes.

---

① McNiff, J. (2013). *Action research: Principle and practice* (*3rd Edition*). Routledge.

Additionally, teachers should actively participate in research projects and seminars focused on intercultural foreign language teaching, facilitating the exchange of ideas and experiences with colleagues and experts (Chan & Erduran, 2023)①. Collaborative learning among teachers enhances teaching knowledge and supports continuous improvement in intercultural teaching practices.

3. Establishing a Professional Learning Community for Foreign Language Teachers

A Professional Learning Community (PLC) is a self-organized group of teachers driven by shared goals and interests, focused on fostering professional growth through collaborative efforts, dialogue, and knowledge sharing. These communities provide support for teachers to improve their teaching practices and adapt to educational reforms and changes (Fan, 2016)②. This study explores the application of PLCs in foreign language education.

①Expert-Guided PLC

Teachers engage in professional development under the mentorship of one or more experts, leveraging the knowledge and experience shared by these experts to enhance their professional competence. This form provides several advantages: A) Strong authority: Experts possess extensive experience and expertise in the field of education, enabling them to offer teachers accurate guidance and advice. Teachers can seek expert advice, attend lectures delivered by experts, and participate in professional research to acquire the necessary expertise and knowledge, thereby elevating the professionalism and authority of their teaching. B) Enhanced professionalism: PLC guided by experts allows teachers to deepen their understanding of the subject matter and teaching methods relevant to their specific courses. With the assistance of experts, teachers can acquire diverse teaching techniques and methods, leading

① Chan, J., & Erduran, S. (2023). The impact of collaboration between science and religious education teachers on their understanding and views of argumentation. *Research in Science Education*, 53 (1), 121-137.

② 范国睿. (2016). 教师共同体是真正的"教师之家". 中国民族教育, (04), 14.

to improved teaching proficiency and effectiveness. C) Heightened effectiveness: Through expert guidance and collaborative exchange, teachers can identify and address challenges and issues encountered in their teaching, thereby refining their teaching approaches and methods.

Approaches to building such a community include: A) Inviting authoritative experts: Selecting authoritative experts with intercultural research or teaching experience to serve as mentors or advisors within the learning community. These experts provide valuable guidance and support to help teachers comprehend cultural differences and similarities, and master effective intercultural teaching strategies. By sharing their experiences and knowledge, experts offer personalized guidance and advice. B) Identifying learning content: Determining the knowledge and skills required for intercultural teaching based on the actual needs and learning goals of teachers. This may include topics such as intercultural communication, cultural sensitivity, and multicultural education. Developing specific learning plans is crucial to guide teachers' professional development. C) Organizing workshop: The learning community can arrange workshop or symposiums where teachers actively participate, fostering communication and interaction among teachers. These activities provide a platform for teachers to learn from one another and engage in fruitful discussions, enabling them to share their teaching experiences and techniques. Ultimately, this collaborative environment enhances each teacher's proficiency and effectiveness. This aspect holds particular significance in intercultural learning, as it necessitates ongoing reflection and communication for adjusting teaching strategies and methods.

②Project-Based PLC

The second form involves project-based PLC. In this form, teachers collaboratively enhance their educational and instructional skills through practical cooperation. This type of learning contributes to improving teaching effectiveness, educational quality, and teachers' professional development. The advantages of a project-based teacher learning community include: A) Clear objectives: Each project has specific goals and tasks that participants need to contemplate and explore according to the project's requirements. Teachers need to establish clear learning objectives and consider how to achieve them through collaborative practices. B) Collaborative success: Project-based PLC requires close cooperation and coordination among participants to collectively accomplish tasks. Through collaboration, teachers can learn from and inspire one another, discussing issues, offering mutual assistance, and growing together to improve educational and instructional competence. C) Practice oriented: Project-based PLC not only promotes communication and cooperation among teachers but also enables them to apply theoretical knowledge into practical contexts, enhancing their practical skills and experience in educational and instructional practices. Through project-based experiences, teachers deepen their understanding of theoretical knowledge and improve teaching effectiveness and quality.

To establish a project-based PLC, specific measures include: A) Selecting suitable projects: Choose challenging and meaningful projects that can promote teachers' learning and growth. These projects can be related to subject teaching, curriculum reforms, educational technology applications, or teaching research. They should be closely connected to teachers' instructional practices and offer a certain level of difficulty and challenge. B) Clearly defining task objectives: Establish specific task objectives and timelines to guide participants, ensuring the quality and timely completion of tasks. These task objectives should align with teachers' actual needs and instructional practices, including aspects such as teaching improvement, curriculum design, or research reports. The specific objectives should match the timeline for task completion to facilitate effective supervision and management of participants. C) Encouraging sharing: Encourage participants to share their thoughts, practices, project outcomes, and experiences. Sharing can be conducted through online or offline methods, such as discussions, exchange sessions, or sharing events. Encouraging participants to share their insights and experiences facilitates communication and collaboration among teachers, collectively improving educational and instructional competence. D) Enhancing communication: Project-based PLC requires close cooperation and communication among participants. It aims to strengthen communication and exchange, avoiding information gaps and misunderstandings. To facilitate effective communication, utilize various communication channels such as email, WeChat, or phone calls, ensuring smooth communication among teachers. E) Summarizing and synthesizing: After project completion, conduct summaries and syntheses, sharing the project's achievements and experiences as references for future instructional practices. Summaries and syntheses can be presented through literature reviews, reports, or papers, consolidating the project's outcomes and experiences as references for future instructional practices. Additionally, these summaries and syntheses can be transformed into teaching cases for other teachers to consult and learn from.

③School-Based PLC

The third form is centered around the establishment of school-based PLC. Within this community, teachers collaborate to explore issues pertaining to the development of ICC, thereby enhancing their professional expertise and practical skills through the sharing of experiences and knowledge. This form of professional development offers several advantages: A) Adaptability: School-based PLC allows for flexible adjustments and arrangements tailored to the specific needs and circumstances of the school and its teachers. Unconstrained by external conditions, it is highly suitable for widespread implementation across diverse regions and school types in China. B) Practicality: School-based PLC integrates relevant theoretical knowledge with practical skills to foster ICC. Through practical activities, case studies, simulated teaching, and other methodologies, teachers continuously improve their abilities and expertise in real-world contexts. C) Interactivity: School-based PLC facilitates direct and profound interactions among teachers, students, and external stakeholders. This collaborative environment enables the collective resolution of challenges and issues encountered in intercultural communication, promoting intercultural understanding and effective communication.

Approaches to establishing school-based PLC include: A) Formation of a learning community: Schools can establish teacher learning communities with a specific focus on ICC. Inviting experts or professionals from within or outside the school to act as mentors or advisors, they provide guidance and support to the community members. B) Determination of learning content: Based on the actual needs and learning objectives of the school and its teachers, the specific theoretical knowledge and practical skills required for intercultural communication and China's external communication are identified. This process informs the development of targeted learning plans and curriculum frameworks. C) Implementation of practical activities: The community organizes teachers to participate in various intercultural exchange activities, develops and implements internationally-oriented curricula, and hosts international academic seminars, among other practical initiatives.

④Virtual Professional Learning Community (VPLC)

Virtual Professional Learning Community (VPLC) functions as a platform that utilizes information and communication technologies to facilitate teachers' learning and collaboration in the context of "Intelligence Plus". It combines both online and offline activities, integrating virtual and real-world teaching research and classroom practices. Through specialized information platforms, such as virtual teaching research office clients provided by higher education institutions, teachers can freely form groups and engage in efficient communication, seamless integration, and rapid knowledge sharing using various forms of communication, such as voice, text, conferences, and live broadcasts. This creates a collaborative "research circle" for teachers (Bedford, 2019)①.

The VPLC offers the following advantages: A) Temporal and spatial flexibility: The VPLC maximizes the utilization of information technology, overcoming limitations of time and space, and breaking down physical barriers on campuses. It provides teachers with convenient access to the latest

① Bedford, L. (2019). Using social media as a platform for a virtual professional learning community. *Online Learning*, 23(3), 120-136.

educational information, enabling them to stay updated with the latest trends in foreign language teaching. This facilitates the enhancement of their educational skills and teaching methods in a more efficient and diverse manner (Carpenter & Munshower, 2020)①. B) Member diversity: Participants in the online learning community can come from different schools, regions, and even countries. This diverse participant base brings forth various perspectives and ideas, fostering exchange and mutual learning among teachers. C) Resource collaboration: Through extensive research and communication, teachers collaboratively develop talent cultivation programs, teaching outlines, knowledge maps, teaching videos, e-learning materials, exercise questions, teaching cases, experimental projects, training projects, datasets, and other teaching resources. This process leads to the creation of a high-quality and shared teaching repertoire.

The development path for VPLC includes: A) Platform construction: To establish an influential teacher network community, it is essential to select a suitable online platform and allocate resources for its construction and maintenance. B) Precise management: The online community requires precise management to ensure active and high-quality participation from teachers. This involves guiding teacher engagement, motivating knowledge sharing, and providing timely responses to their questions. Such management practices contribute to the effective operation and vibrancy of the online community. C) Demonstration and promotion: The VPLC can be led by national-level teaching teams, renowned teachers, and exemplary curriculum models. This enables the promotion of effective talent cultivation modes and curriculum implementation, thereby fostering the professional development of frontline teachers. D) Strengthened cooperation: The online community can engage in collaborative research and teaching activities with other institutions and organizations. This collaboration enhances the depth and breadth of teachers'

① Carpenter, D., & Munshower, P. (2020). Broadening borders to build better schools: Virtual professional learning communities. *International Journal of Educational Management*, 34(2), 296-314.

professional development while expanding the influence and reputation of the online community.

In conclusion, the four forms of PLC mentioned above each possess their own advantages and are suitable for different foreign language education contexts and goals. However, irrespective of the chosen form, active participation and sustained efforts from teachers are crucial for advancing educational improvements and developments. Ultimately, this contributes to enhancing the effectiveness and impact of China's international communication.

6.4 Foreign Language Textbooks

Textbooks are essential in foreign language teaching, serving as the primary source of language input and teaching content in Chinese education. They provide a structured framework for classroom activities, ensuring teaching consistency and facilitating interaction between students and teachers. Tailored textbooks play a crucial role in fostering ICC and meeting the objectives of foreign language education in China.

6.4.1 Current State of Foreign Language Textbooks

According to *Guide 2020*, textbooks serve as crucial conduits for the dissemination of new knowledge, ideas, and concepts. The development of these textbooks should align with the guiding ideology of the new era, reflecting national requirements and educational principles. It is crucial to instill cultural confidence, uphold Chinese culture, assert China's discourse power, and authentically embody Chinese characteristics and styles. Textbooks should integrate socialist core values and traditional Chinese culture, guiding students to develop accurate worldviews and values while embracing global perspectives (NACTELHE, 2020)①. The reform of

① 高等学校大学外语教学指导委员会(The National Administrative Committee on Teaching English Language in Higher Education, NACTELHE). 2020. 大学英语教学指南(2020 版). 高等教育出版社.

teaching content represents the most practical lever for advancing textbook construction and effectively implementing the fundamental task of cultivating virtuous individuals (Liu, 2020)①. However, current textbooks often fall short in meeting these evolving educational needs. Since 2000, scholars have extensively researched "cultural aphasia" in language education, highlighting issues such as the marginalization of local culture and the absence of comparative cultural content in English textbooks. Major publishers such as Foreign Language Teaching and Research Press and Higher Education Press face challenges in adequately addressing these new teaching requirements and objectives (Liu & Yue, 2020)②.

Firstly, textbooks suffer from a significant dearth of Chinese cultural representation and scientific and technological content. In some cases, these elements are completely absent. This deficiency hinders the development of students' ability to convey Chinese stories, promote Chinese culture, and nurture confidence in Chinese cultural heritage. Multiple empirical studies have demonstrated that domestic university foreign language textbooks predominantly focus on Western or Westernized cultures, neglecting the rich diversity of international cultures and Chinese culture. Furthermore, research has uncovered distortions in the presentation of cultural information within textbooks (Liu et al., 2015)③. In the era of globalization, comprehending and acquainting oneself with the development of one's own culture is not only crucial for self-consciousness but also for fostering an understanding of others.

Secondly, existing textbooks do not adequately focus on cultivating moral sentiments. This is evident in two aspects: insufficient emphasis on promoting Chinese traditional culture and contemporary values as guiding principles in textbook development, and fragmented content that lacks organic integration

---

① 刘道义. (2020). 论影响外语教材建设的重要因素. 课程. 教材. 教法, (02), 64-71.

② 刘正光 & 岳曼曼. (2020). 转变理念、重构内容,落实外语课程思政. 外国语(上海外国语大学学报), (05), 21-29.

③ 刘艳红, Lawrence Jun Zhang, & Stephen May. (2015). 基于国家级规划大学英语教材语料库的教材文化研究. 外语界, (06), 85-93.

of Chinese civilization into language learning exercises. While some textbooks include cultural themes in unit designs, these often represent only a small fraction of the content related to intercultural communication. Post-reading annotations typically provide simple cultural knowledge points, limiting the textbooks' effectiveness in moral education and the development of students' ideological and moral awareness.

Thirdly, there is a disjointedness in the structure of teaching activities, language learning content, and exercise designs within each unit, failing to create a cohesive learning experience for students. This fragmented approach hinders holistic and systematic learning, as well as the application of language knowledge in real-life and social contexts. While some textbooks introduce cultural content in short texts, these are often relegated to post-reading materials, which may not engage teachers and students effectively (An & Wang, 2016)①. Textbook design should align with overarching teaching philosophies and educational goals, integrating language knowledge impartation, skills development, quality enhancement, and value shaping into a unified framework.

Fourthly, there is a significant gap between moral objectives and actual textbook materials. Although some textbooks aim to cultivate qualities like "integrity," these objectives are often not fully realized or are superficially addressed. Cultural content often focuses on daily life aspects from a tourist perspective, lacking deeper exploration of values and worldviews. This disconnect underscores the need for deeper understanding among textbook authors on how language learning can integrate with moral education.

These deficiencies indicate that the restructuring of teaching content and the corresponding textbook development are of great significance for the effective achievement of the educational goals of university foreign language courses.

---

① 安琳 & 王蓓蕾.（2016）. 新要求 新视角 新体验——"新目标大学英语"阅读系列教材编写理念与特色. 外语界，(02)，23-30.

6.4.2 New Requirements for Cultivating ICC in Foreign Language Textbooks

According to *Guide 2020*, college foreign language courses are designed to cultivate students' understanding and interpretation abilities of Chinese culture, with the purpose of promoting the dissemination of Chinese culture abroad. The integration of socialist core values into the content of college foreign language teaching is essential. The curriculum should thoroughly explore its ideological and emotional resources, enrich its humanistic content, and achieve a harmonious blend of practicality and humanism (NACTELHE, 2020)①. Textbooks are responsible for selecting, organizing, and presenting knowledge, and they implicitly shape values and transmit ideologies. The development of foreign language textbooks should not only meet the requirements of cultivating professional skills and competencies but also fulfill the new demands of nurturing college students' sentiments and perspectives. Although in China and many other countries, the writing and selection of specific foreign language textbooks are typically carried out by national education departments or authoritative figures (Zhang, 2007)②, as foreign language teachers, we can use these guidelines as a reference for assessing, selecting, and using teaching materials more broadly.

1. Shifting from the "Other" to "Dialogue"

For a long time, the classic foreign language textbooks used in various universities have predominantly adopted the perspective of the "other." These textbooks primarily consist of foreign original texts, which inevitably cater to Western values. However, this "other" perspective fails to reflect the current educational situation in China and does not awaken the genuine aspirations of Chinese students or effectively convey Chinese culture and its positive values.

---

① 高等学校大学外语教学指导委员会(The National Administrative Committee on Teaching English Language in Higher Education, NACTELHE). 2020. 大学英语教学指南(2020版). 高等教育出版社.

② 张红玲. (2007). 跨文化外语教学. 上海外语教育出版社.

In the new era, these textbooks, with their predominantly "other" perspective, no longer meet the needs of Chinese students who actively seek to explore the world and shoulder responsibilities. To establish an invincible position in the world, it is time to shift from the "other" perspective to a mechanism of "dialogue." This form of "dialogue" does not exclude the "other," but rather calls for equal participation of both or multiple parties in cultural exchanges. It aims to foster communication and understanding among different cultures, contributing to the shared destiny and cultural community of humankind.

When developing textbooks, it is crucial to critically evaluate the cultural "dialogue" value of each selected article. Consideration should be given to whether the article's value orientation aligns with the cultivation of talents with a global perspective and humanistic depth in the new era. Additionally, it is important to assess whether the article promotes ethical education and the construction of a shared human destiny. The construction of a "dialogue" mechanism requires an open-minded approach when determining the criteria for selecting teaching materials. Textbook writers should possess a comprehensive understanding of Chinese cultural traditions, heritage, and values. They should emphasize the exploration and rediscovery of outstanding traditional Chinese culture, while focusing on cultivating students' cultural education and humanistic qualities. Simultaneously, foreign literary works with a global perspective should be selected. These works not only possess unique cultural value and humanistic significance but also stimulate intercultural thinking and dialogue. Textbook writers also need to select original materials that align with Chinese cultural values and are compatible with the premise of communication and dialogue between Chinese and Western cultures. They should create a conducive learning environment that guides students towards "dialogue." Apart from knowledge transmission, textbook development should emphasize the cultivation of students' thinking abilities, innovative spirit, intercultural communication skills, and values. Specifically, appropriate cultural interpretations and background introductions can be included in the textbooks. This enables students to understand and comprehend different cultural ways of thinking, behavioral habits, values, as well as the similarities and differences between cultures. Furthermore, by incorporating representative case studies, students can be guided to reflect on and explore potential issues in intercultural communication. Corresponding solutions and suggestions can be provided to better equip students in handling various situations and challenges in practical communication.

2. Shifting from "Instrumentality" to "Humanism"

Language serves as both a tool for understanding the world and a gateway to appreciating diverse cultures. In foreign language education, this dual role highlights its humanistic dimension. Learning a foreign language not only enhances understanding of different lifestyles, thought patterns, and cultural traditions (Wang, 2013)①, but also fosters mutual understanding, tolerance, and respect for diverse national characteristics and cultural diversity. Effective foreign language education should enable students to grasp Western civilization, thought processes, and ways of life, while also promoting awareness of cultural distinctions between China and other nations, thereby cultivating ICC. While emphasizing the practical utility of foreign language education, equal emphasis should be placed on its humanistic implications. This includes guiding students to develop a sound worldview, life philosophy, and values, and nurturing their moral character and sense of social responsibility.

In this interconnected world, Chinese and Western cultures frequently interact. Foreign language education bears the responsibility of nurturing college students as ambassadors of Chinese culture in the new era. To bring China into the global spotlight and effectively convey its cultural heritage, it is essential to cultivate individuals who can contribute Chinese wisdom to intercultural communication, fluently discuss Chinese culture in foreign languages, and share Chinese stories with the world. Therefore, the

① 王守仁. (2013). 坚持科学的大学英语教学改革观. 外语界, (06), 9-13+22.

development of foreign language textbooks should integrate socialist core values and establish a cultural discourse system for foreign language education in China. While imparting language skills, these textbooks should also disseminate Chinese culture, ultimately achieving comprehensive educational goals. The construction of foreign language textbooks should be rooted in the fundamental characteristics of the nation, deeply embedded in Chinese culture while embracing the world. By building upon the foundation of Chinese historical traditions, textbooks should embody the spirit of Chinese culture in a personalized manner, showcasing the distinct Chinese style and strength to the international community. Therefore, in the development of foreign language textbooks, it is crucial to delve into the cultural connotations of the target language. Rich cultural content can guide students in understanding the culture associated with the target language, thereby enhancing their comprehension and proficiency in its usage. Additionally, attention should be given to promoting Chinese culture by integrating traditional values and customs into teaching. This approach helps students understand Chinese cultural traditions and values, while emphasizing the cultivation of their sense of social responsibility and moral character. By doing so, students can better integrate into global cultural exchanges, actively participate in the process of globalization, and contribute to world peace and development.

3. Shifting from "Language for Learning" to "Language in Life"

"Language for learning" alone is no longer sufficient to satisfy students' cognitive needs regarding humanity and the world. Language is evolving to become deeply intertwined with people's thought processes and intellectual development, emphasizing the concept of "language in life" (Li & Wang, 2022)①. This paradigm shift, also known as "language and literature in life" or "language and written expression in life," is central to Chinese language

① 李为为 & 王雪畅. (2022). 课程思政背景下大学英语教材开发的基本原则和方法. 大学, (14), 54-57.

planning (Li, 2016)①. It highlights the integration of language into daily activities, the enrichment of life through language, and the profound impact language has on everyday experiences. Therefore, when selecting texts for foreign language textbooks, it is essential not only to consider language difficulty levels but also whether the content meets teaching requirements, promotes communication, interaction, and practical application, resonates with contemporary college students, imparts values, and contributes to character education.

To achieve these goals, foreign language textbooks need to be updated and relevant, embodying both national or regional characteristics and global features. The content should be closely integrated with China's national conditions, paying greater attention to social realities, introducing materials with distinct contemporary characteristics, exploring emerging Chinese themes, and strengthening awareness of Chinese issues. The selection of textbook content should be closely tied to current hot topics in life, and the activities designed in the textbooks should connect with students' experiences in life, study, and work, reflecting new materials and conveying new ideas. Furthermore, foreign language textbook development should also consider students' interests and needs, using content that is more attractive and engaging to stimulate their learning interests and potential. Through vivid examples and cases, textbooks should guide students to gain a deeper understanding of the cultural, historical, social, and ideological backgrounds behind foreign languages, enabling them to acquire extensive knowledge and enlightenment throughout the process of language learning. Moreover, foreign language textbooks should keep pace with the trends of the times, diversify in types, and adopt a multi-dimensional approach. Texts should combine printed materials, audio, video, and online resources. In terms of specific textbooks, there should be a rich variety of materials, including print versions, accompanying online versions with web links, extended content, and exercises

---

① 李宇明. (2016). 语言生活与语言生活研究. 语言战略研究, (3), 15-23.

available online to assist learners in constructing knowledge. Supplementary materials should also be diversified, providing foreign language readings with abundant content and broad coverage, facilitating students' extracurricular learning and self-improvement. Particularly, many foreign language learners lack opportunities to live, study, travel, and work in countries or regions where the foreign language is spoken. Information technology-based teaching materials showcase a foreign language world to learners, encompassing rich cultural content, opening a window into different cultures, and serving as a substitute for real-life experiences (Perez, 2022)①.

4. Shifting from "Cultural Acquisition" to "Cultural Exchange"

Foreign language teaching has always emphasized cultural acquisition, especially in the case of acquiring the culture associated with a second foreign language. Consequently, for a long time, teachers and students have passively received and read authentic foreign language texts that primarily promote Western values. Little do they realize that many teachers and students unknowingly become "westernized" and believe that all values propagated by the West are correct and desirable. However, over time, people have come to realize that Chinese individuals should not forget their identity as Chinese and the excellence of their traditional culture and socialist core values. Therefore, "cultural acquisition" is no longer limited to acquiring Western culture alone; Chinese traditional culture and the new era culture have also become the content and focus of acquisition. In the contemporary era, the evolution of "cultural acquisition" is imperative for facilitating cultural exchange and dissemination. Cultural exchange entails the communication between two or more entities characterized by substantial cultural disparities (Pan & Zhao, 2021) ②. Boasting a civilization spanning five millennia, Chinese culture has embraced novel and receptive approaches to engage in dialogue and interaction

---

① Perez, M. M. (2022). Second or foreign language learning through watching audio-visual input and the role of on-screen text. *Language Teaching*, 55(2), 1-30.

② 潘雷 & 赵晴. (2021). 孔子学院在中埃文化交流中的作用——以开罗大学孔子学院为例. 中外文化,(01), 168-175.

with other cultures amidst China's ascent in the 21st century. The development of foreign language textbooks must not solely prioritize the imparting of linguistic knowledge, but should also encompass a deliberate selection of texts that serve the purpose of disseminating Chinese culture and fostering intercultural exchange on a global scale. By doing so, an authentic cultivation of perceptive, broad-minded, cultured, and conscientious university students in the new era can be realized. Guided by the aspiration to forge a community with a shared future for mankind, China's leadership on the world stage is undeniably intertwined with its cultural influence. Cultural primacy dictates that we not only comprehend Western culture, but also establish an affinity, inherit, develop, and promote our own cultural heritage. This undertaking necessitates a broader outlook, allowing us to attain a multi-dimensional understanding of ourselves and the world through the cultural conflicts and encounters that arise from multilingual interactions. Simultaneously, the discipline of cultural studies underscores the need for comparing and contrasting cultures to transcend the ingrained patterns of thought, beliefs, and values associated with our own national culture. By adopting a wider perspective and framework, we can appraise ourselves and the world with greater breadth and depth (Liu & Li, 2019) ①. In the realm of language learning, cultural comparisons serve as a means to bring the world and its diverse populations into focus, while providing an effective method for self-discovery, the cultivation of cultural awareness, the establishment of cultural identity, and the nurturing of cultural confidence. By presenting distinct cultural themes from various countries, students are encouraged to embrace a multi-faceted understanding of culture, fostering a diversified cultural consciousness (Liu, 2020)②. Through comparative analysis of our own culture and others, students deepen their comprehension of their own

① 刘正光 & 李易. (2019). 认知语义对比：理论，原则，目标与方法. 外语教学，(04)，1-7.

② 刘亚秋. (2020). 从"文化自觉"到"文化创造性"——理解费孝通文化反思的一条线索. 北京工业大学学报(社会科学版)，(03)，39-46.

cultural heritage, and refine their ability to discern and interpret cultural phenomena.

6.4.3 Methods for Developing Foreign Language Textbooks

Foreign language textbooks serve as a medium and platform for the coexistence and interaction of diverse cultures. As a humanities discipline, their content spans broadly, encompassing classics to contemporary works, Chinese to global pieces, and online to scholarly articles. They offer a rich platform showcasing diverse thought schools across time and borders. Thus, content selection must be judicious, enhancing knowledge, broadening horizons, and fostering humanistic literacy for holistic talent development. While selecting appropriate materials for foreign language textbooks, it is also essential to adopt a intercultural perspective and focus on the dialogue between Chinese culture and other cultures. Teaching materials that are solely centered on Western culture or those that primarily emphasize Chinese culture are contrary to the principles of intercultural "dialogue". Drawing from China's 5,000 years of civilization and traditional culture encourages a tolerant mindset when engaging with global cultures and phenomena, aiming to cultivate individuals through foreign language textbooks who embody qualities such as profound understanding of Chinese culture, a global perspective, and humanistic insight, thus positioning effective in intercultural communication.

1. Integration of Value Shaping and Knowledge Imparting in Textbooks

According to *Guide 2020*, textbooks are pivotal in disseminating new knowledge, ideas, and concepts, serving as primary vehicles for teaching content and essential for achieving educational goals. Cultural confidence, the affirmation of Chinese cultural subjectivity, and the assertion of Chinese discourse authority are crucial in textbook development. Textbooks should authentically reflect Chinese characteristics and style, integrating socialist core values and traditional Chinese culture to guide students in developing accurate worldviews, life perspectives, and values. Rooted in China yet embracing a global perspective, textbooks draw on diverse sources to leverage the strengths of university foreign language courses, reflecting the latest advancements in global science and technology and the achievements of human civilization. This approach aims to cultivate forward-thinking individuals with an international outlook (NACTELHE, 2020)①.

Foreign language textbooks are crucial in shaping students' thoughts and values through their explicit and implicit content (Xu, 2021)②. In today's educational landscape, these materials must align with global trends in educational reform. This alignment encompasses the teaching syllabus, reflecting overall curriculum design, and course materials that emphasize specific cases and core components, integrating value formation, knowledge impartation, and the cultivation of ICC. Historically, mainstream foreign language textbooks have often lacked sufficient content showcasing Chinese culture. In response, teachers should carefully consider the appropriate proportion of Chinese cultural content within textbooks or series of textbooks. To meet national development needs and achieve curriculum objectives effectively, foreign language textbooks must evolve to systematically integrate both native and target language cultures alongside other international perspectives (Fang & Liu, 2021)③. Therefore, during the textbook development process, there should be deliberate efforts to incorporate cultural elements, particularly those highlighting Chinese culture, which have historically been underrepresented. Conversely, critical evaluation is necessary for materials emphasizing Western culture to identify and remove outdated or inappropriate content that may distort students' values. In essence, when selecting materials for university foreign language textbooks, universities should prioritize appropriateness, consider the impact on Chinese culture, and

---

① 高等学校大学外语教学指导委员会(The National Administrative Committee on Teaching English Language in Higher Education, NACTELHE). 2020. 大学英语教学指南(2020 版). 高等教育出版社.

② 徐锦芬. (2021). 高校英语课程教学素材的思政内容建设研究. 外语界, (02), 18-24.

③ 方庆华 & 刘梦歌. (2021). "文化自觉"视角下的大学英语教材文化配置研究. 考试与评价(大学英语教研版), (01), 113-118.

evaluate potential influences on college students.

2. Integration of Language Knowledge and Cultural Knowledge

The organization of content in foreign language textbooks should prioritize cultural themes, with a deliberate integration of both culture and language in each section. This approach, essential for teaching foreign languages for intercultural communication, emphasizes that language content and cultural content are inseparable, serving both as the purpose and means of instruction (Zhang, 2007)①. In textbooks, cultural themes should form the foundational structure, with language teaching content intricately woven into these cultural elements. By thoughtfully selecting relevant content, textbooks can effectively enhance language proficiency while shaping learners' cognitive processes and influencing their values through the learning materials (Pun et al., 2023)②. Therefore, textbooks need to consider comprehensively factors such as students' language learning needs, their language environments, knowledge structures, and proficiency levels. They should cover social customs, history, religion, and particularly values. Moreover, textbooks should introduce cultural elements from diverse Western countries and Chinese traditional culture, including comparative studies between Eastern and Western cultures. This approach empowers students to develop the skills to navigate and appreciate cultural differences effectively.

In contemporary foreign language education, the development of teaching materials should prioritize "cultural awareness." This approach emphasizes not only acquiring and assimilating foreign cultures but also equipping students to use foreign languages effectively for promoting Chinese culture and narrating Chinese stories (Kang & Xu, 2018)③. To remain relevant, teaching materials must be dynamic, align with national development needs, and

---

① 张红玲. (2017). 跨文化外语教学. 上海外语教育出版社.

② Pun, J. K., Fu, X., & Cheung, K. K. C. (2023). Language challenges and coping strategies in English medium instruction (EMI) science classrooms: A critical review of literature. *Studies in Science Education*, 60(1), 1-32.

③ 康莉 & 徐锦芬. (2018). 大学英语教材中的文化自觉及其实现. 外语学刊, (04), 70-75.

achieve curriculum objectives effectively. This involves integrating both native and target language cultures, along with diverse international cultures, within a well-balanced textbook system to counteract "cultural aphasia" regarding Chinese culture. Such an approach fosters students' "cultural awareness" and "cultural confidence," empowering them to tell Chinese stories and engage in meaningful cultural exchanges. Moreover, teaching materials should play a crucial role in developing students' critical thinking abilities. In cultivating ICC, students need to adopt an analytical perspective to critically evaluate aspects of the target language country, gaining experiential insights into cultural differences. Educational materials should convey a positive ethos that inspires students about the richness of human cultures and the importance of moral values, shaping their worldviews and values through language's subtle influence. Furthermore, modern foreign language textbooks should facilitate students' communication in a dynamic global context. They should include cultural knowledge with a global and intercultural perspective, encompassing not only the target language culture but also international cultural knowledge (Templer, 2020)①. This content should be diverse, covering human perspectives, lifestyles, environments, politics, and values comprehensively. Additionally, textbooks should enrich students' understanding of their native language and culture, enabling them to express their unique identity through foreign languages.

Given the intricate and dynamic nature of culture, cultural teaching content in textbooks should transcend traditional lecture-based approaches. A cultural focus in textbooks should adopt a progressive, practical method allowing for flexible teaching cycles. This approach enables students to continuously deepen their understanding and experience of culture. Content presentation should progress from surface-level to deeper insights, external to internal aspects, known to unknown concepts, and concrete to abstract ideas.

---

① Templer, K. J. (2020). Self-enhancement and cross-cultural adjustment: Overclaiming in a global mobility context. *Journal of Global Mobility*, 8(2), 161-182.

Curriculum content should be revisited at different stages, expanding in scope and complexity over time. Textbooks for intercultural studies should demonstrate systematic organization, consistency, hierarchical structure, and incorporate cutting-edge, timely knowledge. They should reflect the humanistic ethos prevalent in Western countries while also responding to evolving domestic perspectives on talent development. This dual focus ensures textbooks balance humanistic nurturing with practical educational needs effectively.

3. Emphasizing the Authenticity and Contextualization of Teaching Materials

Teaching materials are pivotal in offering students practical information, genuine examples, and clear usage rules to aid language development. Authentic language materials can prompt learners to respond at psychological, cognitive, and behavioral levels, enabling genuine experiences in intercultural communication (Bánhegyi & Nagy, 2019)①.

Byram et al. (2002)② argued that foreign language teaching materials should be developed from an intercultural and critical perspective, emphasizing the authenticity of materials and ensuring students' understanding of their contextual use and intended purposes. If the materials present a one-sided viewpoint, students should be encouraged to explore other authentic resources to expose them to different perspectives. This approach promotes critical comparison, analysis, and evaluation of content, focusing on developing students' analytical skills rather than solely acquiring knowledge. Zhang (2017)③ asserted that intercultural foreign language teaching materials must adhere to the principles of authenticity and contextualization. Only authentic materials can genuinely engage learners and evoke responses at the cognitive,

---

① Bánhegyi, M., & Nagy, J. (2019). Teaching cultural differences through Korean Canadians: Teaching material development for English as a foreign language class. *Acta Educationis Generalis*, 9(3), 41-65.

② Byram, M., Gribkova, B., & Starkey, H. (2002). *Developing the intercultural dimension in language teaching*. A practical introduction for teachers. Council of Europe.

③ 张红玲. (2017). 跨文化外语教学. 上海外语教育出版社.

psychological, attitudinal, and behavioral levels, allowing them to have authentic experiences in intercultural communication. Shu and Zhuang (2008)① also advocated for the selection of authentic language materials that reflect real language usage within the target language community. Authenticity should guide the development of foreign language teaching materials, ensuring their usability in real-life situations beyond the confines of the classroom. Taking context into account is crucial for accurate and comprehensive language expression and comprehension. Consequently, when selecting intercultural foreign language teaching materials, it is essential to closely align them with students' lives, identifying their interests and focal points, while also ensuring the authenticity and contextualization of cultural content. This approach allows for the presentation of diverse cultural knowledge and embodies the humanistic spirit. Specifically, texts should be selected for their authenticity, featuring fluent and natural language. Topics should be closely related to main themes, encompassing East-West cultural differences, communication skills, cultural knowledge, and more. All contexts should reflect the environment in which the target language is used, and information should be conveyed within culturally meaningful systems (Xie, 2012)②.

It is worth noting that in reality, as the environment and communication partners change, communication activities also change. In order to cultivate and develop students' ICC, textbooks should not only include information about language context and the social status of the speakers to help learners better understand communicative practices, but they should also contain content that contributes to the enhancement of intercultural consciousness and communicative practices. Teaching materials should incorporate cultural simulations, games, role-plays, dramas, and other exercises to recreate

---

① 束定芳 & 庄智象. (2008). 现代外语教学——理论、实践与方法. 上海外语教育出版社.

② 谢晓晨. (2012). 跨文化交际外语教学教材中的新典范——《跨文化视角外语阅读教程》(1-4册)评价. 庄恩平(Eds). 跨文化外语教学：研究与实践 (pp. 113-119). 上海外语教育出版社.

authentic contexts. This allows students to apply their language knowledge, cultural knowledge, and practical contexts to simulate the process of cultural adaptation. These activities help cultivate students' intercultural sensitivity, tolerance, and flexibility in problem-solving, providing them with opportunities for intercultural communicative practice (Marwa et al., 2022)①. Furthermore, effective language textbooks should systematically integrate the construction of intercultural dynamic interpersonal relationships with intercultural knowledge and practice. They should reflect cultural diversity, multiple perspectives, diverse problems, and flexible answers. Additionally, excellent language textbooks should also emphasize the matching and practice between language forms and functions and the contexts in which they are used. They should be conducive to both teachers and students exercising their agency in teaching and learning processes.

4. Creative Utilization of Teaching Materials

When developing teaching materials, it is essential to follow the principle of "learning knowledge points, exploring points of integration, and integrating practice." This principle ensures the creation of a comprehensive and cohesive structural framework. The content selection should encompass both Chinese and Western cultures, with an emphasis on local and international issues, as well as Chinese-Western comparisons. In addition to developing fundamental language skills, teaching materials should highlight the infusion of culture, values, and ideas, fostering students' cultural sensitivity, national consciousness, and ICC.

As an indispensable foundation for teaching and a primary tool for students' learning, textbooks play a fundamental role in enhancing teaching effectiveness and quality. In educational practice, textbooks are often regarded as the "heart and soul" of teaching, given their direct influence on the quality

---

① Marwa, M., Herdi, H., & Abbas, M. F. F. (2022). Websites use as learning resources in developing intercultural communicative competence in English language teaching classroom. *ELT-Lectura*, 151-162.

of instructional outcomes and students' learning achievements. Consequently, the development of ICC significantly depends on how textbooks are utilized in the classroom, particularly the quality of interaction among students, textbooks, and teachers (Frimpong, 2021)①. Cunningsworth, as cited by Ayu (2020)②, emphasized that each teaching environment is unique and influenced by various factors, including the dynamic nature of the classroom, resource availability, learner expectations and motivation, and curriculum constraints. To better meet instructional needs and fulfill the demand for cultivating ICC, teachers can make necessary adaptations to existing textbooks. They should possess autonomy, flexibility, and creativity in utilizing teaching materials. While textbooks should remain the primary focus in foreign language teaching, supplementary materials can also be employed. Teachers can judiciously modify, add, substitute, or adapt textbooks according to practical requirements, ensuring their systematic use. This approach offers the advantage of providing a standardized framework for classroom instruction, enabling less experienced teachers to rely on them, while also allowing for the incorporation of additional materials to compensate for any shortcomings. Furthermore, teachers are provided with opportunities to explore alternative teaching materials, facilitating diverse instructional activities and the application of teaching techniques. Such flexibility enables more effective fulfillment of students' needs. Therefore, teachers should not only employ core textbooks creatively, aligned with the curriculum and learning objectives, but also independently and selectively develop, utilize, and integrate similar teaching materials, audiovisual resources, online

---

① Frimpong, S. (2021). The role of teaching and learning materials and interaction as a tool to quality early childhood education in Agona east district of the central region of Ghana. *African Educational Research Journal*, 9(1), 168-178.

② Ayu, M. (2020). Evaluation cultural content on English textbook used by EFL students in Indonesia. *Journal of English Teaching*, 6(3), 183-192.

materials, audio-visual materials, newspapers, magazines, and other curriculum resources. This includes supplementing teaching materials and exercises that align with students' proficiency levels and real-life needs, removing or replacing outdated and unengaging content and activities, as well as modifying or adapting exercises and activities that are excessively challenging or too easy. By integrating various teaching resources, teachers can present instructional content in a vivid, comprehensive, and captivating manner. Consequently, students' interest and motivation to learn are enhanced, facilitating a better understanding and mastery of knowledge, and ultimately improving learning outcomes. Additionally, when adapting teaching materials, foreign language teachers should possess a profound understanding of the materials to be adapted and the instructional environment. They should consider students' learning styles, interests, and motivations. Given that students have diverse learning needs and preferences, teachers should leverage their innovative capabilities and employ different teaching methods and strategies, integrating various types of instructional resources to meet students' varying requirements and promote their innovative thinking and practical abilities.

6.5 Application of Information Technology

In 2018, the MOE of China unveiled the *Education Informatization 2.0 Action Plan*, ushering in a comprehensive upgrade of educational digitalization (MOE of the PRC, 2018)①. The *Key Points of the Ministry of Education's Work in 2022* underscored implementing digital strategies in education, fostering demand-driven initiatives, deepening integration, fostering innovation, and bolstering applications, while advancing "Internet + Education" and accelerating education's digital transformation and intelligent

① 教育部. (2018-04-13). 教育部关于印发《教育信息化 2.0 行动计划》的通知. 中华人民共和国教育部政府门户网站. Retrieved July 15, 2023, from http://www.moe.gov.cn/srcsite/A16/s3342/201804/t20180425_334188.html? from=timeline&isappinstalled=0.

evolution (MOE of the PRC, 2022)①. Amid the profound integration of computer information technology and foreign language teaching models, ICC cultivation acknowledges the imperative of modern foreign language information-based instruction. It delves into internet and cloud-enabled teaching modalities and pathways, integrates technology with language courses, and enhances intercultural teaching's quality and efficiency.

6.5.1 Current State of Information Technology Application

The fusion of computer information technology into foreign language education transcends superficial methods like multimedia classrooms, touching the core of language pedagogy: models, curricula, methods, and assessment (Ge, 2019)②. This integration heightens the focus on language proficiency, especially listening and speaking, transforming traditional methods like vocabulary lectures and grammar translation into a blend of classroom and self-directed learning within virtual learning environments. This shift fosters task-oriented, multi-dimensional, and personalized education, elevating computers from mere aids to central players. Attention turns to optimizing and organizing resources for holistic instruction. Assessment evolves from sole summative evaluations to a blend of summative and formative approaches, enhancing self-reflection, evaluation, and instructional adjustment. Currently, cultivating ICC through modern IT confronts three key misalignments:

1. Misalignment Between Mindset and Practice

Some teachers fail to recognize the significant role of information technology in foreign language teaching, viewing it as a mere embellishment and potentially wasting valuable class time. Traditional methods have merits, such as fostering close student-teacher relationships, but they often overemphasize rote memorization and repetitive skills, neglecting language

---

① 教育部. (2022-02-08). 教育部 2022 年工作要点. 中华人民共和国教育部政府门户网站. Retrieved July 15, 2023, from http://www. moe. gov. cn/jyb_xwfb/gzdt_gzdt/202202/t20220208_597666. html.

② 葛军. (2019). 信息技术条件下外语教学中的变与不变. 高等教育研究学报, (04), 99-105.

application and creative thinking. In contrast, information technology, through interactive and collaborative formats like online forums and virtual language labs, actively engages students, enhancing their language expression and application abilities. Secondly, while some teachers acknowledge the importance of information technology, they lack the necessary understanding and skills to use it effectively (Bond et al., 2020)①. The relatively novel application of information technology in foreign language education means many teachers lack the educational background and training to incorporate it meaningfully. Consequently, technology is often used passively, merely as a supplementary tool, without integrating it into the language curriculum, hindering its practical application. Furthermore, some teachers may harbor misconceptions regarding the use of information technology. They may perceive it solely as a teaching tool without considering how to leverage it to enhance instructional effectiveness. This misconception not only squanders the potential of information technology but also compromises teaching quality. Another conceptual issue lies in the belief held by some teachers that using information technology will render the classroom dull and mechanistic, thereby undermining the interaction between teachers and students. They fear that students will excessively rely on electronic devices instead of utilizing their own cognitive abilities. However, in reality, information technology equips teachers with a wider array of tools and resources to design engaging and interactive courses (Castro & Tumibay, 2021)②. Simultaneously, information technology assists students in comprehending knowledge more effectively and improving learning efficiency (Puspitarini & Hanif, 2019)③.

---

① 梅丽莎·邦德，奥拉夫·扎瓦克奇-里克特，马克·尼克尔斯 & 肖俊洪.(2020).重温五十载教育技术研究:基于《英国教育技术期刊》的内容分析.中国远程教育，(01)，1-22+76.

② Castro, M. D. B., & Tumibay, G. M. (2021). A literature review: Efficacy of online learning courses for higher education institution using meta-analysis. *Education and Information Technologies*, 26, 1367-1385.

③ Puspitarini, Y. D., & Hanif, M. (2019). Using learning media to increase learning motivation in elementary school. *Anatolian Journal of Education*, 4(2), 53-60.

2. Misalignment Between National Policies and Specific School Situations

Insufficient policy support remains a significant hurdle in advancing information technology within foreign language teaching. While recent governmental policies aim to promote information technology in education, their implementation lacks effective supervision, enforcement, and assessment mechanisms. Policy execution heavily relies on financial investments, often neglecting essential educational needs and teaching model transformations, thus hindering substantial progress in teaching methodology. Secondly, many educational institutions have limited understanding of foreign language teaching reform objectives and struggle with weak implementation. Despite possessing information technology equipment, these schools fail to integrate it effectively into language education practices. Superficial promotion without proper planning exacerbates these issues, leading to unsatisfactory outcomes. Thirdly, inadequate financial resources impede schools from acquiring necessary information technology equipment for language education, such as multimedia classrooms and electronic devices. High costs and frequent technological updates further strain budgets, compromising the quality and efficiency of information technology education. Fourthly, foreign language teachers often lack proficiency in information technology compared to reform demands. Many are unfamiliar with technology applications and lack the confidence or motivation to incorporate it into their teaching methods. Resistance to change and heavy workloads exacerbate these challenges, highlighting the gap between teachers' skills and current educational needs. Overall, addressing these challenges requires comprehensive policy reform, enhanced institutional understanding, increased financial support, and targeted teacher training to bridge the gap between information technology and effective language instruction.

3. Misalignment Between Technology and Application

Despite the availability of various information technology facilities in some schools, their utilization remains suboptimal. This issue arises from teachers' inadequate comprehension of information technology applications, preventing them from fully harnessing the devices' potential (Zhang, 2020)①. Consequently, even with resources available, some schools fail to maximize their use, creating a misalignment between technology and practical application, significantly diminishing the effectiveness of information technology education. Teachers may restrict themselves to basic functions, overlooking other applications, wasting valuable resources. Technical problems, whether due to device quality or unstable network environments, further impede effective instruction. Maintenance and management of information technology equipment require adequate financial resources and personnel, often lacking in certain schools, leading to higher failure rates and decreased effectiveness. Another issue is the excessive or improper use of information technology. Teachers must integrate students' specific needs and use IT devices accordingly. Over-reliance on technology without considering individual requirements results in mechanical instruction and neglects personalized development. For instance, in foreign language writing instruction, teachers should focus on critical thinking and creativity rather than relying on automated translation functions. This over-reliance leads students to passively accept translations, hindering their language expression, critical thinking, and creativity. Additionally, improper planning and application of information technology devices by some teachers cause confusion among students. Failing to select and apply technology based on students' proficiency and learning needs prevents genuine assistance. A singular teaching approach and lack of diverse strategies limit the utilization of information technology devices, preventing their full instructional potential from being realized.

6.5.2 New Demands for the Application of Information Technology

Modern information technology introduces vivid visuals to foreign

---

① 张静静.(2020).教育信息化2.0背景下农村教师信息化教学能力调查与对策探究.创新创业理论研究与实践,(03),63-64.

language teaching, enriching classroom activities. Multimedia classrooms and software allow teachers to present materials intuitively, aligning with authentic language instruction needs. Text-image integration, paired with dynamic and static elements, creates immersive scenarios for comprehensive language understanding. User-friendly interfaces empower students to actively learn in an interactive multimedia environment, reducing shyness and boosting confidence. Multimedia computer interactions help students refine pronunciation, vocabulary, and syntax, accelerating language proficiency (Jin, 2019)①. Beyond computer-assisted instruction, information technology has become an integral part of the foreign language curriculum, setting new standards for ICC cultivation in language education.

1. Advancing Beyond the Constraints of the Traditional "Classroom + Textbook" Paradigm

Foreign language instruction has embraced information technology as an integral component, evolving it from a tool to a fundamental element, fundamentally transforming instructional frameworks. This approach fosters reciprocal relationships among teachers, students, computers, and instructional content, characterized by interconnections and transformations. Information technology enables flexible and diverse pedagogical methods, contrasting with traditional teacher-led lectures. It enriches education with dynamic multimedia resources like videos, audios, images, and animations, enhancing engagement and intuitiveness, facilitating comprehensive language learning (Qi & Wang, 2019)②.

Moreover, information technology enhances interactivity and engagement. Traditionally, teachers primarily disseminate knowledge, but technology facilitates student-driven interaction via online platforms and forums. This fosters active exchanges, stimulating learning enthusiasm,

---

① 金靓. (2019). 英语教学的信息化及其实践路径. 教学与管理, (12), 105-107.

② 亓明俊 & 王雪梅. (2019). 大学英语阅读网络学习共同体的建构与实施——以某高校大学英语后续课程为案例. 北京第二外国语学院学报, (04), 116-128.

motivation, and autonomy (Ge, 2019)①. Information technology also bridges classroom learning with real-life contexts, enabling practical language applications and cultural insights. By dismantling temporal and spatial limits, it enhances intercultural communication competencies, deepening language mastery and real-world relevance (Nie & Huang, 2020)②. This immersive experience enables students to better understand and master the practical applications of the language in real-life contexts. The incorporation of information technology transcends the traditional boundaries of foreign language teaching, ushering in a new era of instructional practices. By expanding the repertoire of resources and interactive platforms, information technology empowers students to engage in a multifaceted and immersive learning journey, fostering enhanced language proficiency, and a deeper understanding of foreign language knowledge. Ultimately, this integration not only bridges the gap between language instruction and real-life situations but also cultivates students' intercultural communication capabilities, empowering them to excel in an interconnected world.

2. Creating an Ideal Teaching Environment and Approach

Contextualized learning is crucial in integrating information technology into foreign language education. Virtual environments immerse students in simulated and authentic contexts, enhancing teaching effectiveness (Du & Huang, 2020) ③ . This approach not only supports mastery of foreign language knowledge but also cultivates adaptability to diverse language environments and communicative scenarios (Lee & Park, 2019)④. It sparks students' interest in language acquisition by creating an enjoyable learning atmosphere. Traditional methods often focus on teacher-centered instruction,

---

① 葛军. (2019). 信息技术条件下外语教学中的变与不变. 高等教育研究学报, (04), 99-105.

② 聂慧 & 黄柏萍. (2020). VR/AR技术视域下大学英语教学模式创新研究——以理工科院校新工科人才培养为例. 上海理工大学学报(社会科学版), (02), 108-113.

③ 杜岩岩 & 黄庆双. (2020). 在线深度学习的发生机理与促进策略. 中国高教研究, (06), 58-63.

④ Lee, S. M., & Park, M. (2020). Reconceptualization of the context in language learning with a location-based AR app. *Computer Assisted Language Learning*, 33(8), 936-959.

relying on lectures and passive learning. These methods can fail to engage students or meet their individual needs. In contrast, student-centered learning accommodates personalized requirements, using varied teaching approaches to foster motivation, autonomy, and deeper understanding of language proficiency (Wang & Ding, 2023)①. Collaborative learning is another vital aspect of integrating information technology. Through group activities involving cooperation and communication, students gain insights into language knowledge, develop teamwork skills, and enhance language communication (Zhang, 2022)②. Role-playing and discussions in collaborative settings allow students to experience and apply language knowledge creatively. Furthermore, information technology offers open access to abundant educational resources. Platforms provide access to foreign language movies, journals, instructional videos, and online dictionaries, enriching learning experiences and promoting critical thinking and problem-solving in language learning (Yan, 2021)③. Integrating information technology into foreign language education enhances learning by providing diverse resources and fostering interactive, collaborative, and contextualized learning environments. These approaches empower students to explore practical language applications, develop critical thinking skills, and gain deeper insights into foreign language knowledge.

3. Restructuring Foreign Language Teaching Structure

The evolution of information technology is reshaping learning methods, particularly in foreign language education. Firstly, the integration of computer networks has shifted the instructional approach towards emphasizing student-centered teaching and leveraging modern technology to foster autonomy and

---

① 汪萍 & 丁妍西. (2023). 高校外语教学数字化转型探索研究. 广州广播电视大学学报, (02), 29-33+108.

② 张恒超. (2022). 交流合作学习认知特征. 武汉科技大学学报(社会科学版), (03), 338-348.

③ 阎光才. (2021). 信息技术革命与教育教学变革: 反思与展望. 华东师范大学学报(教育科学版), 39(7), 1-15.

independent learning (Yu, 2020)①. In traditional methods, teachers typically acted as knowledge transmitters, with students as passive recipients. However, information technology empowers students to take a more active role in their learning process, engaging in self-directed exploration and inquiry. In technology-integrated classrooms, although the teacher's visible role may diminish, their role transforms into that of organizers, coordinators, and facilitators (Tian et al., 2023)②. Teachers utilize information technology to provide personalized learning resources and plans tailored to individual student needs, thereby enhancing motivation and learning outcomes. Online platforms and multimedia technologies support remote teaching, fostering communication, discussions, and collaboration between teachers and students. Secondly, the establishment of online learning platforms through modern information technology facilitates self-directed learning among students (Huang et al., 2020)③. Students can independently discover, select, and process information based on their proficiency level, needs, and interests. Unlike traditional teaching materials, information technology provides comprehensive and diverse resources such as foreign language movies, music, literature, news, and magazines from around the world. These resources not only enhance language skills but also deepen cultural understanding and awareness of social contexts. Interactive learning tools like speech recognition, machine translation, online dictionaries, and grammar checkers further support convenient language learning. Online platforms encourage educational interaction through dynamic conversations and concept

① 郁宇. (2020). 信息技术背景下应用型本科院校大学生自主学习状况调查分析. 创新创业理论研究与实践, (17), 28-29+39.

② 田小红, 季益龙 & 周跃良. (2023). 教师能力结构再造: 教育数字化转型的关键支撑. 华东师范大学学报 (教育科学版), (03), 91-100.

③ 黄荣怀, 汪燕, 王欢欢, 逯行 & 高博俊. (2020). 未来教育之教学新形态: 弹性教学与主动学习. 现代远程教育研究, (03), 3-14.

construction (*Gromova*, 2021)①. Overall, the integration of information technology in foreign language education promotes student-centered learning, facilitates self-directed inquiry, and enriches cultural understanding through interactive and collaborative online platforms. This approach encourages deeper engagement in intercultural learning and enhances students' overall language proficiency and cultural competence.

In summary, information technology integration in foreign language education revolutionizes teaching, offering convenient, efficient, and diverse learning resources. It dismantles traditional frameworks, fostering flexible models centered on students. This environment empowers students in intercultural exchanges, boosts language proficiency and cultural understanding, achieving holistic learning. Teachers must adapt, by mastering language skills, teaching techniques, and information technology to craft student-centric, multidimensional learning environments, acting as organizers, designers, and facilitators.

6.5.3 Implementation of Information Technology

Foreign language education should fully leverage information technology's impact on teaching, exploring integration pathways and practical models. Emphasizing problem-solving, online inquiry, and group collaboration in teaching models optimizes information resources, fostering student autonomy and inquiry in language learning. This approach integrates classroom teaching with online self-directed learning, empowering students to take charge of their language education effectively.

1. Elucidating the Objectives of Integrating Information Technology in Foreign Language Teaching

The primary goal of language teachers is to facilitate students' acquisition

① Gromova, T. V. (2021). Information technologies significance in higher education in context of its digitalization. In S. I. Ashmarina, & V. V. Mantulenko, (Eds.), *Current achievements, challenges and digital chances of knowledge based economy*. (pp. 19-26). Springer.

of knowledge and skills, nurturing their autonomy in foreign language learning and preparing them to be culturally aware global citizens (Godwin-Jones, 2015)①. Establishing clear teaching objectives guides the integration of information technology into foreign language education. It is essential for teachers to align technology use with specific course and lesson goals, ensuring coherence across classroom, extracurricular, and online learning contexts. To achieve these objectives, teachers should integrate intercultural learning with language skill development. By incorporating authentic language materials, multimedia resources, and intercultural communication activities, teachers enhance students' listening, speaking, reading, and writing abilities within diverse cultural contexts. Furthermore, teachers can effectively use information technology to support ICC. Through flexible approaches like online video teaching, teachers help students understand the contextual use of foreign languages and communication styles. Utilizing platforms for instructional videos provides insights into cultural backgrounds and societal nuances, creating an engaging learning environment. Moreover, information technology in foreign language teaching should prioritize the cultivation of cultural sensitivity and adaptability. Teachers can design scenario-based tasks or role-playing activities that allow students to engage in language practice within virtual intercultural environments and address challenges encountered during intercultural communication. Additionally, teachers can incorporate learning activities such as case studies, cultural comparisons, and cultural interpretations to nurture students' sensitivity and adaptability toward different cultures. Encouraging reflection and discussion among students, teachers can foster an awareness of biases and stereotypes within their own culture, while promoting respect and appreciation for the diversity present in other cultures.

2. Designing Innovative Instructional Content

With the continuous advancement and widespread adoption of information

---

① Godwin-Jones, R. (2015). Contributing, creating, curating: Digital literacies for language learners. *Language Learning & Technology*, 19(3), 8-20.

technology, more foreign language teachers are integrating innovative technologies into their teaching practices to enhance student learning outcomes. Information technology offers a plethora of tools and possibilities for designing creative instructional content that engages and motivates students. Teachers can start by incorporating multimedia technology to create interactive teaching activities that spark students' curiosity. Platforms like online teaching platforms and presentation software enable the presentation of course content in animated formats, utilizing engaging visuals and dynamic banners, thereby enhancing student interest and improving learning outcomes (Yu et al., 2024)①. Furthermore, emerging technologies such as virtual reality (VR) and augmented reality (AR) can be utilized to develop innovative instructional content that enhances students' ICC. AR, for instance, can create immersive language learning experiences that deepen students' understanding of foreign cultures, thereby improving their ability to communicate across cultural boundaries (Al-Ansi et al., 2023)②. Teachers can also employ highly interactive methods like online gaming to immerse students in virtual language environments, allowing them to explore communication behaviors and cultural traditions from diverse backgrounds (Chen & Yuan, 2021)③. Gaming serves as an engaging and interactive instructional tool that captures students' attention and ignites their interest and enthusiasm (Jiang & Chen, 2023)④. Language learning games in particular engage students and develop their language skills while fostering critical thinking and intuition. Moreover, integrating creative elements that

---

① 于兆吉，房一宁 & 鲍卉. (2024). 教育、科技、人才"三位一体"赋能高等教育新质人才培养的逻辑、挑战与进路. 现代教育管理，(09)，34-44.

② Al-Ansi, A., Jaboob, M., & Garad, A. (2023). Analyzing augmented reality (AR) and virtual reality (VR) recent development in education. *Social Sciences & Humanities Open*, 8(1), 100532.

③ 陈先红 & 袁文霞. (2021). 信息 · 情感 · 意义:"短视频讲故事"的集体对话. 新闻与写作，(10)，90-95.

④ 蒋立兵 & 陈佑清. (2023). 技术赋能学习中心教学的逻辑与路径. 课程. 教材. 教法，(05)，56-63.

reflect Chinese cultural characteristics into instructional content can enhance student engagement and cultural understanding. For example, incorporating traditional Chinese music like Beijing Opera when teaching pronunciation allows students to appreciate the rhythm and melody of foreign languages while immersing them in Chinese culture. This approach encourages students to compare and contrast their own cultural background with Chinese culture, fostering cultural confidence and identification. Information technology also offers opportunities for effective teaching assessment and feedback. Online platforms and assessment tools enable teachers to collect and evaluate student assignments efficiently, providing timely feedback that enhances learning outcomes (Du, 2024)①. Additionally, teachers can design a variety of instructional quizzes and exercises using technology, offering students diverse and practical learning experiences.

3. Establishing a Student-Centered Learning Environment

An increasing number of teachers are embracing student-centered learning environments to offer personalized, autonomous, and interactive learning experiences. Understanding each student's unique learning needs allows foreign language teaching resources to be tailored effectively, enhancing engagement and overall learning outcomes. Firstly, teachers utilize online learning platforms to provide a wealth of teaching resources and tools. These platforms establish an open and collaborative mechanism for publishing and accessing foreign language teaching materials, ensuring timely availability and utilization. Teachers can upload course materials, assignments, and tests, enabling students to access them flexibly anytime, anywhere (Wen & Wang, 2024)②. Interactive features such as learning tasks and online discussions on these platforms foster student autonomy and meaningful interaction (Xu &

① 杜嘉.(2024).高校在线课程教学效果评价模型的构建与应用.中国电化教育,(09),122-128.

② 温军英 & 王伟宜.(2024).数智赋能高等教育教与学的现实向度与伦理限度.高教发展与评估,(05),92-104+123-124.

Zhu, 2020)①. Secondly, prioritizing student participation and immersive experiences within the classroom setting is crucial. Information technology enhances classroom interactivity through tools like interactive projectors and whiteboards that present multimedia resources. Interactive games and role-playing activities engage students directly in the learning process. Cooperative learning methods such as group discussions promote interaction, cooperation, and knowledge sharing among students. Moreover, teachers cater to individual learning needs by employing diverse teaching methods and resources based on students' learning styles. Integrating elements of Chinese culture into foreign language teaching enriches students' understanding and appreciation of Chinese cultural nuances, enhancing language skills across listening, speaking, reading, and writing. Multimedia resources can spotlight Chinese cultural landmarks, traditional practices, and historical contexts. Furthermore, personalized learning support and guidance are essential. Teachers use information technology to monitor students' progress closely, identifying and addressing learning issues promptly (Zhao, 2020)②. Customized learning tasks and resources based on students' performance promote their individual development and growth. In essence, by leveraging information technology effectively, teachers create dynamic learning environments that cater to diverse student needs, foster engagement, and promote intercultural understanding, preparing students for success in a globalized world.

4. Constructing an Open Teaching Communication Platform

The advancement of digital and intelligent education has prompted the development of open teaching communication platforms. Information platform-based foreign language teaching enables convenient and seamless communication between teachers and students, providing them access to an

---

① 徐喆 & 朱萍. (2020). 基于超星网络教学平台的线上教学策略探究. 创新创业理论研究与实践, (18), 22-23.

② Zhao, Y. (2020). A personalized English teaching design based on multimedia computer technology. *International Journal of Emerging Technologies in Learning* (*iJET*), 15(8), 210-222.

open and unrestricted platform for communication and exchange. This, in turn, creates favorable conditions for diverse foreign language education. First and foremost, the establishment of an open teaching communication platform necessitates the selection of a suitable platform. Presently, numerous open-source learning management systems such as Moodle and Canvas, as well as commercial online learning platforms like Coursera, are available. It is of paramount importance to choose a platform that aligns with the teaching content and methods. Additionally, factors such as platform stability, security, and user-friendliness should be taken into account during the platform selection process. Secondly, a user-centered design is essential for the platform. The platform should offer convenience to both students and teachers, ensuring that its operation is straightforward and easily comprehensible. Furthermore, the platform should cater to the diverse needs of its users by providing a wide range of functions to fulfill various teaching requirements. For instance, it can facilitate online communication for students, enable online assignment grading for teachers, and offer students access to diverse forms of course resources. Moreover, an open teaching communication platform should prioritize the effectiveness of communication. Different teaching strategies should be adopted based on specific learning objectives to maximize the platform's efficacy. For example, oral and listening skills can be taught using online videos, while reading and writing skills can be enhanced through online document editing tools. Teachers should select appropriate teaching strategies based on the learning objectives and the individual circumstances of their students. Lastly, the construction of an open teaching communication platform should emphasize the evaluation of its usability. Teachers and students should assess the platform, provide feedback on their user experience, and offer suggestions for continuous improvement and optimization of the platform's functionality and design.

In conclusion, the construction of an open teaching communication platform entails the selection of a suitable platform, prioritizing user experience, employing diverse teaching strategies, and conducting regular evaluations and improvements. By doing so, teachers and students can enhance their communication and interaction, thereby improving the effectiveness of ICC cultivation. Additionally, by combining the unique characteristics of China's international communication and information technology, teachers and students can utilize this platform to effectively promote Chinese culture and bolster international influence.

6.6 Summary

This chapter provides an in-depth examination of the practical application of ICC cultivation models in foreign language education at Chinese universities.

The researcher begins by examining current classroom instruction in foreign language courses. This analysis informs the proposal of effective content and approaches for fostering ICC, aligning with emerging ICC frameworks. In universities, foreign language education should embrace the dual objectives of "SLA + ICC," aiming to cultivate individuals with a global perspective, a comprehensive understanding of the world, national pride, and a commitment to promoting Chinese culture. These individuals should be equipped to engage in intercultural communication, manage discourse in critical moments, and uphold the image of the Party and the nation. Classroom teaching should reflect the complexities of intercultural communication, requiring an open-minded attitude, acceptance of linguistic variations, and respect for cultural differences to prevent misunderstandings and conflicts. Creating authentic language contexts within the classroom is crucial, allowing students to experience, understand, and apply intercultural communication. The teaching process should incorporate universal human values, humanistic care, target language conventions, and other relevant factors to facilitate effective communication and encourage innovative discourse. Additionally, instilling a sense of mission among students is vital, emphasizing the importance of two-way communication between their own culture and foreign cultures. Students should not only use foreign language proficiency to learn advanced Western technology and culture but also tell China's story in a manner that resonates globally, using foreign languages as a medium. Intercultural teaching in foreign language classrooms should harmonize SLA and ICC. Foreign language education encompasses more than acquiring authentic language skills and understanding foreign cultural traditions; it also involves disseminating Chinese culture to non-Chinese-speaking foreign audiences, using foreign languages as a conduit. This aligns with the current demand for intercultural communicative talents who can effectively bridge domestic and international contexts.

After exploring extracurricular activities in foreign language education and their role in fostering ICC, three key findings emerge. Firstly, extracurricular activities allow students to engage with diverse cultural backgrounds, enhancing their ICC. This engagement can occur through various channels such as domestic and international social media platforms, intercultural exchange programs, and exposure to cultural products. Secondly, these activities emphasize the social functions of language and meet the demands of international communication by focusing on experiential learning, cultural awareness, and practical skills. Thirdly, effective approaches include: A) leveraging social media platforms for interactive communication with people from different countries. This fosters mutual understanding, respect, and enhances China's international influence and image; B) organizing domestic intercultural activities to boost students' international perspectives and cultural literacy, increasing their awareness of global affairs and elevating China's discourse power in external communication. in external communication; C) participating in intercultural exchange activities abroad to broaden students' horizons, enrich their experiences, and enhance their ICC, strengthening China's competitiveness on the international stage; D) utilizing online courses, books, newspapers, magazines, and other cultural products for indirect exposure, deepening understanding and respect for different cultures and social backgrounds.

Faculty members are the soul of teaching and essential to improving educational quality and reforms. Research on foreign language faculty in Chinese universities reveals the following findings: Firstly, there are still issues with the development of ICC among foreign language faculty in Chinese universities. The main reasons include: A) teachers not meeting standards for language and intercultural teaching in knowledge, skills, and consciousness; B) insufficient emphasis placed by foreign language teachers on cultivating ICC; C) ICC development not deeply engaging with target language cultures, limited to superficial cultural aspects; D) lack of confidence in teaching intercultural communication, language, culture, and related subjects, especially in disseminating Chinese culture, often resulting in narrow cultural representations. Secondly, professional competence for foreign language teachers should be dynamic and interconnected, integrating contemporary wisdom to express Chinese culture, exploring cultural connotations to enhance cultural confidence, and using cultural commonalities for strong appeal. Teachers need to strengthen educational beliefs, understand talent goals in foreign language education, establish cultural confidence, and be aware of their roles and tasks in intercultural education. They should promote integrity in teaching and learning, engage in action research to understand students' intercultural needs and improve teaching quality, and develop students' ICC. Creating PLCs within the classroom can support teachers in refining practices and responding to new challenges through various learning community forms, such as expert-guided PLC, project-based PLC, school-based PLC, and VPLC.

Textbooks are essential for disseminating new knowledge and achieving educational objectives. In foreign language education, textbooks must meet specific ICC cultivation requirements. Currently, these textbooks often inadequately reflect Chinese culture and scientific content, lack emphasis on moral values, focus on fragmented content, and exhibit a degree of disconnection. To address these issues, textbook development should shift from focusing on the "other" to fostering "dialogue" by selecting authentic materials that align with Chinese cultural values, facilitating exchanges between Chinese and Western cultures, and creating an atmosphere for meaningful "dialogues." Additionally, a transition from an "instrumental" to a "humanistic" approach is needed, emphasizing deeper cultural connotations, the dissemination of Chinese culture, and nurturing social responsibility and moral character. This helps students integrate into global cultural exchanges. Textbooks should also move from "language for learning" to "language in life" by employing engaging materials that stimulate interest and potential, allowing students to acquire extensive knowledge and inspiration. Furthermore, the shift from "cultural acquisition" to "cultural exchange" should be promoted, enhancing students' diversified cultural awareness through comparative analysis with foreign cultures and fostering cultural reflection. Effective textbook development and utilization should integrate value shaping and knowledge transmission, merge linguistic and cultural knowledge, emphasize the authenticity and contextualization of materials, and creatively employ textbooks by leveraging and integrating teaching resources practically.

The application of information technology in foreign language education must fully integrate with teaching to cultivate students' ICC. Currently, there are three areas of misalignment: between concepts and practices, national policies and specific school situations, and technology and its application. To address this, the objectives of information-based foreign language teaching must be defined, creating an ideal teaching environment and approach. This involves reshaping the structure of foreign language education and designing multidimensional, student-centered information-based learning environments. Four methods can innovate this integration: A) explore diverse teaching strategies to promote cultural exchange and understanding, B) design creative instructional content for diverse and practical learning experiences, C) establish student-centered learning environments to enhance interest and outcomes, D) build open communication platforms to facilitate teacher-student exchanges.

The next chapter is the conclusion, which provides an overall review of the research, summarizing the findings, identifying study limitations, and offering suggestions for further research.

Chapter 7
Conclusion

This chapter provides a concise review of the research problem and process, summarizes the main findings of this study, and finally identifies the limitations of the research and provides suggestions for further study.

7.1 Research Overview

Foreign language education plays a crucial role in national strategies, higher education missions, and the global dissemination of Chinese culture. This study focuses on cultivating ICC within China's foreign language teaching. The main goal is to develop a model for nurturing ICC in Chinese universities, drawing on established ICC research and its application in foreign language education. This research aims to offer insights into ICC development's conceptualization and methodologies, contributing to both theoretical and practical aspects of ICC in Chinese higher education.

This study reviewed relevant literature and theories, then determined the research design and methodology. An integrated approach combining empirical and theoretical research was used. Grounded theory initially explored ICC components and established a universal framework. A survey of students in five Hunan Province universities then assessed their existing ICC levels, with the data categorized, summarized, and analyzed. This study outlines the concepts, principles, objectives, content, and stages of constructing the ICC cultivation model. It formulates theoretical models for fostering ICC in foreign language education and practical models for classroom implementation.

Additionally, it explores the specific application of the ICC cultivation model in Chinese university foreign language education.

7.2 Research Findings

This study conducted an in-depth analysis of the research questions, yielding key findings in three areas: the ICC framework, the current ICC levels among university students, and the ICC cultivation model in foreign language education. Additionally, the study explores the specific application of this model in Chinese universities' foreign language education.

7.2.1 Framework of ICC

A key focus of this study was investigating the ICC framework, specifically exploring its components and their interrelationships. The objective was to establish a comprehensive framework for ICC, providing a foundation for further research on its development. Using grounded theory, this study analyzed and categorized existing literature through open, axial, and selective coding, along with saturation tests. This analysis led to the construction of an ICC framework tailored to China's international communication context.

This study developed an ICC framework consisting of four main components: intercultural consciousness, knowledge, skills, and behavior. Intercultural consciousness acts as the trigger, key to overcoming communication barriers, encompassing a global perspective, intercultural awareness, and motivation. Knowledge functions as a tool, providing a reservoir for communication through declarative knowledge (linguistic, paralinguistic, and cultural) and strategic knowledge (reduction and achievement strategies). Skills ensure effective communication, including plurilingual, pluricultural, communication and cooperation, and adjustment and adaptation skills. Behavior fortifies practical application through intercultural experience, speculative training, and interactive practice. This four-element framework, integrating globalization and localization, reflects the organic connection between language, society, and communication, tailored for China's contemporary international communication landscape.

7.2.2 Status Quo of College Students' ICC

This study, using a 5-point Likert scale, reveals that respondents exhibit high levels of overall ICC and its four dimensions: intercultural consciousness, knowledge, skills, and behavior. Significant differences in ICC levels are found when grouped by age, gender, year level, and major. Correlation analysis shows a significant relationship between the demographic profile and ICC levels. Multiple response set analysis highlights critical thinking ability, comparison of cultural differences, and opportunities for intercultural contact as the top challenges faced by students in becoming interculturally competent.

7.2.3 ICC Cultivation Models in Foreign Language Education

A key focus of this study was constructing an ICC cultivation model for foreign language education in Chinese universities. The goal was to create a model defining the conceptual framework, objectives, principles, content, and stages of ICC development. The study proposed three guiding principles, three fundamental objectives, and three levels of focus, emphasizing four aspects of ICC cultivation. All teaching components were designed to work synergistically. Based on this, the study developed a theoretical model for ICC cultivation and a practical model for classroom implementation, aiming to foster ICC at both macro and micro levels.

The cultivation of ICC integrates overall objectives with systematic and dynamic approaches, linking various stages of foreign language education to form a comprehensive ICC development system with the goal of "SLA + ICC". Guided by three principles—integrating instrumental and humanistic aspects, aligning language and cultural teaching, and balancing local and foreign cultures—the process aims for sustainable ICC development. It aligns with national educational guidelines focused on nurturing talent, addressing the impact of Chinese cultural aphasia, and enhancing cultural identity. The ultimate goal is to improve students' intercultural consciousness, knowledge, skills, and behavior, addressing challenges in effective communication and credibility in international contexts. ICC cultivation involves internal components like curriculum guidelines, course design, textbooks, teaching methods, faculty, and assessment, as well as external components such as extracurricular activities.

This study on ICC cultivation in foreign language education emphasizes the integration of internationalization and localization, developing both theoretical and practical models. The theoretical model includes three levels: the platform layer, the forming layer, and the competence layer. The platform layer consists of foreign language courses, interdisciplinary studies, and resource acquisition. The forming layer involves internal processes like curriculum design, teaching pedagogy, materials, faculty qualifications, and assessment, as well as external processes such as intercultural interactions via social media, exchange activities, and cultural products. The competence layer follows the conscious-competence model, progressing from intercultural consciousness and knowledge to skills and behavioral competence. The practical model for classroom teaching includes objectives, activities, methods, and assessment, bridging the gap between theoretical ICC concepts and practical implementation in the classroom.

7.2.4 Application of ICC Cultivation Models

The fourth focal point of this study is the application of ICC cultivation models in foreign language education. It explores how to implement the theoretical and practical models to develop ICC in Chinese university foreign language education. Key findings were made in classroom teaching, extracurricular activities, faculty, teaching materials, and the use of modern information technology.

Based on the current state of foreign language teaching in Chinese universities and the new ICC framework requirements, the researcher proposed content and methods conducive to ICC cultivation. Foreign language teaching should clarify the dual objectives of "SLA + ICC," reflect the complexity of intercultural communication, create authentic language contexts in the classroom, and inspire students' sense of mission. Intercultural teaching involves learning authentic foreign languages, understanding foreign cultural traditions, and using foreign languages to communicate Chinese culture to non-Chinese-speaking friends. This approach meets the demand for intercultural communicative talents required by current domestic and international situations.

Exploring the current situation, new requirements, and specific methods of extracurricular activities for ICC cultivation revealed that domestic and foreign social media, intercultural exchange activities, and cultural products are key avenues for enhancing ICC. Extracurricular activities emphasize the social function of language, cultural experiences, practical skills development, and cultivating cultural consciousness for external cultural dissemination. Methods include: using social media for interactive communication to enhance China's international influence; conducting domestic intercultural activities to improve students' understanding of international affairs and China's discourse power; participating in foreign intercultural exchanges to broaden perspectives and enhance China's global competitiveness; and engaging with cultural products like online courses, books, and magazines to deepen understanding and respect for different cultures and social backgrounds.

Faculty is the soul of teaching and key to improving quality and educational reform. Many foreign language teachers in Chinese universities have not met the "foreign language and intercultural teachers" standards in knowledge, skills, and consciousness, feeling inadequate in teaching intercultural communication, language and culture, and communication skills. Particularly in disseminating Chinese civilization, they are constrained by "tradition," stuck in the "symbolism", and limited to surface "differences". Foreign language teachers should integrate contemporary wisdom to reconstruct new expressions of Chinese culture, explore cultural connotations to enhance cultural confidence, and utilize cultural commonalities to make Chinese culture more appealing. To enhance faculty development, teachers should fortify their teaching beliefs, emphasize ideological construction, cultivate their character through moral values, foster their character through continuous learning, and demonstrate their character in teaching practices. They should engage in action research to better understand students' intercultural needs and improve teaching quality. Creating learning communities in foreign language classrooms, such as expert-guided, project-based, school-based, and virtual PLCs, can support and assist teachers in adapting to changing environments and new challenges.

Teaching materials are essential for achieving educational objectives, yet current foreign language materials lack adequate representation of Chinese culture, emphasis on moral values, and coherence in content design. To address these issues, materials should shift from focusing on the "other" to fostering "dialogue" by incorporating authentic materials that reflect cultural values and Chinese culture. This includes moving from an instrumental to a humanistic approach, nurturing students' social responsibility and character, and facilitating their integration into global cultural communication. Additionally, the focus should transit from "language for learning" to "language in life," aligning with contemporary trends and broadening students' knowledge and enlightenment. Finally, materials should shift from "cultural acquisition" to "cultural exchange," fostering diverse cultural awareness and critical cultural analysis. The development and use of teaching materials should unify values and knowledge transmission, integrating language proficiency with cultural understanding. Emphasis should be placed on authenticity and contextualization, creatively selecting, utilizing, and integrating teaching resources.

Modern information technology has transcended its role as an auxiliary tool in foreign language education. However, there are discrepancies between conceptual understanding and practical implementation, as well as misalignments between national policies and specific school contexts, and a gap between technology and application. In this new era, cultivating ICC in foreign language education requires innovative integration of information technology. This involves setting clear objectives for digitalized teaching, designing engaging content, establishing student-centered learning environments, and creating open platforms for effective communication and collaboration.

7.3 Research Limitations and Suggestions for Future Research

7.3.1 Research Limitations

ICC is a complex and multifaceted competence. Its cultivation involves various aspects, and foreign language education encompasses multiple stages and factors. Conducting thorough research on ICC cultivation in higher education foreign language teaching is challenging. Despite innovative efforts, limitations due to constraints in expertise, time, and resources are evident. These limitations primarily manifest in three aspects:

A) Scope of empirical research: The study's empirical research, conducted through a survey of students from five universities in Hunan Province, is limited in scope. Factors such as time, resources, and student availability constrained the sample selection, affecting its representativeness. Expanding the research to include a broader range of universities is necessary for a comprehensive understanding of ICC at the student level.

B) Research content: Constraints on the researchers' time and the length of the paper limited the investigation of key foreign language education elements, such as curriculum requirements, course design, and assessments. These aspects need thorough exploration in future studies on the ICC cultivation model in higher education.

C) Depth of research: While the study addresses the perceptions, qualities, development, and structure of foreign language faculty, further exploration of specific research questions is needed. Investigating the precise role of foreign language faculty in cultivating ICC would be particularly valuable.

7.3.2 Suggestions for Future Research

Due to the aforementioned subjective and objective factors, this study has several limitations and deficiencies. The proposed viewpoints also have significant limitations, indicating the need for broader and deeper research. This study aims to serve as a comparative platform for future research, encouraging more scholars to engage in intercultural foreign language teaching and guide foreign language education in China. Future research can focus on the following aspects:

A) Expand the research scope: Future studies should select schools from different levels and regions to enhance the scientific validity of the research. Incorporating interviews with teachers, students, and experts, increasing the sample size of the survey, and conducting regional comparative analyses can further enrich the research.

B) Increase research content: Future research should explore other aspects of foreign language education, such as curriculum standards, course design, testing, and evaluation, to systematically cultivate ICC.

C) Deepen research dimensions: Further in-depth research can focus on specific teaching methods and approaches for cultivating ICC in the classroom and investigate the role of teachers in this process.

D) Implement dynamic tracking: ICC cultivation in foreign language education is a lengthy process. Future studies should implement the ICC cultivation model in teaching and use tracking methods to understand its effectiveness. As the demands for ICC evolve, tracking and analyzing data over time will help adjust strategies based on students' proficiency and changes in intercultural contexts, aiming for continuous improvement of the ICC cultivation system.

APPENDIX

Questionnaire

Chinese College Students' Intercultural Communication Competence Self-Evaluation Questionnaire (Modified Version)

Dear students,

The questionnaire is an empirical survey of Chinese college students' ICC (intercultural communication competence). The questionnaire includes two parts: personal information and ICC self-assessment. This questionnaire is anonymous. The content of the questionnaire is mainly to investigate the status quo of Chinese college students' ICC. The results of the questionnaire are only used for academic research, and your personal information is absolutely confidential. Please complete every question in the questionnaire carefully.

Thank for your support!

Part Ⅰ Personal Information

Directions: please make a choice according to your actual situation.

1. Age: A. <18 years old B. 18～20 years old
   C. 20～22 years old D. >22 years old
2. Gender: A. male B. female
3. Year level: A. freshman B. sophomore
   C. junior D. senior

4. Major:

A. philosophy B. economics
C. law D. education
E. literature F. history
G. science H. engineering
I. agriculture J. medicine
K. management L. art

Part Ⅱ ICC Self-evaluation

Directions: this part is the Chinese college students' ICC self-assessment scale, including four aspects (consent/consciousness, knowledge, skills, and behavior). Please choose a number from "1" to "5" according to your actual situation. See the following for details:

SCALE	STATISCIC LIMIT	RESPONDE MODE	VERBAL INTERPRETATION
1	1.00～1.80	Very Unsatisfied	Not Manifested (NM)
2	1.81～2.60	Unsatisfied	Slightly Manifested (SM)
3	2.61～3.40	Neutral	Moderately Manifested (MM)
4	3.41～4.20	Satisfied	Highly Manifested (HM)
5	4.21～5.00	Very Satisfied	Very Highly Manifested (VHM)

No.	**Please judge to what extent the following statements are in line with your current situation of ICC.**	**Please select one and check it (√)**
Consciousness:		
a	I realize that in the context of globalization, intercultural communication is the affirmation, respect and understanding of the cultural characteristics of different nations.	1 2 3 4 5
b	I realized that intercultural activity can help me understand and identify with my own culture, and cultivate myself to take the historical responsibility for the development of my own culture.	1 2 3 4 5

c	I realize that human beings coexist in a multi-cultural environment, and different cultural characteristics have the phenomenon of mutual penetration.	1 2 3 4 5
d	I realize that I can rationally analyze cultural differences in intercultural communication.	1 2 3 4 5
e	I realize that when communicating with foreigners, I should maintain an open and tolerant attitude and respect each other's culture.	1 2 3 4 5
f	I realize that the two cultures have different styles, different language use, and different cultures and languages have had an impact on society.	1 2 3 4 5
g	I realize that overcoming prejudice, eliminating stereotypes and maintaining cultural relativism can help achieve more effective intercultural communication.	1 2 3 4 5
h	I realize that the more I respect cultural differences, the more motivated I am to practice communicating across cultures.	1 2 3 4 5
i	I realize that the stronger the sense of global citizenship, the stronger the willingness to participate in intercultural communication.	1 2 3 4 5
j	I realize that maintaining a positive and lasting communication motivation can make intercultural communication more smoothy and efficient.	1 2 3 4 5
Knowledge:		
a	I get the language knowledge such as pronunciation, vocabulary, grammar, discourse and pragmatic knowledge used in intercultural communication.	1 2 3 4 5

b	I understand the nonverbal knowledge used in intercultural communication, such as facial expressions, gestures, gestures, hugs and other body language.	1 2 3 4 5
c	I master my country's history, geography, sociopolitical and cultural knowledge and values.	1 2 3 4 5
d	I know my own way of thinking, basic norms and behavioral knowledge.	1 2 3 4 5
e	I master the history, geography, social politics and cultural knowledge and values of other countries.	1 2 3 4 5
f	I know the way of thinking, basic norms and behavioral knowledge of other countries.	1 2 3 4 5
g	I have learned the comparative knowledge of significant differences between different cultures.	1 2 3 4 5
h	I understand the different strategies for treating high context culture and low context culture.	1 2 3 4 5
i	I know the achievement strategies for successful intercultural communication (reporting, asking for help, procrastination, etc.).	1 2 3 4 5
j	I know the avoidance strategies for successful intercultural communication (avoiding topics, avoiding language forms, etc.).	1 2 3 4 5

Skill:		
a	I have mastered the skills of using foreign languages to communicate successfully with people from different social and cultural backgrounds and fields.	1 2 3 4 5
b	I have mastered the skills of nonverbal communication, such as facial expression, gesture and posture.	1 2 3 4 5
c	I have mastered the skills to understand and express meanings by combining specific contexts, using structured knowledge.	1 2 3 4 5
d	I have mastered the skills to consider other countries' political, economic, religious and other events from different cultures and perspectives.	1 2 3 4 5
e	I have mastered the skills to interpret cultural concepts and phenomena, and help resolve cultural conflicts.	1 2 3 4 5
f	I have mastered the skills of integrating language, culture and thinking from the perspective of holism.	1 2 3 4 5
g	I have mastered the cooperation skills of maintaining different cultures, actively breaking the silence and creating collaboration opportunities.	1 2 3 4 5
h	I have mastered the communication skills to effectively avoid offending the other party in terms of language and behavior in intercultural communication.	1 2 3 4 5
i	I have mastered the adaptive skills of adjusting my own behavior and handling the frustration encountered in intercultural communication.	1 2 3 4 5
j	I have mastered the adjustment skills of giving up, transforming and selectively absorbing language and cultural elements.	1 2 3 4 5

Behavior:		
a	I have practical experience in updating language systems (such as vocabulary and reference) in intercultural communication.	1 2 3 4 5
b	I have the experience of successfully communicating with people from different cultural backgrounds and fields.	1 2 3 4 5
c	I have the experience of experiencing and updating cultural knowledge through intercultural activities.	1 2 3 4 5
d	I have the practice of accepting, comparing and evaluating different cultures.	1 2 3 4 5
e	I have the experience of conducting intercultural reflection and seeking appropriate ways to solve intercultural conflicts.	1 2 3 4 5
f	I have the experience of noticing the problems in my own language system, consciously analyzing language forms, and then producing corrected output.	1 2 3 4 5
g	I have the practice of regarding language and culture as a whole and negotiating with each other on meaning.	1 2 3 4 5
h	I have the practical experience of combining knowledge and customs in different fields to build and adjust my own cultural identity.	1 2 3 4 5

Closed question: What issues or challenges do you usually encounter to be able to become intercultural communication competent? Directions: Please select 3～5 of the following 20 options that suit your own situation and check them (√).		
1	linguistic knowledge	
2	cultural knowledge of foreign countries	
3	global perspectives	
4	cultural integration skills	
5	nonverbal knowledge	
6	communication motivation	
7	cultural understanding skills	
8	strategy knowledge	
9	opportunities for intercultural contact	
10	cultural knowledge of the native country	
11	adjustment and adaptation skills	
12	opportunities for meaning negotiation	
13	critical thinking ability	
14	cultural differences comparison	
15	cultural heritage awareness	
16	language knowledge application skills	
17	opportunities to regulate identity	
18	awareness of cultural equality	
19	adapt & adjust skills	
20	communication & cooperation skills	